"On his eightieth birthday, J. I. Packer said the greatest challenge for the twenty-first-century church was to recatechize and disciple believers. These contributions from two of our best Christian thinkers help us to do precisely what Packer said is needed. It will help you to see how to make not just converts but, as Jesus tells us, disciples."

—**Chuck Colson**, founder, Prison Fellowship

"Nothing could be more practical than the urgently needed wisdom that J. I. Packer and Gary Parrett provide in this book. More than a call to recover a neglected practice, *Grounded in the Gospel* provides concrete advice to us all for dedicating ourselves anew to rooting the next generation in the great truths of the faith."

—**Michael Horton**, J. Gresham Machen Professor of Theology, Westminster Seminary California

"Having been initially formed by Lutheran catechetical practices, I heartily endorse J. I. Packer and Gary Parrett's efforts to encourage evangelicals to adopt similar procedures for training both young and old in the foundational elements of faith. I want to prod parishes of all denominations to listen to Packer and Parrett's cries and constructive proposals to better equip new believers. This is an urgently needed book!

—**Marva J. Dawn**, author of *Is It a Lost Cause?* and *Talking the Walk*; teaching fellow in spiritual theology, Regent College

"At last, a book that tells local churches how to fulfill *all* of the Great Commission! It's important that we 'go' and that we 'make disciples,' but it's also important that we 'teach' new believers and help them grow in the faith. I highly recommend this book to pastors and church leaders who want to encourage Christian intelligence and maturity in their people."

—**Warren W. Wiersbe**, author of the "BE" commentary series

"This book considers one of the 'ancient ways' as vital for the present and future health of the church but emphasizes two critical factors: learning is important and catechesis is about the holistic development of the whole people of God. Christian learning needs to make a comeback in the church. This book will help."

—**Linda Cannell**, academic dean, North Park Theological Seminary

"J. I. Packer and Gary Parrett offer a diagnosis and prescription to remedy our shallow faith and practice. While the prescription might not be popular in our individualistic, do-it-yourself contemporary church culture, it's precisely the remedy needed to reverse the pandemic of narcissistic spirituality and lethargy plaguing the church."

—**Walt Mueller**, Center for Parent/Youth Understanding

"Many thoughtful Christian analysts have pinpointed the lack of maturity and of a biblical mindset among the vast majority of Christians as one of the most serious problems today in the church worldwide. Few have presented a concrete remedy for this problem as effectively as J. I. Packer and Gary Parrett have in this book."

—**Ajith Fernando**, national director, Youth for Christ Sri Lanka

"Packer and Parrett argue that recovering the practice of catechesis can go a long way toward curing anemic Christianity. The book's biblical grounding and theological structure should go a long way toward encouraging evangelicals to resurrect this ancient church practice."

—**Mark Galli**, senior managing editor, *Christianity Today*

GROUNDED
in the
GOSPEL

Building Believers the Old-Fashioned Way

J. I. PACKER *and*
GARY A. PARRETT

BakerBooks

a division of Baker Publishing Group
Grand Rapids, Michigan

Published by Baker Books
a division of Baker Publishing Group
P.O. Box 6287, Grand Rapids, MI 49516-6287
www.bakerbooks.com

Printed in the United States of America

Library of Congress Cataloging-in-Publication Data
Packer, J. I. (James Innell)
    Grounded in the Gospel : building believers the old-fashioned way / J. I. Packer and
Gary A. Parrett.
        p. cm.
    Includes bibliographical references (p.   ) and indexes.
    ISBN 978-0-8010-6838-6 (pbk.)
    1. Catechetics—Protestant churches. I. Parrett, Gary A., 1957– II. Title.
BV1534.2.P33 2010
268′.804—dc22   2009051892

To
David Wells,
who diagnoses so clearly
the malaise for which
catechesis is the remedy

Contents

Introduction

We who worked together on this book are separated generationally, ecclesiastically, and culturally. Parrett is an American, a free churchman, and a younger man than Packer by some decades. Packer is a veteran Anglican presbyter, English by extraction, and Canadian by choice. The discovery, however, that we were both passionate about catechesis brought us together.

As evangelical Christian educators, we see catechesis as integral to the all-age Christian nurture that every congregation should be practicing. Together we mourn its current eclipse, perceiving this as the deepest root of the immaturity that is so widespread in evangelical circles, and we unite in seeking the recognition, restoration, and indeed enhancement of it as a basic discipline of Christian life.

In this we find that we see eye to eye with the late Pope John Paul II and his successor, Benedict XVI, and we are happy to be in their company at this point. Both have been clear and emphatic that in order to be fully useful, Christians must know their faith well. We could not agree more.

Surveying evangelical congregations in the Western world today, we believe that what confronts us is a case of being so close yet so far away. Conservative evangelical congregations regularly excel in the number and variety of forms of Sunday instruction and midweek group experiences provided for their adherents. Yet the hustle and bustle ends up like a shower of arrows that all hit the target yet miss the bull's-eye. Although these congregations have done well in so many ways, something more is needed.

What exactly is the problem? Look at it this way. During the past century mechanization and technology have increased the pace of Western life, leaving us all wanting to do things more quickly so as to get on with whatever we see as next business. The hurrying mindset has led to the fast-food revolution, in which we wolf snacks as we go along rather than treat meals as big deals in the way our grandparents did. And out of this fast-food revolution has come the junk food predicament: we are offered, and gobble down, what quickly makes us feel full, but it isn't a balanced diet. It doesn't give us the vitamins we need but loads us up with unnecessary fats. As a result, we end up obese, flabby, and out of shape. Something similar seems to happen in our churches; the food we get and give in our learning and teaching, though no doubt tasty, does not nourish us as spiritual food should. Before anything else, adjustments in our diet are needed, or we shall never be lithe, virile, upright Christians— strong, resilient, and passionate for God in the way that evangelical Christians in days past were.

After J.I.'s heart attack he was given a document entitled "Guidelines for a 'Heart-Healthy' Life . . . Low Saturated Fat Diet." One way in which his spouse helps him is by regularly reminding him of what the document directs and deprecates. A spiritually heart-healthy diet, we think, is the primary need of present-day Western congregations. And the foundation of that diet, we believe, is good catechesis. We came to hope that by pooling our resources we might make a helpful difference at that point. Hence the present volume.

Obstacles

We are well aware that in advocating a renewal of catechesis we fight an uphill battle and swim against the stream. Why should this be? For several reasons, which we now review.

The first and biggest factor that inhibits catechesis, and the hardest to counter or circumvent, is the *turn away from external authority* in Western culture. This became potent in the nineteenth century. As a cultural force, it grew out of the anti-Catholic-church fury of the French Revolution that burst out in 1789 with the storming of the Bastille. To be sure, this fury was, at least on the surface, political rather than directly religious. The maddened mob believed the French Roman Catholic hierarchy and the attached church system were buttressing the irresponsible royal autocracy and sought to bring both power structures down in flames together. Deists and atheists gave their support, and the aftermath was the slow but inexorable crossing of a western European and American cultural barrier: leading thinkers in the West began to see themselves as pioneers of a new, post-Christian era in which the Christian heritage of belief might be questioned and critiqued like any other human point of view. This was a radical turn from a millennium and a half of acknowledging the truth and authority of God's written Word as set forth in and by the church.

The clearest discernment of this shift was in Holland, where men like Groen van Prinsterer and Abraham Kuyper analyzed it realistically as an antitheistic flow of thought, and the Antirevolutionary political party and the Free University of Amsterdam were founded to stand against it. But because all this was done in the Dutch language, it had no impact outside of Holland. Elsewhere, ripples of the Revolution, linked with the burgeoning egocentricity of the Romantic movement in literature and the arts, carried intellectuals on both sides of the Atlantic over the watershed, thus preparing the ground for critical biblical scholarship and theological liberalism. This turn away from external authority led straight to the post-theistic perspective of Nietzsche, though few traveled so far or so disruptively. Many Protestant leaders remained largely unaware that the real roots of Christianity—namely, belief in the Trinity, the incarnation, salvation in Christ, and the supernaturalness of the church—were being replaced by the idea that those who adhered to the church system and kept up religious appearances were still free to believe or disbelieve as their personal judgment might suggest. This liberal mindset undercuts catechesis completely, for catechesis assumes the existence of authoritative truth that needs to be taught. Liberalism, in the church as in today's wider culture, says there is no such thing. At best, therefore, catechesis will only be a minority interest among conservative Christians—Protestant, Catholic, and Eastern Orthodox—one which many are likely to deride both in and outside official church structures.

The second inhibiting factor, a corollary of the first, is *resistance to authoritative instruction* within the Christian community. This is particularly apparent in Western Anglicanism. For three and a half centuries, partly out of reaction against the highly catechetical character of Puritanism and partly in the belief that liturgical conformity is what really matters, the assumption has held sway that, once confirmed, congregants need to learn no more for the rest of their Christian lives. But similar resistance breaks surface in other circles too. In children's and youth work across the board, today's agenda is learning Bible stories rather than being grounded in truths about the Triune God.

In group Bible studies generally, participants are led to look directly for personal devotional applications without first contemplating the writers' points about the greatness, goals, methods, and mystery of God. In putting together Christian books and magazines for popular reading and in composing, preaching, hearing, and thinking about sermons, the story is the same: it is assumed that our reaction to realities is more significant than any of the realities to which we react. Thus we learn to cultivate a mode of piety that rests upon a smudgy, deficient, and sometimes misleading conception of who and what the God we serve really is. Brought up on this, we now reflect the subjectivist turn of the Western thought-world of more than a century ago: personal guesses and fantasies about God replace the church's dogma as our authority, a hermeneutic of habitual distrust and suspicion of dogma establishes itself, and dogma becomes a dirty word, loaded with overtones of obscurantism, tunnel vision, unreality, superstition, and mental enslavement.

It would be quite unrealistic to expect a welcome for catechesis within such a context. We must expect to have to fight for a hearing in order to say what is on our hearts. It is countercultural not only in secular terms, but in church terms also. And so we expect to have a struggle on our hands, even with some whom we might otherwise count as friends.

A final factor inhibiting catechesis emerges here: *preoccupation*. In most evangelical churches, the Sunday and weekly programs are already as full as can reasonably be managed. To make room for catechesis, some familiar elements of church life will have to be pushed into the background, if not, indeed, terminated. Otherwise the good will be found blocking out the best. That resentment and resistance will result when such a rearrangement is attempted is, unhappily, a foregone conclusion.

Our book, therefore, must and will combine exposition with advocacy. Nothing we say will be meant, nor must be read as, negative criticism of faithful evangelical pastoral ministry that is already going on. Our sole purpose is to see the good made better, under God and for his glory. We ask our readers to bear this in mind, and to focus simply on weighing what we have to say by the scriptural standard.

Foundations

Underlying our argument, first to last, is a particular view of human nature, and how God shapes it for himself. This view, though largely overshadowed in today's church, not to mention today's world, has a long history; we find it in C. S. Lewis, Calvin, Thomas Aquinas, Augustine, Irenaeus, both Testaments of our Bibles, and most fully and explicitly in the teaching of Paul and John—Paul especially. It has in fact been the mainstream Christian view throughout. In thumbnail-sketch form, it is as follows:

Human Nature and God

Created by God through human agency, each human individual is a psychophysical entity, an embodied soul or (one could say) an ensouled body. Intellectually, emotionally, and volitionally, actively and reactively, we are self-conscious units who live in and through our physical bodies—bodies that grow, mature, wear out, and finally cease functioning altogether. While they function, they sustain and condition our conscious life, but not always in the best way. Our physical makeup can cause problems—sometimes very acute problems. Instinctively we know that controlling and directing our bodies in our interactions with people and things so that we achieve goals and avoid disasters is the path of fulfillment. We act accordingly, though in important ways our bodies are always somewhat beyond our control. With resurrection bodies in glory we may expect our experience of "body management" to be different, but here on earth this is how it is.

Human life is a matter of consciously acting to fulfill decisions made in obedience to desires and determinations that are fueled partly by a sense of obligation, partly by a prospect of pleasure and satisfaction and avoidance of trouble, and partly by a sense of need. Some of these latter desires are triggered by felt physical and personal needs for relief of some kind, and others by pressures arising from circumstances and possibilities imaginatively envisaged. But all our desires stem from the central core of selfhood within the soul, which Scripture speaks of as the *heart*, and all come with a moral quality which that power of the mind that we call *conscience* discerns, approvingly or disapprovingly as the case may be.

All truth, that is, all our knowledge of reality at every level, enters our heart through our mind, as our minds receive and process the products of different modes of awareness of various sorts of things—animate and inanimate, good and bad, beautiful and ugly. This is how we come by such knowledge as we have of our own selves, other selves, and God. In the case of God, it is through the impact of his works in creation, providence, and grace, plus the input of his Word, made effective to us by his Spirit, that we come to know what we do in fact know of his reality (which knowledge, though much in itself, is, we may be sure, not much in relation to all that he is and knows himself to be in himself). All the knowledge of God we have is given to us by God, and has as its purpose our responsive obedience to him in worship and work. Then, as we give God pleasure by obeying his will revealed to us and by matching our works and ways to his as our sovereign Creator, royal Covenanter, and universal Companion, we bear his image and display his likeness. Thus, at least, it was meant to be; but this, unhappily, is not what actually goes on.

Human Sin and Divine Grace

Human life, as we live it ourselves and observe it in others, is tragically far from what it was meant to be. It is distorted, disfigured, marked by disaffection to God and inner disintegration of our various personal powers. God made us all for fellowship with himself in love, worship, and service, but a perverting force, which Scripture labels *sin*, now controls us, and has so twisted our hearts that self-service (egocentricity) rather than God's service (God-centeredness) is all that is natural to us now. Total unawareness of God is impossible—God sees to that!—but the pride and self-will, envy and greed, that now rule in our hearts go far to blanket this awareness, or alternatively to falsify it beyond recognition. Irreligious self-assertion and idolatrous religiosity both result from damage done by sin to our hearts and minds.

Regarding religiosity: we need to realize that pride and self-will are compatible with a great deal of meticulous religious observance (witness the Pharisees of Jesus's day). What they are not compatible with is the humility of conscious worthlessness and amazement at discovering that God lavishes love on so unworthy a person as oneself. In all the world's major religions apart from Christianity, and among many on the fringes of the Christian churches, such observances are assumed to commend us to whatever divine being or beings there may be, and to secure for us a right to, and a place in, the divine favor. This self-deception, a regular by-product of our pride, constantly confirms an inner confidence that winning our way into God's good graces is a real possibility. From this flows a complacent stubbornness that makes people all over the world very slow to surrender this assumption. Christianity, however, is unique in insisting that God's favor toward humanity is already forfeit, that it cannot now be earned or secured by any action on our part, and that we have only condemnation and final rejection to look forward to. Nevertheless, Christianity continues, God receives lost sinners into his favor, pardons, adopts, and literally remakes them, through the grace and mercy that are mediated via Jesus Christ the Lord, God's incarnated, crucified, risen, reigning, returning Son.

Paradoxical? Certainly, yet true. Fantastic? Certainly, yet factual. Beyond comprehension? Certainly, yet real nonetheless. We confront here the mind-blowing, heart-stirring wonder of the redeeming love of God, that which makes the Gospel genuinely and uniquely good news.

Let us be clear on this. Christianity is not in essence a moral code or an ascetic routine, as so many down the centuries have mistakenly supposed. Rather, it is a supernaturalizing personal relationship with a supernatural personal Savior. Christianity centers upon Jesus Christ the Lord who, today and every day through the Holy Spirit, confronts everyone to whom the Gospel comes, summoning us to recognize and respond to him. He calls on us, not just to acknowledge his reality and the salient facts about him, but to exercise *faith* in him—that is, on the basis of the facts, to *trust* him—for the forgiveness of our sins; to *repent*—that is, to leave behind our present natural life of sin-driven bondage, and enter a new life of Christ-led freedom; and to become *disciples*—persons, that is, who conscientiously, as our life project, walk with him, learn from him, worship him and the Father through him, and maintain obedience to him, conforming ourselves to his recorded attitudes and example up to the limit of the Holy Spirit's enabling.

It is the Holy Spirit, the third person of the Godhead residing in each believer's inner being, who, having invisibly but effectively united believers to Christ, now sustains them in that union, working in them the motivation and compassion of Christ, and mediating to and through them the power of his risen life. He illuminates their minds to understand Christ's teaching, and biblical teaching generally, to see how it applies to them personally, and to envisage and pray for Christian advance. He reshapes their outlook, habits, and character by energizing their efforts at faithful obedience across the board.

Every Christian thus becomes a work in progress, a lifelong reconstruction site, with the Holy Spirit as architect and craftsman at every point, first to last.

Following the Bible, we call the Spirit's engendering of faith, repentance, and the commitment to discipleship *regeneration* or *new birth* (John 3:1–8; Titus 3:5; 1 Peter 1:22–23; 1 John 2:29; 3:9; 5:1, 18), and we speak of the consequent whole-souled pursuit of holiness and righteousness as *sanctification, growth in grace*, and *glorification begun* (Rom. 8:30; 2 Cor. 3:18; 1 Thess. 5:23; 2 Peter 3:18).

Christian Discipleship and Teaching

Teaching is a universal human activity, found in families, schools, all forms of task-oriented communities, and among friends and colleagues in every mode of society. It consists of transmitting knowledge and skills. Biblical religion required teaching from the start and in every new generation; priests, Levites, and parents were solemnly charged to do this, and in Jesus's day this was the life's work of the scribes. Jesus himself was a teacher par excellence, and when he gave his marching orders to his first disciples before withdrawing from this world he specified that a teaching ministry corresponding to his own must go on. Go, he said, "and make disciples of all nations, baptizing them in the name of the Father and of the Son and of the Holy Spirit, teaching them to observe all that I have commanded you" (Matt. 28:19–20). We speak of this, rightly, as Christ's Great Commission to his church. God's children are called and charged to be people who, having themselves learned, now reach out to teach what they have learned.

It is apparent that the Christian pioneers took the terms of Jesus's commission very seriously, for there is a kind of drumbeat with regard to teaching that resonates throughout the New Testament. Teaching, not just for the correcting of current errors (though there was much of that to be done), but for the maturing of the faithful in themselves, was at the heart of their church life. The mindset involved is shown by Paul's words to Timothy: "What you have heard from me [as your teacher] in the presence of many witnesses commit to faithful men who will be able to teach others also" (2 Tim. 2:2). The church is to be a learning-and-teaching fellowship in which the passing on of what we learn becomes a regular part of the service we render to each other. Surely this is a realization that today's churches urgently need to recover.

A teacher, of course, is a person from whom others do in fact learn. Real teaching, whether at home, at school, in the pulpit, or wherever, will engage attention, strike sparks in the mind, and evoke some kind of interactive response. Where this does not happen, the correct verdict is that one has tried to teach but has not succeeded, thus verifying the schoolteacher's time-honored tag: "no *im*pression without *ex*pression." While teaching comes naturally and instinctively to some, it is an art that can be mastered to a degree by anyone who can think and speak clearly about things and is concerned to get them across. Paul sees teaching as a spiritual gift (that is, a capacity to serve Christ by some form of Christian expression; see Rom. 12:7), but that does not mean that there is no need to stir up, develop, and hone the skill by reflection, preparation, practice, and submission to competent assessment. The reverse is true, and it is only pride and stubbornness that will make improvement here impossible. Many, if not most of us, can learn to teach adequately, at least in an informal setting, if that is what we really desire to do.

Building Believers

This phrase appears in our subtitle, and before we plunge into our argument we would like to comment on its meaning and fittingness as an expression of our goal.

The Greek *oikodomē* and its cognate verb *oikodomeō*, which in the New Testament signify spiritual maturing and consolidation, have given rise to the English phrases "build up," "built up," and "building up," which are regularly used in pastoral contexts as variants for "edify" and "edification." ("Built up" as a rendering of *oikodomeō* is found in 1 Peter 2:5 KJV.) They are words taken from the building trade and used metaphorically to denote the desired outcome of pastoral care and the pastoral process. In identifying with this desire, we would observe that the little adverb "up" in these renderings tends to mislead. It seems to suggest that the goal of the pastoral process, of which catechesis is part, is to produce some form of height, distinction, or dignity. But the true associations of the word lie elsewhere, in ideas of sound workmanship, thoroughness of construction, solidity, stability, and utility with no weak spots, defects, or malfunctions that might reduce the building's quality. It is important to see this.

Not too long ago, during a building boom, a couple purchased one of a pair of houses that were virtually identical in design and were to be put up side by side on a vacant lot. The wife visited the site most days and watched the house go up. The result was a structure the housing inspector described as remarkably well built, and it has proved trouble free ever since. Leaks and cracks in the house next door, however, have revealed shoddy workmanship. The effects of faulty assembly can be long term. And so can the consequences of deficient discipling, which is our point here.

Superficial smatterings of truth, blurry notions about God and godliness, and thoughtlessness about the issues of living—careerwise, communitywise, familywise, and churchwise—are all too often the marks of evangelical congregations today, particularly, if we may dare to say it, some newly planted ones. (We pick on evangelical groupings because we ourselves belong to them, and thus know something about them from the inside. We do not imply that other brands of contemporary Christianity are free from the same faults.) We think that as long as catechesis, which was the strength of Christian nurture in the past, continues to be out of fashion, these shortcomings are not likely to disappear. As we contemplate today's complex concerns, hopes, dreams, and ventures of Christian renewal, discipleship impresses us as the key present-day issue, and catechesis as the key present-day element of discipleship, all the world over. The Christian faith must be both well and wisely *taught* and well and truly *learned*! A far-reaching change of mindset about this is called for, without which such well-worn dictums as "American Christianity is three thousand miles wide and half an inch deep" will continue, sadly, to be verified. Recovery of the educational-devotional discipline that we are advocating cannot, to our mind, come a moment too soon.

Agenda

It is our belief that in today's congregations there is a need to give the same sort of training to a new generation of catechists that we now give to Bible study group leaders and Sunday school teachers. Catechists are teachers whose special task is to ground worshipers of every age in the truths Christians live by and in the ways Christians are to live by those truths. Why is this necessary? Because all congregants, adults no less than the young, need a full initial grounding in these things, followed by regular revisiting and deepened exploration of them. As we regularly revisit books of the Bible we have gone through before and find new wisdom and relevance in them because of the new experiences that we bring to the study, so it is with truths about God, his ways, and his goals. This is the basic territory of discipleship. In most evangelical churches today the need for lifelong Bible study, the value of Bible study groups for everyone, the beneficial ways good books can augment one's experiences, and the necessity of expository preaching are pretty well established. But the attention to the comparable value of catechesis—truth-in-life study, as we may fairly call it—is not appreciated; indeed, attention to doctrine is sometimes actually avoided, lest it induce contention and coldheartedness and thereby diminish devotional ardor.

Here is our starting point. In the following chapters we shall seek to correct this imbalance, showing catechesis to be complementary to, and of no less value than, Bible study, expository preaching, and other formational ministries, and urging upon our readers that congregational strategy must find room for this biblically based and historically affirmed ministry if full spiritual health among the faithful is to be advanced. And we shall offer suggestions for implementing this insight.

Concerning the Collaboration

A Few Words from J.I.

From my standpoint, there is little to say about the providential way in which Gary and I teamed up to become joint authors of this book. As so often with God's special providences, the sense of God's preplanning and preparation of us both for the task has been very strong. Though Gary had been a student of mine shortly after I came to Canada, I had lost touch with him since he finished at Regent. I had no idea that he now held an academic doctorate and a professorship in educational ministries, had become an international lecturer and author (add into the bargain that he is a hymn-writer also), and was planning his own book on catechesis, a good deal of which was already drafted. It only took us a few minutes to decide—or perhaps I should say discover—that we were heaven-sent colleagues for birthing the present volume, with materials in hand that were complementary for the purpose. By vigorous and wonderfully harmonious to-ing and fro-ing we completed the book in a very few months, and I think we are both happy with it; I know I am. We have plans for more, but this is not the place to reveal them.

A Few Words from Gary

It is truly a great joy and privilege to have been able to partner with J.I. on this project. I was one of his students at Regent College during the early 1980s. Soon after I joined the faculty of Gordon-Conwell Theological Seminary, J.I. spoke at our school and I was able to renew acquaintance with him. On several occasions over the past decade or so I have sought his counsel about how to advance the cause of catechesis. My passion for this critical ministry developed primarily as a result of my studies under J.I. and by reflecting on his own ministry as a catechist, a ministry that he modeled both in the classroom and in so much of his writing through the decades.

In the fall of 2006, Beeson Divinity School hosted a conference in honor of J.I.'s eightieth birthday. The conference was entitled "J. I. Packer and the Evangelical Future."[1] I had written a hymn of thanksgiving to God for J.I.'s ministry, and Timothy George kindly invited me to join the conference for the hymn's "debut."[2] Just before the hymn was sung, J.I. had the opportunity to respond to all the conference presenters and to offer his own thinking about "the evangelical future." His response was, it seemed clear to me, a clarion call to catechize. J.I. mentioned that he had long wanted to do some writing in this area, but that he would really need a partner to pull it off. No sooner had the conference been formally closed than I approached my beloved former professor to express my eagerness to be that partner. Perhaps a month later, I had occasion to visit with Bob Hosack, acquisitions editor for Baker Books, and I asked him if he would be interested in receiving a proposal for such a project. He immediately said that he would be. Thus the wheels were set in motion for the book that is now in your hands. We are very thankful to Bob, as well as to our project editor, Robert Hand, and to all the others at Baker Books for their kind support of this project.

A portion of my contributions to this current book, especially in chapters 5 and 6, represents an expansion of ideas that I have presented in another recent project: *Teaching the Faith, Forming the Faithful*, which I coauthored with my Gordon-Conwell colleague and dear friend, Steve Kang.[3] That book surveys a larger umbrella of formative and educational ministries, one of which is catechesis—*the entire focus* of the present volume. Words cannot adequately express my gratitude to J.I. for his willingness to have me partner with him in the task of promoting a recovery of so vital a ministry.

A Final Word of Warning

The reader will soon discover that both of us have a fondness for what J.I. has sometimes called "apt alliteration" or "artful alliteration." There are plenty examples of such in this book, along with other aids for memory and organization—hymns, acrostics, acronyms, and so on. Some may think we have gone a bit over the top with such devices, but our defense is simple: these have always been among the tools employed by catechists. And since we are both catechists at heart, we really can't seem to help ourselves! (Nor have we any desire to do so.)

Building Believers the Old-Fashioned Way

Thus says the LORD: "Stand by the roads, and look, and
 ask for the ancient paths,
where the good way is; and walk in it,
 and find rest for your souls."
But they said, "We will not walk in it."

Jeremiah 6:16

Some years ago, flying home from a conference of church educators, I (Gary) found myself engaged in a lively conversation with the affable gentleman seated next to me on the plane. Learning that I was a professor of Christian education, he began to tell me of his own religious journey. He had been raised nominally Catholic and had married a woman who was a nominal Jew. It all worked fine, he explained, until the couple had children. At some point, his wife said to him, "You know, we really should choose a religion for the sake of our children." And so, "I told her, 'I could change.'" (Apparently, his commitment to Catholicism was not very deep.) I was especially struck by what he told me next. In order for him to become Jewish, he explained, he had to meet weekly with the local rabbi over a period of many months. The rabbi guided him toward familiarity with the basics of Jewish practices and beliefs. Only after receiving this instruction, and after experiencing a *mikvah*—a ritual immersion to solemnize his conversion—was he received into the community as a Jew.

This story reminded me of my sister's story. She, like me, had been raised a nominal Protestant and had married a nominal Roman Catholic. They too were fine with this arrangement until children came. In this case, it was my sister who agreed to change. Once again, this adult conversion could not occur without systematic instruction. My sister was instructed by the local priest for several months. Then, in a rite of initiation, she was received into the Catholic church.[1]

Compare such stories to what happens in many evangelical churches today. How might we greet a visitor at the doors of one of our own churches? If we noticed the newcomer at all, we might bid her welcome, hand her a bulletin, and point her to a seat. If she visited the church a second or third time, some well-intentioned member of the church might be found already trying to persuade this new "member" to become a Sunday school teacher. But the recruiter might find himself competing with the choir director (or praise team leader), or the manager of some other understaffed ministry in the church who had also spied the candidate. What is unlikely to occur is that anyone would make serious inquiry into the newcomer's own spiritual condition, or offer her a carefully conceived opportunity to be instructed in the Christian faith.

In some churches, of course, a plan may well be in place to introduce "seekers" to the Christian faith. Programs such as Alpha and Christianity Explored are proving very helpful in this regard.[2] But an interesting phenomenon is occurring in many places where these ministries are undertaken. These evangelistic ministry efforts are attracting large numbers of church members as well as inquirers. It seems that many who already count as believers are hungry—famished, really—for a rudimentary knowledge of the faith. Have they never been taught Christian beliefs in a serious way? Seemingly not.

Historic Practices of Disciple Making

Historically, the church's ministry of grounding new believers in the rudiments of Christianity has been known as *catechesis*. It is a ministry that has waxed and waned through the centuries. It flourished between the second and fifth centuries in the ancient church. Those who became Christians often moved into the faith from radically different backgrounds and worldviews. The churches rightly took such conversions very seriously and sought to ensure that these life-revolutions were processed carefully, prayerfully, and intentionally, with thorough understanding at each stage.

With the tightening of the alignment between church and state in the West, combined with the impact of the Dark Ages, the ministry of catechesis floundered in large measure for much of the next millenium.[3] The line between natural and spiritual birth virtually disappeared. According to the centuries-old practice, infants baptized into the church were, in theory, to be catechized later in the faith. But too often nothing of the sort occurred. As a consequence of such neglect, great numbers of persons who claimed to belong to Christ had very little idea of what that might even mean.

The Reformers, led by heavyweights Luther and Calvin, sought with great resolve to reverse matters. Luther restored the office of catechist to the churches. And seizing upon the providential invention of the printing press just decades before their time, Luther, Calvin, and others made every effort to print and distribute catechisms—small handbooks to instruct children and "the simple" in the essentials of Christian belief, prayer, worship, and behavior.[4] Catechisms of greater depth were produced for Christian adults and leaders. Furthermore, entire congregations were instructed through unapologetically catechetical preaching, regular catechizing of children in Sunday worship, and, in many cases, through the renewed practice of congregational singing of psalms and hymns.

The conviction of the Reformers that such catechetical work must be primary is unmistakable. John Calvin, writing in 1548 to the Lord Protector of England, declared, "Believe me, Monseigneur, the Church of God will never be preserved without catechesis."[5] The church of Rome, responding to the growing influence of the Protestant catechisms, soon began to produce its own. The rigorous work of nurturing believers and converts in the faith once for all delivered to the saints, a didactic discipline largely lost for most of the previous millennium, had become normative again for both Catholics and Protestants.

It could well be argued that the spirit and power of healthy catechesis was hampered by the hostile tone that entered the picture as Protestants and Catholics began increasingly using their catechisms to hurl attacks at one another. Nevertheless, this rebirth of serious catechetical discipling was a momentous step forward for all concerned.

The critical role of catechesis in sustaining the church continued to be apparent to subsequent evangelical trailblazers of the English-speaking world. Richard Baxter, John Owen, Charles Spurgeon, and countless other pastors and leaders saw catechesis as one of their most obvious and basic pastoral duties. If they could not wholeheartedly embrace and utilize an existing catechism for such instruction, they would adapt or edit one or would simply write their own. A pastor's chief task, it was widely understood, was to be the teacher of the flock.[6]

Recent Departures from Catechesis

Today, however, things are quite different, and that for a host of reasons. The church in the West has largely abandoned serious catechesis as a normative practice. Among the more surprising of the factors that have contributed to this decline are the unintended consequences of the great Sunday school movement. This lay-driven phenomenon swept across North America in the 1800s and came to dominate educational efforts in most evangelical churches through the twentieth century. It effectively replaced pastor-catechists with relatively untrained lay workers and substituted an instilling of familiarity (or shall we say, perhaps, *over*familiarity) with Bible stories for any form of grounding in the basic beliefs, practices, and ethics of the faith.[7]

Thus for most contemporary evangelicals the entire idea of catechesis is largely an alien concept. The very word itself—*catechesis*, or any of its associated terms, including *catechism*—is greeted with suspicion by most evangelicals today. ("Wait, isn't that a Roman Catholic thing?") Ironically, as noted above, it was the Reformers who impelled the church of Rome to once again take catechesis seriously. In recent decades, while the Catholic church has renewed its catechetical labors with vigor, most evangelicals have not likewise returned to their own catechetical roots.[8] (Where Roman Catholics once learned from the evangelicals, it now appears that it is we evangelical Protestants who have much to learn from them.)

In offering this book we hope to contribute to a much-needed evangelical course correction in these matters. We are persuaded that Calvin had it right and that we are already seeing the sad, even tragic, consequences of allowing the church to continue *uncatechized* in any significant sense. We are persuaded, further, that something can and must be done to help the Protestant churches steer a wiser course. The part we hope to play with this particular project is that of making the case for a recovery of significant catechesis as a nonnegotiable practice in specifically evangelical churches.

What we are after, to put it otherwise, is to encourage our fellow evangelicals to seriously consider the wisdom of building believers the old-fashioned way. Many contemporary evangelicals profess a predilection for being on the "cutting edge" of our cultural surroundings. We frequently look for new or novel ways to do things. We long to be relevant. We're ready to change course on a dime in order to "meet people's needs." What we've been doing hasn't worked, we reason. Therefore everything must change. The old models and programs have not produced the anticipated results, we discover. So we commit to new models and new programs that "the best research" suggests might get the job done. Or we look at what other "successful" churches are doing and convince ourselves that imitating them offers the best prospect for success.

Looking Backward to Move Forward

While the intentions that drive such attitudes are understandable, it manifests a lack of wisdom on our part when we are guided primarily by such thinking.

The fact is, we tire ourselves out by constantly striving to reinvent the wheel. Is the current state of discipleship lamentable? It may well be so in many of our churches. But rather than looking for the latest technique, program, marketing scheme, or impressive model, we would do well to stop, take some deep breaths, and carefully reconsider our course. God's words uttered through the prophet Jeremiah many centuries ago seem apt for us today:

> Thus says the LORD: "Stand by the roads, and look, and ask for the ancient paths,
> where the good way is; and walk in it,
> and find rest for your souls."
> But they said, "We will not walk in it."

Jeremiah 6:16

We agree with the widespread conviction that many evangelical churches are in need of deep change today. Indeed, the fact that we share this conviction will be very obvious throughout this book. Our premise, however, is that the surest way forward is to carefully contemplate the wisdom of our past. We are not, as it turns out, the first ones who have ever had to wrestle with the issue of how to grow Christian communities and Christian individuals in contrary cultures. We are not the first to wonder about how to nurture faith in the living God and foster obedience to his way. It is not only contemporary church leaders who can teach us how to be "relevant" and "effective" in ministry today. We urge concerned church leaders to, in the language of Jeremiah 6:16, "stand by the roads, and look, and ask for the ancient paths, where the good way is; and walk in it."

In the Scriptures of the Old and New Testaments we find an abundance of wisdom for building believers who will live to the glory and honor of our God. There are models and mandates, principles and practices that are as relevant for ministry today as they ever were. Church history also provides us with numerous examples of vibrant, fruitful seasons in the lives of God's people, when true disciples were truly being made, when whole communities were alive with and for God's glory. We do not disdain the idea of looking around at contemporary models to find guidance for our own ministries of disciple making. But we do suggest that this not be our only source for wisdom, or even our primary source. Instead, we would counsel, let us look *back* before looking *around*. Our first gaze, of course, must be to the testimony of the Scriptures themselves. Whether we are considering historic practices or contemporary ones, as professed evangelical Christians all our thinking and efforts should be vetted by diligent study of, and contemplation upon, the Bible.

From this biblical basis, how shall we best proceed? Perhaps we could apply a version of C. S. Lewis's familiar counsel. Lewis argued that for every book we read by an author who is still living, we should read one by an author who has died. Or, if that is too much for us, then for every three books we read by living authors, we should read one by a dead author.[9] Our counsel here is that for every new method we meet that purports to promote congregational health today we look back to the well-tried methods that promoted congregational health in the past. Such an approach will serve us well in many areas, but perhaps none so important as that of making disciples for Jesus Christ. There is so much wisdom for us in the practices of those who have gone before us if we will only humble ourselves to listen and learn. Sadly, too many evangelicals are like the people of Judah to whom Jeremiah spoke. We hear the counsel to look to the old paths and walk in the good way. But, convinced that newer ideas are always better than those of the ancient and good way, we stubbornly resolve (as we read at the end of Jer. 6:16), "We will not walk in it."

Signs of Return and Renewal

Happily, however, many young believers are beginning to recognize that newer does not always mean better. In what may well be a function of the so-called "postmodern turn," it seems that some are now rejecting the modernist myths about inevitable progress. In the broader culture, examples of such thinking are readily apparent. Many new automobiles, though employing the very latest technology, are specifically designed to look like older, "classic" models. Baseball stadiums that were symbolic of the modernist "functionality" (Shea Stadium in New York, the Kingdome in Seattle, the Astrodome in Houston, Riverfront Stadium in Cincinnati) have been torn down or imploded and replaced with high-tech and high-comfort facilities that are self-conscious evocations of the old-time, classic ballparks.

Perhaps it is not surprising, then, that there is a movement afoot among younger evangelicals to re-embrace ancient paths from Judeo-Christian faith traditions. This trend has many and varied manifestations. It can be seen in the sometimes random eclecticism of the so-called emerging churches. It can be seen with a more thoughtful and sustained apologetic and rationale in the "Ancient-Future" vision of Christianity Robert Webber championed in his prolific writing and teaching ministry. Evangelical publishers have developed series of books dedicated to *ressourcement* based upon ancient practices of the church. Many individual congregations are finding their own ways "backward" (if we may put it like this), newly embracing the historic Christian calendar, moving toward more regular celebration of the Lord's Supper, rediscovering historic hymns, and so on. Some believers have apparently concluded, with justification, that modernism—with its insatiable appetite for what appears newer, bigger, better—has effectively robbed us of many great treasures from our own Christian history. And so they are starting to look back with a mix of curiosity and longing.

We applaud much of this trend, though we would offer one cautionary remark. Some of this latching on to ancient practices is ad hoc in nature, and not sufficiently grounded in theological understanding or rationale. Just as it is unwise to take up new practices just for the sake of being different, so it is unwise to simply take up old practices because, though old, they have an appeal of novelty to us. We need to understand the contexts—historical, cultural, and theological—within which they arose so that we may properly assess their suitability for use today. Above all, as we have already said, we need to test those practices against the teaching of the Scriptures.

Sadly, the recommended habit of looking back has not yet led many evangelicals toward a reassessment of the practice of catechesis. It remains, for most, a hidden treasure. But a rediscovery of this particular treasure has the potential for a double blessing. It is a practice that, in its own right, will prove to be of great benefit to the church. And, what is more, because of its concern with grounding believers in the essentials of the Christian faith, it will also serve to make us wiser and more discerning about other practices we may encounter in our journeys backward.

What Is Catechesis?

Before we offer definitions or descriptions of catechesis, let us consider the term itself, as well as a number of related terms. Catechesis derives from a New Testament word for teaching—the Greek verb *katēcheō*. The primary definitions of this term are "to share a communication that one receives" and "to teach, instruct." Its overtones point to the weight and solemnity of the instruction being given. In classical usage, the term was used of poets addressing their hearers from a stage.[10] In the New Testament, *katēcheō* is one of a number of words referring to the giving of teaching or instruction. In chapter 2, we look at its usage in the New Testament, along with other biblical terms that have implications for the ministry we now refer to as catechesis.

At this point, we simply note that the word *catechesis* is biblical in origin. By the second century of the church, from that same Greek root a range of terms had arisen to describe various aspects of this vital ministry of teaching and formation that was becoming increasingly central to the life of the Christian community. These terms include:

- *catechesis*—a "catchall" word for this particular form of ministry; sometimes used to refer specifically to the *process*
- *catechize*—a verb referring to the *process* of teaching in this particular manner
- *catechism*—sometimes a designation for the actual *content* in which persons are catechized; often used today to refer to content in some

particular printed format; sometimes, another "catchall" word for this form of ministry

- *catechist*—the teacher; the one who catechizes others
- *catechumen*—the learner; the one being catechized
- *catechumenate*—the sometimes formal, sometimes not-so-formal school of the faith that emerged in many churches to prepare new believers for their baptism and for full participation in the church's life
- *catechetical*—an adjective with many possible applications; one use is in regard to the "catechetical schools" for Christian higher learning established in some cities, such as Alexandria, in the second and third centuries
- *catechetics*—the study of the art and science of catechesis (as *homiletics* refers to the study of preaching, and as *liturgics* refers to the study of worship)

Numerous definitions of Christian catechesis have been offered over the many centuries of its practice. Before proposing our own for consideration, we present a brief sampling of other definitions and/or descriptions of this vital ministry that we have found helpful. That catechesis is really a comprehensive and complex ministry becomes evident when surveying the breadth and variety of these suggestions. Catechesis is:

- "The brief and elementary instruction which is given by word of mouth in relation to the rudiments of any particular doctrine . . . as used by the church, it signifies a system of instruction relating to the first principles of the Christian religion, designed for the ignorant and unlearned."[11]
- "The process by which persons are initiated into the Christian community and its faith, revelation, and vocation; the process by which persons throughout their lifetimes are continually converted and nurtured, transformed and formed, by and in its living tradition."[12]
- "The shaping of religious emotions and affections in the context of teaching doctrine."[13]
- "Our coming to know who and whose we are. . . . our learning to be followers of the Incarnated One. . . ."[14]
- "The essential ministry of the Church through which the teachings of Christ have been passed on to believers throughout the ages."[15]
- "The totality of the Church's efforts to make disciples, to help men believe that Jesus is the Son of God so that believing they might have life in his name, and to educate and instruct them in this life, thus building up the body of Christ."[16]

Most of the authors we have cited above actually use multiple descriptions of catechesis in their works on the subject. Indeed, it is very difficult to find one definition of catechesis that fully captures all that catechesis can and should be. But, in order to have a simple and concise place from which to begin our deliberations in this book, we suggest the following: *Catechesis is the church's ministry of grounding and growing God's people in the Gospel and its implications for doctrine, devotion, duty, and delight.*

Throughout this book, we will be considering this definition and building upon it, adding nuances and offering variations as we go. We will discover that catechesis is sometimes thought of in very narrow terms (primarily concerned with preparing new believers for baptism or confirmation) and sometimes in much broader terms (as the neverending ministry of nurturing believers in the faith). We will also discover that many have argued for the value of a pre-Christian catechizing of those who are intrigued by the call of the Gospel but are not quite prepared to heed it. All this leaves us with at least three distinctions in categorizing catechetical ministry, as follows:

- *Procatechesis* (or *protocatechesis*): This refers to catechizing those whom many contemporary church leaders would call "seekers" and whom the ancients might have called "inquirers."
- *Catechesis proper:* This refers to the formal catechetical work of preparing children or adult converts for baptism or confirmation—that is, for their full inclusion in the life of the church.
- *Ongoing catechesis:* This refers to the ministry of teaching and formation that really is neverending as believers are continually nurtured in the way of the Lord.

An Overview of Our Explorations

We will be considering all these aspects of catechesis and more throughout the chapters of this book. For now, we would simply drop the following hints about the assertions we will be making as we proceed:

- *Catechesis is a thoroughly biblical idea and practice,* and we (that is, the evangelical movement as a whole) have strayed grievously from the mandates and models of Scripture in this regard. (The focus of chapter 2.)
- *The practice of rigorous catechesis has proven to be essential and effective* at numerous critical junctures in the life of the church, and there is much to be learned from this history for ministry in contemporary contexts today. (The focus of chapter 3.)
- *Many forces have conspired to distract most of today's evangelicals from the biblical business of catechizing,* and there are significant consequences

that have resulted from our failures in regard to this ministry. (Discussed in the Introduction and further in chapter 3.)

- *Happily, there are a number of contemporary efforts under way to renew catechetical ministries.* These are worthy of our serious observation and, in some cases, emulation. (As noted, especially, in chapter 7.)

- *Catechesis involves instruction that is both ancient and essential.* It focuses on the primary doctrines of "the faith that was once for all delivered to the saints" (Jude 3), and especially upon the glorious Gospel of the blessed God. Thus it aims to celebrate and preserve the unity of the church. (A focus of chapters 4 through 6; also of chapter 8.)

- *Catechesis involves instruction that is holistic.* It touches the entire person (and the entire community)—head, heart, and hands; doctrine, experience, and practice. (An emphasis of chapters 9 and 10.)

- *Catechesis involves instruction that is highly relational and interactive.* It is a ministry *of the church* and must be carried on in the context of the community of faith. (Another emphasis of chapters 9 and 10.)

- *Catechesis involves instruction that is timely and culturally relevant.* This ancient faith must always be presented vis-à-vis those alternative claims regarding truth, worldview, and lifestyle that dominate the age and culture in which the church lives. (A focus of chapter 8.)

- *Catechesis involves instruction that is foundational for faith development throughout one's life.* While catechesis is often associated (and rightly so) with grounding persons in the basics of the faith, it also envisions practices for ongoing learning upon and within those very foundations that have been laid. (An emphasis of chapters 7 and 9.)

A Word about Words

The ministry of catechesis can, in fact, be meaningfully conducted without being labeled "catechesis." The word itself is, as we have seen, derived from a biblical verb (we will argue further in the next chapter that the concept itself is thoroughly biblical). Nevertheless, some evangelical churches may be hesitant about speaking of catechesis today, lest it should appear that they are being led by church tradition rather than Holy Scripture. Some churches are, for similar reasons, resistant to the use of creeds. We have likely all seen church bulletins or road signs outside church buildings proclaiming, "No creed but Christ; no law but love; no book but the Bible." Overlooking the obvious irony that such a statement, in fact, constitutes a rather concise and dogmatic creed in its own right, we should be sensitive to the cultural realities of various evangelical communities of faith. How, then, shall we best proceed?

On the one hand, we do well to avoid the "magic word syndrome," that is, the supposition that you cannot engage in a certain practice without parading the word itself as a label for what you are doing. When all is said and done, what matters most is that we are obedient to the mandates of God's Word. If haggling over the use of a particular term hinders our essential obedience from moving forward, then we should really count the cost before we engage in such fighting. In some contexts, insisting on retaining the *term* catechesis may actually prevent us from fulfilling the *task* of catechesis. If the term itself is to be such a stumbling block—because of personal or community-wide sensibilities—we really can manage quite well without it. We can simply call our task of grounding and growing believers in the faith by some other name: "faithful formation," "maturity teaching," "going for growth," the "Truth and Wisdom Project," or something similar.

On the other hand, reclaiming words carefully and patiently can be a powerful act of instruction all by itself. For example, many evangelical churches that recite the Apostles' Creed have altered "I believe . . . in the holy catholic Church" to read "*holy Christian Church*" or "*holy universal Church.*" Such a choice can easily be defended, of course, by appeal to cultural sensitivities and by a desire for clarity over confusion. But other evangelical churches have determined that the word *catholic* is a beautiful term that captures and communicates more than "universal" does, and something beyond what "Christian" does, in this context. They further recognize that this ancient word actually predates the distinctions between the Eastern and Western churches, or between Protestants and Roman Catholics. And so, with the help of sound and sustained teaching, they retain the term in their recitation of the Creed.

In the spirit of the latter approach, we have opted in this book to use the word *catechesis* rather than substitute something in its place. Our strategy is to *retain and explain*, rather than to *reject and replace*. Our rationale for our *retain and explain* strategy includes the following points:

1. As we have already demonstrated, *catechesis* is a biblically based term.
2. Retaining the term encourages us to connect with two thousand years of our own history as Christians—something we reckon to be both honest and wise.
3. Retaining the term encourages a properly ecumenical spirit, allowing us to build bridges to link ourselves up with other Christian communities that have retained this biblically based and historically affirmed language of the church's ministry of teaching and formation.
4. As we noted above, there is clear and mounting evidence of renewed interest in the ancient practices of the church, especially among younger evangelicals. Rather than turning people off, retaining and explaining

the language of catechesis will, we believe, actually be very attractive to many in and near our churches today.

5. Finally, it seems clear to us that the term *catechesis* embraces a wider range of meaning than any available alternatives.

We might use *instruction, teaching, nurture, formation,* or invoke some other related term. But each of these actually represents a piece of the ministry that is catechesis; no one of them captures the whole of it. The words *discipleship* and *discipling* might be as close as we could come to familiar terms that parallel the less familiar (to evangelicals) *catechesis*. But *discipleship* and *discipling* arguably are larger words that embrace the ministry of catechesis within a range of ministries that includes, for example, training in evangelism and missionary endeavor as well.

Although we are determined to thus *retain and explain* the word *catechesis*, we do not begrudge those who, for reasons they believe to be quite valid, choose the alternate strategy of *reject and replace*. Instead, we enthusiastically support and celebrate faithful efforts of catechesis wherever we see them, regardless of how those labors may be labeled.

In the chapters that follow, we turn our attention to a fuller exploration of this labor of love, this task of teaching, this very good work of grounding and growing, forming and fashioning the people of God.

2

Catechesis Is a (Very!) Biblical Idea

> One who is catechized must share all good things with the
> one who catechizes.
>
> Galatians 6:6 (a literal rendering)

It will doubtless surprise a good number of evangelical Protestants to hear
that catechesis is not only a biblical idea, but a very biblical idea. Many
of us—especially those of us who grew up in North American evangelical
cultures in recent times—rarely if ever heard the words *catechesis* or *cate-chism*. If we did hear them, it was likely to be from a Catholic school friend
who had to decline an invitation to play on a Saturday morning because, "I
have to go to catechism."

Beyond this association with Roman Catholicism, we may have found the
word in use among Lutherans or Episcopalians—groups often seen as outside
mainstream American evangelicalism. Within evangelical circles, conservative
Presbyterians and other Reformed believers probably represent the only major
groups that have regular acquaintance with the notion of catechesis, primarily
in the form of the Westminster Shorter and Heidelberg Catechisms. For most
of what we might call "garden variety" evangelicals, however, catechesis has,
up to now, been a largely foreign concept.

The fact is, however, that catechesis is an exceedingly biblical notion. We will attempt to demonstrate this in the present chapter by means of several lines of argument. First, we will look at Old Testament precursors to the sort of faith training that a rigorous catechesis envisions. Next, we will turn to several terms in the New Testament that point us toward catechesis. We will then survey possible New Testament examples of early catechetical ministry. Then we will consider the fact that some of the New Testament documents themselves appear to be examples of early catechetical writings. Finally, we will observe several passages that have the force of catechetical imperatives.

Old Testament Precursors to Catechesis

Catechesis, as we saw in chapter 1, should be understood as a ministry of rigorously grounding and growing believers in the Christian faith. This includes a comprehensive concern for our beliefs about God, our communion with God, and our obedience to God. We will be unpacking all of this further throughout the course of this book. For now, we simply assert that such determined attention to faith formation is a biblical constant that was established early on in the Old Testament. The New Testament takes this idea further and centers it on the person and work of Jesus Christ. But the concept of diligent teaching about our beliefs, our obedience, and our relationship with God was already in place many centuries before the time of Christ.

There are numerous Old Testament terms and passages that make all this very clear. In chapters 6 and 11 of Deuteronomy, the Israelites are commanded to instruct their children about God's redemptive deeds and holy commands. This instruction was declared to be especially important for the sake of younger generations who had not personally witnessed what God had done for Israel (e.g., Deut. 6:20; 11:2). God's ways were to be wholly embraced and his laws obeyed by the older generation, and then all of this was to be diligently passed on to the younger generations (Deut. 6:6–7; 11:18–19). The word rendered as "teach . . . diligently" in Deuteronomy 6:7 is the Hebrew verb *shanan*, of which the dictionary definition is "whet or sharpen," and which here suggests teaching in such a way as to make a deep impression upon the learner. Some versions (e.g., the NIV) begin verse 7 thus: "Impress [these commands] upon your children." How was such deeply impressive teaching to be done? It would need to be intentional, multisensory, and constant. The passage continues:

> You shall teach them diligently to your children, and shall talk about them when you sit in your house, and when you walk by the way, and when you lie down, and when you rise. You shall bind them as a sign on your hand, and they shall be as frontlets between your eyes. You shall write them on the doorposts of your house and on your gates. (Deut. 6:7–9)

The heart of the curriculum for the faith training of children, and indeed of all the Israelites, was the *torah*. This beautiful Hebrew term has typically been rendered into English as "law," but this is really an inadequate translation. While "law" captures the authority aspects of the term and concept, *torah* has broader connotations than our English "law." *Torah* comes from a Hebrew root that signifies "shooting" (as in shooting an arrow) or "casting" (as in casting lots). The true connotation of *torah* is more "direction" or "guidance" or "instruction" than mere legislation. In many Jewish translations of the Bible and in biblical commentaries, therefore, it is more typical to see the word rendered "instruction" or "guidance" rather than "law," and it is more common still to see the word simply left untranslated—as "the Torah of the LORD."

Torah certainly includes the commands of the LORD, but whereas the modern English speaker thinks of law as a binding and restrictive thing, the Hebrew Scriptures portray the *torah* as a divine gift that illumines God's path or way (*derek* in Hebrew). There is a path of the wicked that leads to destruction. But the way of the LORD leads to life and blessing. This is the path men and women and communities and nations have been created to walk in. How do we discern that path from among the manifold options presenting themselves to us? We discern God's *derek* by rejecting the counsel of the godless and, instead, by carefully and diligently meditating upon the LORD's *torah*. The first Psalm clearly makes the case:

> Blessed is the man
> > who walks not in the counsel of the wicked,
> nor stands in the way of sinners,
> > nor sits in the seat of scoffers;
> but his delight is in the *torah* of the LORD,
> > and on his *torah* he meditates day and night.
>
> He is like a tree
> > planted by streams of water
> that yields its fruit in its season,
> > and its leaf does not wither.
> In all that he does, he prospers. The wicked are not so,
> > but are like chaff that the wind drives away.
>
> Therefore the wicked will not stand in the judgment,
> > nor sinners in the congregation of the righteous;
> for the LORD knows the *derek* of the righteous,
> > but the *derek* of the wicked will perish.
>
> Psalm 1[1]

Far from proving restrictive in a negative or oppressive manner, God's gift of *torah* illumines the path upon which we must walk (Ps. 119:105; the more general term for "word"—*dabar*—is used in this instance—"Your word is a lamp to my feet and a light to my path"—but the entire psalm is plainly a celebration of God's *torah*). Secure in the knowledge of being on God's path, our hearts are set free to run in the way of his commands (Ps. 119:32). The *torah*, which we have called the curriculum for Israel's religious instruction, is not any kind of abstract notion. It is, notably and critically, a behavior pattern, to be embodied in the lives of teacher and parent as an illustrative model for the young. Indeed, from the same Hebrew root that gives rise to *torah* come words for teacher, *moreh*, and for parent, *horeh*. These persons are to be living guides in the way of the LORD. A key Hebrew verb for teaching—*yarah*—also arises from the same root. To teach, then, involves pointing others to, and leading others in, the way.[2]

Aside from these principal comments about *torah*, we should also note that the term is most commonly used to refer to the entirety of the "five books of Moses": Genesis, Exodus, Leviticus, Numbers, and Deuteronomy. In those books, we certainly find God's holy commands—the Decalogue, for example, is recorded twice, in Exodus 20 and in Deuteronomy 5—but these are set within the larger context of the narrative of God's redemptive work on behalf of Israel. The Torah, in other words, embraces both God's mighty deeds and his holy commands. In fact, even the Decalogue has both of these features in view. While many Christians refer to the "Ten Commandments," many Jews call this passage the "Ten Words." Indeed, the Bible itself refers to these as the "Ten Words" (*debarim* in Hebrew; see Deut. 4:13; 10:4). And the first of the ten words is not a command but rather God's statement about his divine, covenant identity and redemptive deeds: "I am the LORD your God, who brought you out of Egypt, out of the house of slavery." Obedience to the commands is thus set forth as a response, the only fitting response, to who God is and to what he has done.

This pairing of mighty redemptive deeds and holy commands is also in view in another important passage in the Old Testament. In Psalm 78 the psalmist pleads with his people to faithfully pass on to future generations the record of God's mighty deeds and holy commands (Ps. 78:4–5). He is persuaded that diligent attention to impressing this twofold message upon children and grandchildren would help those future generations to "set their hope in God and not forget the works of God, but keep his commandments" (Ps. 78:7). Thus they would not become "like their fathers, a stubborn and rebellious generation, a generation whose heart was not steadfast, whose spirit was not faithful to God" (Ps. 78:8).

The message of such a psalm is fitly juxtaposed against the backdrop of passages like Judges 2. There we read—in some of the most tragic language to be found in the Bible—of the generation that arose after Joshua and his contemporaries: "And there arose another generation after them who did not know the LORD or the work that he had done for Israel. And the people of

Israel did what was evil in the sight of the LORD and served the Baals. And they abandoned the LORD, the God of their fathers, who had brought them out of Egypt" (Judg. 2:10–12). The text does not only say that this new generation did not know the LORD. It says, further, that they did not know "the work that he had done for Israel." Moses had instructed the Israelites to teach their children diligently, specifically noting that "your children . . . have not known or seen" these things (Deut. 11:2). But those in Joshua's generation had apparently failed in their task. It is this sort of failure that the psalmist warns against in Psalm 78. Even with our best efforts to teach our children God's mighty deeds and righteous commands, we have no guarantee that they will grow up to truly know the Lord. But if we fail to teach what we have known and seen of God's ways, we will be without excuse when God calls us to account for how we raised our children.

For the present, we will add just one final thought about Old Testament precursors to the concept of catechesis. On a broad scale, one might argue that there were three major types of teaching in the Old Testament that are reflected in the three divisions of the Hebrew Bible.[3] Jews refer to their collected Scriptures as the *Tanakh*. This word is an acronym built upon the following threefold division:

Torah—the books of Moses
Nevi'im—the Prophets
Kethuvim—the Writings

The threefold division is acknowledged in the New Testament. The risen Jesus said the following to his disciples: "These are my words that I spoke to you while I was still with you, that everything written about me in the Law of Moses and the Prophets and the Psalms must be fulfilled" (Luke 24:44). (The Psalms are the first and largest book in the third section of the Tanakh—the Writings.) Corresponding to this threefold instruction were three types of teachers in ancient Israel—priests, prophets, and sages. And, further, there is a correspondence here to three dimensions of faith within Judaism—learning, worship, and action. The goal of all Jewish education, wrote Rabbi Abraham Joshua Heschel, is reverent obedience to the LORD.[4] It is not knowledge as abstraction that is sought through faith training. It is, rather, that God's people will actually *walk in the way* of the LORD.

We will later be considering some implications of the above threefold pattern for discipleship today. For now, we note only that the faith training envisioned in the Hebrew Bible is comprehensive in its concern and range, dealing with all dimensions of human life and experience. We shall see that catechesis has historically shared this concern. Indeed, we will argue that there can be no faithful catechesis apart from such a commitment to the formation of whole persons and whole communities. Further, we will discover that in early

Christian catechesis, in the New Testament and beyond, the same concern for conforming to God's way that we find in the Old Testament is still very much present.

The Term *Katēcheō* in the New Testament

In the New Testament, the notion of catechesis becomes sharper still, particularly in terms of its focus on the person and work of Jesus Christ. In the first place, we begin with some biblical terms that emerge related to catechesis. The term *catechesis* itself, as we said earlier, comes from the Greek verb *katēcheō*. At first glance, this is simply one of numerous New Testament words for "teaching" or "instruction." It appears numerous times in various forms in the New Testament and has been rendered in English versions of the Bible by a variety of terms. We have placed the appropriate translated word in italics in each of the citations that follow. In many of these cases, the term seems simply to mean "to impart information," or "to teach" in a general sense. It is used in Acts 21:21 with reference to false rumors being spread about the apostle Paul. Paul himself, however, always uses the term to refer to giving instruction about the content of the faith. In 1 Corinthians 14:19, for example, he writes that although he spoke in tongues more than all the Corinthians, "in church I would rather speak five words with my mind in order to *instruct* others, than ten thousand words in a tongue."

In some of the New Testament instances of the term, we may already have evidence of an emerging use of *katēcheō* as a standard (we would say technical) term for imparting basic Christian knowledge. While none of these are definitive, we find the three following examples to be at least suggestive of what would become known as catechesis in the centuries immediately succeeding the New Testament era.

The first instance is in Luke 1:3–4, part of the author's preface to the third Gospel. Luke, writing to "most excellent Theophilus," explains that he offers here a well-researched, orderly account, "that you may have certainty concerning the things you have been *taught*." There are important interpretive questions about the verse. First of all, is Theophilus an actual individual, or is this a symbolic name for all believers who are the intended readers (*Theophilus* means "lover of God")? This is disputed, but many contemporary scholars take the former view and suggest that Theophilus was also likely the patron for Luke's work. Secondly, is Theophilus already a faithful believer and follower of Jesus, or is he an inquirer or an early-stage catechumen? Our answer to this question may help us understand the catechetical implications of Luke's account. If Theophilus was not yet fully a believer, then we may understand whatever earlier instruction he had received as a sort of procatechesis, which Luke now supplements with a narrative of Christ conceived and composed as a more formal catechetical account. (This appears to be part, at least, of the rationale for all four Gospels, as we shall shortly see.) If, on the other hand, Theophilus was a believer already, then *katēcheō* here might refer to a past experience of some sort of catechesis, to which Luke now adds his confirming testimony. These issues are much debated among commentators, and it is probably unwise to be too dogmatic about our own answer, though we tend toward the latter view.

The second instance where we may see something of a technical usage of *katēcheō* also comes from the pen of Luke. Introducing his readers to Apollos—a new character in the unfolding drama of the still emerging church—Luke writes, "He had been *instructed* in the way of the Lord. And being fervent in spirit, he spoke and taught accurately about Jesus, though he knew only the baptism of John" (Acts 18:25). Again, the term here may simply mean that Apollos had been instructed in a general sense about the way of the Lord. But given the fact that "the way of the Lord" is itself a technical term for full-scale Christianity both in Scripture and in the language of the ancient church, it seems to us to be a strong possibility that *katēcheō* here carries a more technical sense. Apollos had, in fact, been catechized in the way of the Lord, albeit only to a limited extent. He was in need of further catechesis about the person and work of Jesus, including apparently the sacramental ordinances that Jesus instituted, and God was about to provide this through the ministry of Priscilla and Aquila, who had themselves been catechized by the apostle Paul. This further catechesis helped Apollos become a source of deep blessing to the believers (see Acts 18:1–4, 18–21, 26–28).

Our third and final example of a possible technical usage of *katēcheō* in the New Testament is in Galatians 6:6. As Paul moves toward the closure of this particularly spirited letter, he writes, "One who is *taught* the word must share all good things with the one who *teaches*." If we were to use the language of the early church (see chapter 1 for our outlining of the various terms) in rendering the key words in this verse, our reading might be, "The catechumen must share all good things with the catechist." While we cannot say definitively that this is in fact an intentionally technical use of the term, many have argued that it is the clearest example of such usage in the New Testament.

It is in any case clear that if *katēcheō* cannot be indisputably understood as a technical term within the New Testament itself, it became such a term soon afterwards. One example from the middle of the second century is often cited. In 2 Clement 17:1, we read: "Let us repent, therefore, with our whole heart, lest any of us should perish needlessly. For if we have orders that we should make it our business to tear men away from idols and to *instruct* them, how much more wrong is it that a soul that already knows God should perish?" (emphasis added).[5]

Other New Testament Terms Related to Catechesis

The case for catechesis as a New Testament reality, however, is not primarily dependent upon the biblical term *katēcheō*. There are other terms that appear throughout the New Testament that are quite explicit when it comes to the practice of grounding and growing believers in the essentials of the faith. In the first place, there are several words that relate unambiguously to the matter of catechetical content. These include "the Gospel," "the Faith," "the teaching(s)" or "the doctrine(s)," and "the tradition(s)." The first two of these terms—the Gospel and the Faith—we will explore in greater detail in chapters 4–6. For now, we simply point out that these terms and their frequent usage in the New Testament clearly indicate that certain Christian truths and practices were regarded as essential and nonnegotiable material for preaching and teaching in the church.

"The teaching(s)" or "the doctrine(s)" are terms frequently used to render the Greek words *didachē* or *didaskalia* in the New Testament. A key example for our purposes is Acts 2:42. There we read of three thousand newly baptized believers who earnestly committed themselves to "the *teaching* of the Apostles, the fellowship, the breaking of bread and the prayers." "Teaching" is *didachē* in this instance. Together, the fourfold commitment seems to represent an outline of essential content in this early school of Christian disciples (that is, an early sort of *catechumenate*, to use another term introduced in chapter 1). The converts were drilled in an understanding of apostolic doctrine, in the discipline of authentic Christian fellowship, and in the communal practices of worship and prayer.

The teaching of the apostles—the first of these fundamental commitments—no doubt focused on the Gospel of Jesus Christ and other essential aspects of the Faith, all derived from the apostles' own Spirit-led exposition of the Holy Scriptures in the light of Christ. There are a number of other New Testament examples of phrases such as "the teaching(s)." In Romans 6:17, Paul thanks God for the fact that the Roman believers had become "obedient from the heart to *the standard of teaching* [*tupon didachē*] to which you were committed." *Tupos* in Greek literally means "die-stamp," and thus metaphorically a fixed pattern functioning as a benchmark or standard. Paul writes to Timothy about being faithful in his own teaching ministry. By doing so, he would be "a good servant of Christ Jesus, being trained in the words of *the faith* and of *the good doctrine* that you have followed" (1 Tim. 4:6). Here we have the apostle using both "the faith" and "the . . . doctrine" (in this instance, the Greek word is *didaskalia*) in a single verse. In Titus 2:10, Paul exhorts Titus to teach the believers godly living, "so that in everything they may adorn *the doctrine* [*didaskalia*] of God our Savior." This verse thus aptly finishes the passage that began with Paul's urging Titus to "teach what accords with *sound doctrine*" (Titus 2:1).

The apostle John, likewise, makes reference to the importance of "the teaching." In 2 John 9–11 he writes, "Everyone who goes on ahead and does not abide in *the teaching* of Christ, does not have God. Whoever abides in *the teaching* has both the Father and the Son. If anyone comes to you and does not bring *this teaching*, do not receive him into your house or give him any greeting, for whoever greets him takes part in his wicked deeds."

Another important set of terms we must consider are words deriving from the Greek noun *paradosis*. These are usually rendered as "tradition" or "traditions" in English versions of the New Testament. In some instances, the word is used with negative connotations, referencing the traditions of men that stand over against the teaching of God in Scripture and through the apostles. Thus Jesus rebukes the religious leaders of his day for "making void the word of God by your *tradition* that you have handed down" (Mark 7:13). Paul too warns the Colossians against falling prey to "human *tradition*" (Col. 2:8). Before he surrendered to Jesus as his Lord, Paul himself had been "extremely zealous . . . for *the traditions* of my fathers" (Gal. 1:14; some of these traditions doubtless reflected God's Word, while others contradicted it).

In other places, however, *paradosis* is used in a very positive sense. In 2 Thessalonians 2:15, Paul urges the believers to "stand firm and hold to *the traditions* that you were taught by us, either by our spoken word or by our letter." Later in the same epistle, Paul warns the believers to "keep away from any brother who is walking in idleness and not in accord with *the tradition* that you received from us" (2 Thess. 3:6).

The Greek verb *paradidōmi* is closely related to the noun *paradosis*. Alongside all the implications of the verb *katēcheō* and other New Testament words for teaching, *paradidōmi* represents a critical dimension of the catechetical process. It is typically rendered in English versions of Scripture as "deliver," "commit," "hand over," or "pass on." Luke writes in the opening verses of his Gospel of "the things that have been accomplished among us, just as those who from the beginning were eyewitnesses and ministers of the word have *delivered* them to us" (Luke 1:1–2). Paul and Timothy *delivered* to the believers for observance the decisions that had been reached by the apostles and elders in Jerusalem. "So the churches were strengthened in *the faith*, and they increased in numbers daily" (Acts 16:4–5). We noted earlier Paul's praise for the Roman believers' having "become obedient from the heart to the standard of teaching to which you were *committed*." Apostolic teaching hands the learners over, as it were, to the truth that must henceforth rule their thoughts and lives. And the apostle Peter warns about false teachers for whom "it would have been better . . . never to know the way of righteousness than after knowing it to turn back from the holy commandment *delivered* to them" (2 Peter 2:21).

Perhaps the most striking use of *paradidōmi* in the catechetical sense we are focusing on is found in Paul's first letter to the Corinthians. Twice in chapter 11 of that letter Paul uses the term to describe critically important teaching he had given during his eighteen months of ministry in Corinth. First, speaking in general terms, he commends the Corinthian believers "because you remember me in everything and maintain *the traditions* even as I *delivered* them to you" (1 Cor. 11:2). Then later in the chapter Paul speaks specifically of instructions regarding the Lord's Supper: "For I received from the Lord what I also *delivered* to you, that the Lord Jesus on the night when he was betrayed took bread" (1 Cor. 11:23). The words Paul uses in the following verses are very similar to those recorded in Luke's account of the Last Supper (Luke 22:19–20). Paul had not made up these words. He had received (*parelabon*) them. Before these words were recorded in either Luke's Gospel or Paul's letter, they had passed verbally from Jesus to the apostles and, in turn, had been handed down by the apostles to the various followers of Christ.

Then in 1 Corinthians 15:3–5, Paul introduces the Gospel as he preached it among the Corinthians. "For I *delivered* to you as of first importance what I also received [*parelabon*]: that Christ died for our sins in accordance with the Scriptures, that he was buried, that he was raised again on the third day in accordance with the Scriptures, and that he appeared."

Paul's use of the term *parelabon* in these passages is both intriguing and instructive. He does not indicate how he had received these teachings. To say that he had received them from the Lord does not require that he had done so by direct revelation. It is more likely that he had received this teaching "from the Lord" through the teaching of the other apostles. In similar fashion, we who worship the Lord today receive God's Word through the ministry of preachers and teachers and through our own reading and study of the Scriptures. Beyond the issue of how Paul received this instruction, however, is the simple but crucial fact *that* he received it. If "passing on" or "delivering" describes the catechetical process from the vantage point of the teacher or catechist, "receiving" describes the same process from the vantage point of the disciple or catechumen. In fact, all who engage in the ministry of catechizing others are continually exercised in both directions—they pass on what they have received. Catechesis, then, is not concerned with novelty—certainly not in terms of content. It is concerned, rather, with faithfulness in both learning and teaching the things of God.

Taken together, these various New Testament terms—the teaching(s) or doctrine(s), or the tradition(s) that we both receive and pass on—reveal important truths about the Faith that was once for all delivered to the saints.[6] This Faith is not only to be earnestly contended for. It is also required that believers diligently study it (Acts 2:42), abide in it (2 John 9–10), obey it (Acts 6:7), and—as the numerous verses we have considered above indicate—faithfully pass it on to others. Catechesis represents a convergence of these commitments. It is the intentional passing on of the Faith, not merely for cognitive apprehension, but for the holistic transformation of individual believers and for the maturing of those believers together as the body of Christ.

Examples of "the Teaching," "Sound Doctrine," "Tradition," and "Passed on" in the New Testament

"And they devoted themselves to the apostles' *teaching*." (Acts 2:42)

"Watch out for those who cause divisions and put obstacles in your way that are contrary to *the teaching* you have learned." (Rom. 16:17 NIV)

"Now I commend you because you remember me in everything and maintain *the traditions* even as I *delivered* them to you." (1 Cor. 11:2)

"For I received from the Lord what I also *passed on* to you: The Lord Jesus, on the night he was betrayed, took bread, and when he had given thanks, he broke it and said, 'This is my body, which is for you; do this in remembrance of me.'" (1 Cor. 11:23–24 NIV)

"For what I received I *passed on* to you as of first importance: that Christ died for our sins according to the Scriptures, that he was buried, that he was raised on the third day according to the Scriptures." (1 Cor. 15:3–4 NIV)

"So then, brothers, stand firm and hold to *the traditions* that you were *taught* by us, either by our spoken word or by our letter." (2 Thess. 2:15 NIV)

"Keep away from every brother who is idle and does not live according to *the teaching* you received from us." (2 Thess. 3:6 NIV)

"So that you may charge certain persons not to teach any different *doctrine*." (1 Tim. 1:3)

"Let all who are under a yoke as slaves regard their own masters as worthy of all honor, so that the name of God and *the teaching* may not be reviled." (1 Tim. 6:1)

"If anyone teaches a different doctrine and does not agree with the sound words of our Lord Jesus Christ and *the teaching* that accords with godliness, he is puffed up with conceit and understands nothing." (1 Tim. 6:3–4)

"For the time will come when they will not endure *sound doctrine*." (2 Tim. 4:3 NASB)

"He must hold firm to the trustworthy word as *taught*, so that he may be able to give *instruction* in *sound doctrine* and also to rebuke those who contradict it." (Titus 1:9)

"But as for you, teach what accords with *sound doctrine*." (Titus 2:1)

"Show that they can be fully trusted, so that in every way they will make *the teaching* about God our Savior attractive." (Titus 2:10 NIV)

"It would have been better for them not to have known the way of righteousness, than to have known it and then to turn their backs on the sacred command that was *passed on* to them." (2 Peter 2:21 NIV)

"Anyone who runs ahead and does not continue in *the teaching* of Christ does not have God; whoever continues in *the teaching* has both the Father and the Son." (2 John 9 NIV)

Catechetical Documents in the New Testament

There is yet another line of argument that establishes the biblical basis of cat-echesis: many, if not all, of the New Testament writings themselves are in effect catechetical documents. Indeed, in the general sense of the term—catechesis as instruction—all the New Testament writings plainly served catechetical purposes. The Gospels and the narrative of Acts, the letters and the book of Revelation, were all vitally important teaching documents within the life of the early church.

Beyond this general sense, however, can it be argued that any of the New Testament books were *explicitly* catechetical documents? As a matter of fact, many have made this very case. The Gospels are often viewed as a starting point of instruction. Each of the evangelists, it is argued, was presenting an account of Jesus's life and teaching to particular communities of professed believers. The result is four carefully crafted and culturally contextualized cat-echetical documents. We dealt earlier with some of the interpretive questions surrounding the opening verses of Luke's Gospel. Our tentative conclusion was that Luke's account may be more a work to confirm an earlier catechesis that Theophilus had received than primarily a catechetical work in its own right. It is entirely possible, however, that Luke-Acts represents an intentional effort of initial or ongoing catechesis.[7]

Many have suggested that Matthew's Gospel is more explicitly catechetical. R. V. G. Tasker, though not himself arguing that catechesis was the primary purpose of Matthew's writing, joins many in noting the educational value of the evangelist's "systematic arrangement of his material according to subject matter rather than in strict chronological sequence."[8] He goes on to quote J. H. Ropes's remarks about Matthew: "A well-educated man of distinguished literary ability, he undertook to provide for the instruction of Christians a systematic compendium or handbook of what was known about the deeds and words of the Founder of the Christian Church."[9]

Matthew's arrangement of narrative portions followed by extended pas-sages of Jesus's teaching, and the book's similarities to early catechetical works like *The Didache of the Apostles* and the *Epistle of Barnabas*, are also frequently noted in support of the view that his work is distinctly catechetical in nature and intent.

Of Mark's Gospel, suffice it to say that it serves extremely well as the basic text for the current catechetical course Christianity Explored, to which we shall return later, and this in itself strongly suggests that it was actually writ-ten, among its other purposes, for catechetical use. As for John's Gospel, the absence of any direct account of Jesus's baptism, transfiguration, and institu-tion of the Lord's Supper, which might undergird the profound Trinitarian teachings on the new birth and the Bread of Life that John records so fully, would seem to support the time-honored guess that John was intentionally writing a higher catechetical supplement to initial Christian instruction, such as the Synoptic Gospels provide.

To the degree that some or all of the Gospels are, in fact, catechetical works, there are some key implications for those of us who would catechize today. In terms of content, the books point, of course, to Christocentricity in catechesis. Jesus's person and his reconciling work—in both life and in death—are the central foci of each of these works. The account of his passion, death, and triumphant resurrection is especially prominent in each narrative. But critical too is the account of Jesus's living faithfully and obediently in the will and way of his heavenly Father. Who Jesus was, and how he lived, suffered, died, and rose, are the substance of all four Gospel records. We will argue through the course of the book that this emphasis on proclaiming Christ is always proper and primary for Christian catechesis.

In terms of catechetical process, the Gospels together may argue for the wisdom of taking a narrative approach. Even Matthew's account, which, as we noted above, may be seen as more topical than chronological in arrangement, is fully concerned to trace the outline of the story of Jesus from initial promise, to birth, to life and ministry, and on to death, resurrection, and ascension. Such an emphasis on telling *the Story*, we will later suggest, may be especially important for renewed catechetical work in our time.

Beyond the Gospels and Acts, we can easily see how the apostolic epistles are exceedingly important catechetically—if not explicitly, then certainly by implication. The majority of the letters were evidently occasioned by circumstances, crises, or questions that arose in the various Christian communities. As we shall see later in this book, catechesis can and must be a responsive ministry at times. When Paul responds to heresy among the Galatians or to abuses and questions arising among the Corinthians he is doing important catechetical work. The same can be said regarding the letters of Peter, John, and Jude, and of the letter to the Hebrews.

Catechesis, however, is not always responsive. Indeed, it is in the first instance more of a preemptive ministry. It seeks to lay spiritual, moral, and theological foundations that can help grow a church and its individual members toward maturity, so that they will not be easily swayed by deceptive doctrines or moral compromises that will, invariably, arise to trouble them (see Eph. 4:11–16). It aims, in other words, to prevent struggles before they begin, anticipating them and, as we say, nipping them in the bud.

Some of the New Testament letters combine preemptive and responsive elements of teaching. In any case, the line between these emphases is a fuzzy one at best. In the letter of James, for example, the author appears to be responding to abuses that are already observable in the communities he is addressing. It seems likely that sins of spiritual laziness, of partiality toward the rich, of internal fighting, and more are already at work in the lives of his readers, and James writes to correct these things. On the other hand, James's writing has much in common with many early Christian works of catechesis, especially his way of emphasizing the moral outworking of the Christian faith in daily obedience to the Word and way of God. His letter, then, is probably as much preemptive in purpose as it is responsive.

At least three of Paul's letters seem to be of primarily preemptive catechetical import. These are the letters to the Ephesians, the Colossians, and the Romans, by common consent the three greatest and most significant letters he ever dictated. Their expository styles differ: Romans proceeds by what has been called the "diatribe" method, that is, by perpetually raising and resolving questions, while Ephesians and Colossians follow the "proclamatory" method of letting each point grow out of what preceded it, building each new thought logically and analytically on and out of what went before. But in doctrinal content the three letters complement each other, laying out different elements of the one truth about the grace of God, which is expressed and enjoyed through the Lord Jesus Christ in the new life that he brings. In all three, Paul shows that he has the mind of a theologian, for he relates everything systematically to God's purpose revealed and redemption achieved through and in Christ, thus spelling out in full what he understood to be the Gospel. Equally, however, he shows himself to have the mind of a catechist as he lays out his material in clear doxological and devotional format. He relates it to those whom these pastoral letters, sermons on paper as they are, seek to disciple by indicating the faithful obedience and obedient faithfulness that Gospel truths require of them in all departments of life. In Paul, theologian and catechist are one.

Thus to the Romans, who he knew had differences among themselves regarding Jew and non-Jew together in the church, and to whom he knew he had probably been misrepresented already by Judaizers who thought the Gospel required Gentiles to become Jews, Paul presents in detail the theme of *knowing and sharing Christ's salvation*. And to the Colossians, confused by devotional proposals that for Paul entailed christological heresy, he offers a presentation on the theme of *living faithfully and authentically in Christ*, in which his correction of the errant devotional proposals (worshiping angels and attending to visions) becomes almost incidental to his main thrust. Ephesians seems to bear the marks of an encyclical, a circular letter growing out of Colossians, addressed to a group of churches whose copies Tychicus delivered, and from the Ephesian copy of which our present text derives; but be that as it may, the letter's catechetical theme is clear and explicit: *live up to your calling in Christ* in face of the world, the flesh, and the devil. As a group, all three letters are teaching the same Gospel—centered on Christ; oriented toward new life; attuned to faith, hope, love, and good works; and focused on the church as central in God's plan of grace. Each, however, adds something distinctive to what is in the other two (Christology in Colossians, ecclesiology in Ephesians, and soteriological detail and Old Testament fulfillment in Romans, for starters). In each, Paul expounds high doctrine not as rarefied abstractions for

Christian eggheads, but as practical truths to be grasped, responded to, and lived out by everyone. Moving thus on a preemptively catechetical wavelength, the apostle is unapologetically didactic, and what he writes, apart from its compression (writing is always more compressed than direct speech, and Paul on paper is a truly marvelous compressor), must surely have corresponded to what he would give to churches viva voce.

Catechetical Imperatives in the New Testament

One of the most important arguments for ministries of catechesis today derives from the simple fact that believers have been commanded to teach others catechetically. As we saw to be the case in the Old Testament, so in the New, parents are commanded to teach their children. Paul, citing the responsibility of fathers in particular, writes, "Fathers, do not provoke your children to anger, but bring them up in the discipline and instruction of the Lord" (Eph. 6:4). Paul himself actually models the teaching of children in the same letter, when he specifically addresses children in the believing community (Eph. 6:1; see also Col. 3:20).

In the pastoral epistles especially we find numerous exhortations to exercise ministries of substantive teaching. It is clear that Timothy and Titus were to see such teaching as central in their own ministries. Here are some of Paul's exhortations to them:

- "Charge certain persons not to teach any different doctrine, nor devote themselves to myths." (1 Tim. 1:3–4)
- "If you put these things before the brothers, you will be a good servant of Christ Jesus, being trained in the words of the faith and of the good doctrine that you have followed." (1 Tim. 4:6)
- "Command and teach these things." (1 Tim. 4:11)
- "Devote yourself to the public reading of Scripture, to exhortation, to teaching." (1 Tim. 4:13)
- "Keep a close watch on yourself and on your teaching. Persist in this, for by so doing you will save both yourself and your hearers." (1 Tim. 4:16)
- "Teach and urge these things. If anyone teaches a different doctrine and does not agree with the sound words of our Lord Jesus Christ and the teaching that accords with godliness, he is puffed up with conceit and understands nothing." (1 Tim. 6:2–4)
- "O Timothy, guard the deposit entrusted to you." (1 Tim. 6:20)
- "Follow the pattern of the sound words that you have heard from me, in the faith and love that are in Christ Jesus. By the Holy Spirit who dwells within us, guard the good deposit entrusted to you." (2 Tim. 1:13–14)

- "What you have heard from me in the presence of many witnesses entrust to faithful men who will be able to teach others also." (2 Tim. 2:2)
- "Remind them of these things, and charge them before God not to quarrel about words. . . . Do your best to present yourself to God as one approved, a worker who has no need to be ashamed, rightly handling the word of truth." (2 Tim. 2:14–15)
- "The Lord's servant must not be quarrelsome but kind to everyone, able to teach, patiently enduring evil, correcting his opponents with gentleness." (2 Tim. 2:24–25)
- "Preach the word; be ready in season and out of season; reprove, rebuke, exhort, with complete patience and teaching. For the time is coming when people will not endure sound teaching." (2 Tim. 4:2–3)
- "But as for you, teach what accords with sound doctrine." (Titus 2:1)
- "Show yourself in all respects to be a model of good works, and in your teaching show integrity, dignity, and sound speech that cannot be condemned." (Titus 2:7–8)
- "Declare these things; exhort and rebuke with all authority." (Titus 2:15)
- "Remind them to be submissive to rulers and authorities, to be obedient, to be ready for every good work." (Titus 3:1)

Beyond the teaching ministries that Timothy and Titus themselves were to engage in, they were also to ensure that other leaders and mature believers would likewise engage in teaching. Overseers (*episkopoi*) were required to be "able to teach" (1 Tim. 3:2). Each overseer was to hold firmly to the deep truths of the Faith "so that he may be able to give instruction in sound doctrine and also to rebuke those who contradict it" (Titus 1:9). Mature men were to be enlisted who could teach others (2 Tim. 2:2), and the mature women were likewise "to teach what is good" (Titus 2:3).

In light of this testimony from the pastoral epistles, what might Paul think of the state of affairs in too many of our churches today, with pastors who do not regard teaching as a central feature of their ministries and with other church leaders who are largely ignorant of the Faith they have been charged to pass on to others? May God grant to those of us in such leadership roles a spirit of repentance to take up a serious ministry of teaching once again. Returning to a vision of rigorous catechesis will go a long way toward such a course correction.

Here we may appropriately observe that Christians who are developing in a natural, healthy way—regenerate persons, that is, who are now indwelt, led, and energized in mind and heart by the Holy Spirit—will welcome this kind of ongoing instruction in which attention is focused on the self-revealed Triune God: who and what he is; what he has done, is doing, and will do; his works, ways, will, wisdom, and how he wants to be worshiped; in short, everything he shows us with regard to himself throughout Scripture. Children between two and twelve in ordinary, healthy families will again and again manifest curiosity about what their parents are up to, and will often follow them around and stand watching them at work. When you love someone, you want to know everything about them. Similarly, children of God whose spiritual instincts have not been blunted or twisted will, in the natural course of things, show strong theological interests; they will want to learn all they can about their heavenly Father, their gracious Savior, and the sanctifying Holy Spirit, and will always welcome opportunities to find out more about their glorious God. Theirs is not the sinful curiosity that seeks to pry into things unrevealed, but the affectionate curiosity of admiration, gratitude, and love.

Reading between the lines of the heavy letters of Paul and the book of Hebrews, and the profundities of Jesus's teachings in John's Gospel, one gets the sense that those at the receiving end of these documents must have been excited already about God's loving purposes and the fresh taste of life lived in and under Christ in the Spirit's power. They were willing to think hard about it all. Theologically, Romans, Colossians, Ephesians, Hebrews, and John are dense and deep, but the writers are clearly confident that their addressees, hearing these documents read in church, will be able to grasp their meaning. It looks as if these early Christians lived in a sustained theological buzz, constantly discussing and debating divine things in a lifelong learning endeavor that was one of their many spontaneous expressions of newness of life in Christ.

But if that is so, then the general dumbing down of doctrinal instruction in today's Western churches, the widespread suspicion and skepticism about the trustworthiness of the Bible and the Christian heritage, and the bland assumption of so many that learning biblical theology is in any case not needed for Christian well-being are both telltale symptoms and continuing causes of the weakness, woolliness, and waywardness that outsiders nowadays too often discern in us. A change of heart in Christians and a conscious course correction in church practice is, as was said above, most urgently needed for our good.

Nor is that all. We close this chapter with a supremely weighty and compelling thought, more demanding and decisive than any we have expressed thus far. We catechize because of the model and mandate of our Lord Jesus Christ. Jesus was and is the model catechist. He was the Teacher of teachers. It is not only his example that moves us to catechize, however. We catechize by command of Jesus. Jesus charged his followers with the task of teaching on several occasions during his earthly ministry (e.g., Matt. 10:14; 13:52). Just before ascending to the Father's right hand in glory, the risen Christ commanded his followers to disciple all the nations. This task requires the ministry of serious, sustained, systematic, and substantive teaching—"teaching them to observe all that I have commanded you" (Matt. 28:20). Catechesis is a faithful and fruitful ministry that flows directly from this "Great Commission" of Jesus.

Catechesis is, indeed, a very biblical idea! More than that—the ministry of catechesis is actually a biblical imperative. Tragically, however, the church has very often been unfaithful in working out God's will in regard to this critical ministry. In the next chapter, we turn our attention to our checkered past in this respect as we consider the waxing and waning of catechetical endeavors in the history of the church. This will make for realism as we attempt to see the way ahead.

The Waxing and Waning of Catechesis

Believe me . . . the Church of God will never be preserved
without catechesis.[1]

John Calvin

As the quote at the head of this chapter makes clear, Calvin, like the
other great catechetical figures in Christian history, was persuaded that
a faithful catechesis was absolutely essential to the healthy continuance
of Christ's church. As the first decade of the twenty-first century now draws to
a close, Christians of all sorts once again seem intent on testing this thesis.

Although there are signs of catechetical renewal in certain circles—particularly
among Catholics and Anglicans—most of the evangelical Protestant world still
lags behind, and meantime the consequences of an uncatechized church are readily apparent. Survey data gathered over the past decade or so consistently reveals
high levels of biblical and theological illiteracy among self-identified American
evangelical Christians. Beyond the "hard data," however, we see evidence all
around us of serious unhealthiness in too many of our congregations.[2]

For some time voices have been warning of "the coming evangelical col-
lapse." In a 2009 article by that title, Michael Spencer suggested that among
the reasons for the coming demise is the following:

We Evangelicals have failed to pass on to our young people an orthodox form of faith that can take root and survive the secular onslaught. Ironically, the billions of dollars we've spent on youth ministers, Christian music, publishing, and media has produced a culture of young Christians who know next to nothing about their own faith except how they should feel about it. Our young people have deep beliefs about the culture war, but do not know why they should obey Scripture, the essentials of theology, or the experience of spiritual discipline and community. Coming generations of Christians are going to be monumentally ignorant and unprepared for culture-wide pressures.[3]

His argument is really a modern-day counterpart of Calvin's: without catechesis, the church cannot be sustained. We know, of course, that Jesus promised that the church he was building would endure, that the gates of hell cannot prevail against it (Matt. 16:18). But throughout the two millennia of Christian history, the health of Christian communities has, in fact, often been linked to the presence or absence of serious catechetical ministries.

In this chapter, we will look at three seasons in church history during which catechesis flourished—among ancient churches of the second through fifth centuries, within the continental and British Reformations of the sixteenth century, and among the English Puritans of the seventeenth century. In each of these seasons, we will highlight one feature of catechesis that especially marked catechetical ministry at that time, giving particular attention to a notable catechist of the period. This is not intended to be a full-scale survey of the history of catechesis. Others have undertaken that task and for more details we would refer readers to their works.[4]

After looking at these three seasons of catechetical flourishing, we will consider some of the many factors that have contributed to the decline of catechesis after such seasons and to its relative absence in our own times.

Here, in brief, is the overview of the three seasons of flourishing we will be considering:

Period	Notable Feature	Notable Catechist
Ancient churches of the second through fifth centuries	Development of the catechumenate	Augustine of Hippo
Continental reformers of the sixteenth century	Golden age of the catechism	Martin Luther
English Puritans of the seventeenth century	Pastoral duty of family catechizing	Richard Baxter

Development of the Catechumenate

By "catechumenate," we refer to what might be called a sort of school of the Faith—sometimes more formal, sometimes less so—in which, during the early Christian centuries, new believers were prepared for baptism and thus welcomed into the full life of the church. Our knowledge of the catechetical practices of this age is drawn from a variety of sources. These include early catechetical manuals or other documents, such as the late first- or early second-century *Didache of the Apostles*, Irenaeus's *Demonstration of the Apostolic Teaching*, and the third-century *The Apostolic Tradition* of Hippolytus. We also have catechetical lectures and other materials from such ancient catechists of the church as Tertullian, Chrysostom, Cyril of Jerusalem, Theodore of Mopsuestia, Gregory of Nazianzus, Ambrose of Milan, and Augustine of Hippo.

The notion that there needed to be a journey toward baptism, one that included a lengthy period of instruction, will no doubt seem strange to many contemporary evangelicals. After all, we read in the book of Acts of numerous converts who, in most instances, were baptized almost immediately after their professions of faith. But within the first several centuries of the church's history, after Christianity had for the most part left Jerusalem and the synagogues behind, it became increasingly the case that those coming to faith in Jesus Christ came with little knowledge of the God of Israel or of the Hebrew and Christian Scriptures. Such conversions to Christ were truly radical, worldview-altering, life-transforming journeys. These were quite different experiences, therefore, from most of the conversion accounts and baptisms recorded in the New Testament. There we read of three thousand observant Jews who were baptized on the day of Pentecost (Acts 2). We read of the Ethiopian eunuch who, while studying the scroll of the prophet Isaiah, was assisted toward faith in Christ by the Spirit-prompted teaching of Philip (Acts 8). We read, in the same chapter, of many Samaritans coming to faith. They would have regarded at least the books of Moses as sacred and authoritative. We read later (Acts 10) of the gentile Cornelius coming to faith, together with friends and members of his family. He and his household were already "devout and God-fearing" (Acts 10:2). So too was Lydia, generally regarded as the first believer on European soil (Acts 16:14). Indeed, the Philippian jailer and his family stand alone in the book of Acts as having come to faith and to the waters of baptism with no apparent background in the faith of the Jews. This family, though, did have the benefit of significant instruction from Paul and Silas prior to their baptism.

As the Gospel spread to primarily gentile and pagan peoples, the church came to regard conversion to Christ as so revolutionary that it requires a significant time of instruction and drilling in other spiritual activities prior to the conferring of baptism upon new believers. The development of the catechumenate reflected this view.

Evidence strongly suggests that the basic idea of a catechumenate was in place by the second century, but the practices that would mark the journey toward baptism developed over time and varied from place to place.[5] There seems to have been movement from less formal to more formal structures, corresponding to the shifting realities of the church as a whole. By the fourth century, Christians no longer represented a persecuted minority in the Roman Empire. This generally meant greater emphasis on structure and hierarchy in most aspects of congregational life, including the ministry of catechesis. Whereas in earlier days the principal catechists might have been mature believers, whether elders or not, in the more formalized church structures the catechist was typically a pastor or the bishop. The numbers of those needing to be catechized also greatly increased as persecution decreased. Instructing larger numbers of would-be Christians led to more formal settings. Small group interactions in the home of a believer gave way to lectures held within church buildings.

A Catechumen's Journey

The following represents the outline of a catechumen's journey toward baptism. It is based on evidence drawn from descriptions of the catechumenate as conducted in several settings in the fourth and fifth centuries. Not all of what follows would have occurred exactly the same way in each of these settings, but the composite picture that emerges reflects at every point practices typical of the era.

Those who were interested in becoming Christians were brought by a friend, or sponsor, to church leaders. The leader, typically a bishop or pastor, would interview the *inquirers* to discern both their current spiritual condition and motives for wanting to join the church. Sponsors would testify on behalf of the inquirers about their sincerity and resolve. In some cases, a person was disqualified based upon style of life, or was asked to leave a profession that was deemed incompatible with being a Christian. For some catechists, improper motives might also be taken as grounds for refusal. Inquirers would often receive some general introduction to the Christian faith, perhaps in the form of an overview of the Bible's redemptive story.[6] Afterward, if all parties agreed, inquirers would then become *catechumens*.

Catechumens became "hearers of the Word," worshiping with believers each Lord's Day and participating in other opportunities for fellowship and instruction. In some cases, the catechumens were regarded as Christian believers of sorts already, but not yet counted fully among the faithful. The liturgy of the church was generally divided into two major sections: a service of the Word and a service of the Table. All were welcome to take part in the service of the Word. There they would hear the Scriptures read and explained and would join in the prayers and hymns. Typically, catechumens would then be dismissed with prayers of blessing prior to the celebration of the Lord's Supper. In some cases, this dismissal was marked by a formal closing of the doors—recalling God's closing of the door on Noah's ark—thus reminding the catechumens that they were not yet truly among the saved. The celebration of the Eucharist was reserved for those who had been baptized.

During the catechetical journey, catechumens were expected not only to be hearers of the Word, but also doers of the Word. The new life into which they were entering was to be characterized by love and good deeds. Faithfulness in hearing, doing, and in prayer would all be taken into account when the catechumens finally put their names in as candidates for baptism. The sponsors would once again give testimony on behalf of the catechumens with regard to all these areas. If the candidacy was approved by church leaders, the catechumens would then enter a final, more intensive phase of catechesis.

In this final phase of catechesis, the candidates for baptism might be called by one of several titles—*electi, illuminati, competentes* ("the qualified": common in the West), or *phōtizomenoi* ("the enlightened": common in the East). This final phase was increasingly scheduled to correspond with the season of Lent, the period of reflection and repentance that prepared believers for the celebration of Holy Week. During this final phase (if it had not already occurred earlier in the process), the *competentes* were often marked off within the congregation. Standing or sitting in a special location during the liturgy, they were now the visible objects of much prayer and attention. They would gather daily to pray and be prayed for. The daily prayers would include prayers of exorcism—that God would deliver these souls from every influence of evil. They would engage in certain ascetic exercises, including fasting. And they would be catechized, now more formally, by the pastor or bishop.

The daily instructions would often include an exposition of the ancient Creed[7] and of the Lord's Prayer. The Creed was "handed over" (*traditio symboli*) to the *competentes* by means of oral, line-by-line presentation, repetition, and exposition. The Creed was not to be written down, nor were the *competentes* to rehearse the Creed in the presence of ordinary catechumens, let alone outsiders. It was a treasure reserved for this stage of the journey, and not before, just as baptism was reserved for those who had already passed through this stage and the Lord's Supper was reserved for those who had been baptized. This holding back of treasured teaching and rites was an application of the *disciplina arcani* ("discipline of secrecy"). This principle and practice seemingly was based upon the proverb forbidding the casting of pearls before the swine (Matt. 7:6) as well as upon Jesus's practice of teaching in parables. As Jesus explained to his disciples when asked why he taught in parables, "To you it has been given to know the secrets of the kingdom of heaven, but to them it has not been given" (Matt. 13:11). Only as Jesus, on request, explained, his parables would understanding dawn, and only as the Faith was explained, step-by-step, to the *competentes* would its full significance for their lives be grasped.

Sometime before the actual baptism, perhaps a day or several days earlier, a candidate would profess the Faith by repeating the words of the Creed that she had committed to memory and upon which she had been meditating for many days. This was the giving back, or returning, of the Creed (*redditio symboli*). Augustine's own conversion was encouraged in part by his having heard the story of the profession of Victorinus who, like Augustine himself, was an African and a noted rhetorician. Augustine reflects upon this episode in his *Confessions* (which are, from beginning to end, written in the form of prayer).

> At Rome those who are about to enter into your grace usually make their profession in a set form of words which they learn by heart and recite from a raised platform in view of the faithful. . . . So when he mounted the platform to make his profession, all who knew him joyfully whispered his name to their neighbors. There can have been none who did not know him, and the hushed voices of the whole exultant congregation joined in the murmur, "Victorinus, Victorinus." They were quick to let their joy be heard when they saw him, but just as quickly came a hush as they waited to hear him speak. He made his declaration of the true faith with splendid confidence, and all would gladly have seized him in their arms and clutched him to their hearts.[8]

Between the *redditio symboli* and the actual experience of baptism, there was typically a final round of catechesis. Included now would be some instruction about the elements of the baptismal ritual that would ensue in a few days' time. In some cases, the *competentes* would be catechized about the spiritual meaning of the baptism they were soon to experience. In other cases, however, these things were kept hidden from the candidates until after the actual experience had occurred; prior to the event, it was deemed necessary only that they knew the minimum about what to expect.

This divergence of practice represents a debate about application of the *disciplina arcani*. Such catechists as Chrysostom and Augustine seem to have believed that candidates would be better served by being catechized about the mystery of baptism prior to the experience. Cyril of Jerusalem, on the other hand, represented the other opinion. In a postbaptismal catechesis on the mysteries of the sacrament (*mystagogy*), he explained his rationale as being built "on the principle that seeing is believing."[9] William J. Harmless summarizes Cyril's apparent convictions on the matter:

> Cyril believed that the discipline of secrecy [*disciplina arcani*] simply enshrined a good pedagogical principle: that in matters of mystery, experience must precede explanation. Cyril trusted that being stripped naked, dunked, then oiled from head to foot was itself splendid catechesis. Only after his initiates had drunk in and savored the rich, elusive power of such symbols did instruction assume its proper place. Only then would the resonances of theological reflection have sufficient poignancy.[10]

56

As the quote from Harmless suggests, the baptism itself would have numerous ritual components. The following description is of baptisms under the ministry of Augustine.

Men and women would typically be separated for the ceremony because they would be baptized naked. The ceremony would be held during the great Easter vigil. At some point prior to their disrobing, the candidates would face the west, extend their hands, and renounce the devil and all his works. Then, facing the east, they would repeat their profession of the faith. The baptismal fonts were designed in such a way that "living water" would flow into them. The water should not be standing, stagnant water, for it represented the cleansing power of the Holy Spirit. The fonts typically held enough water to facilitate full immersion, though it is unclear how the candidates were actually immersed. Before entering the font, candidates would strip off their old clothes—goatskin sackcloth, which they trampled under their feet. There were three immersions, each one preceded by a question about faith in the persons of the Trinity, to which the candidate would respond, *"credo"*—"I believe." The newly baptized were anointed with oil, and the presence and power of the Holy Spirit was invoked over them. They were prayed for with the laying on of hands.

The *competentes* were now *neophytes*. Emerging from the font, they were clothed with new robes of white linen, which they wore for the next eight days. Special sandals were also worn to keep their feet from touching the earth. Then all who had been part of the baptism ceremony would return to the main basilica where they would be greeted by the faithful in a spirit of joyous celebration. Now, for the very first time, the *neophytes* would experience the ritual speech, prayers, and actions of the Lord's Supper. "The neophytes experienced all this—seeing, hearing, partaking in 'what took place on the altar'—without comment or catechesis. Augustine's silence was deliberate. He would not take up the deeper implications of Eucharist—'what it is, what it means, and the great mystery it holds'—until the next morning."[11]

While there was some disagreement among catechists of the era regarding whether or not baptism should be explained prior to the event, there seems to have been consensus about withholding catechesis regarding the Lord's Supper until after it was experienced. Postbaptismal catechesis typically centered upon explanation of the mysteries of the sacraments (*mystagogy*), and could last for several days or weeks. The *neophytes* were now greatly celebrated and strongly challenged. They were new creatures in Christ and now, by God's grace, they must earnestly aim to live as such.

Evaluation and Consideration

Of course, much of the above may seem to a contemporary evangelical believer in North America like a journey through foreign lands. But we would suggest that some of these catechetical practices are worthy of deep consideration, if not outright emulation. In particular, we note three aspects of the ancient catechumenate that could encourage enriching practices in contemporary efforts of catechetical renewal.

First of all, the deliberate concern for the spiritual readiness and ongoing development of those becoming Christians deserves our attention. If we take seriously the task of discipling people for Jesus Christ, such attention is really necessary. Discipleship involves meeting people where they are and helping them go where they must go. All of this envisions faith as a journey, an idea apparent in both Testaments of the Bible (more on this in chapter 7). Those making disciples serve as guides in this journey, and this means that we need to know where we are going. We will also need to know the health and condition of our fellow travelers. Such knowledge is necessary for every aspect of our preparation and leadership—what sort of nourishment will be needed, what challenges may arise to hinder the journey, and what stops and adjustments may be necessary along the way. The plan of the ancients may seem a bit too elaborate for us, but perhaps they were actually far ahead of the game, relative to us, in terms of understanding the nature of the Christian pilgrimage as a significantly new way of thought and life.[12]

Secondly, we see great value in the holistic approach to instruction that is reflected in *how* and *where* catechesis occurred. Thoroughness of plan and performance is integral to the discipling of inquirers. Helping people become like Jesus surely involves every aspect of our humanity, and the ancients knew it. Thus their catechetical vision required the engagement of eyes and ears, minds and hearts, hands and feet. We will say much more about the wisdom of such a vision throughout the course of the book.

Thirdly, the combination of sobriety and celebration that attended the journey of a catechumen toward full inclusion in the life of the church is surely a model for us moderns to match. Many evangelicals today have unwisely dismissed the notion of rites of passage, perhaps fearing a fall into the trap of empty ritualism. But who says that our rituals must be empty? The Bible itself prescribes potent rituals—evident, again, in both Testaments. It is up to church leaders to keep such ritual acts filled with meaning in their own minds and in the minds of congregants. We will be addressing this also at various points throughout the book.

The Reformers and a Return to Roots

With the strengthening of the relationship between the church and the state came the rise of a medieval "Christian society." This had profound impact on the catechumenate as it had been previously experienced. With the masses suddenly becoming a part of the church, "the early Christian community was now transformed into a crowd of nominal Christians (a transformation described as a real tragedy by Chrysostom in his famous sermons at Constantinople)."[13] Infant baptism became normative and was only rarely followed up with the intended catechizing of children in the faith. The rigorous catechizing of individual adults coming to faith in Christ likewise became a very rare occurrence. The literacy of those filling the cathedrals was often very low, and access to the Scriptures was very limited in any case. Those deeply desirous of growth in the spiritual life may have sought it through a personal disciple-elder relationship. The monastic life was one expression of this. Otherwise, what catechetical work did occur was typically done in very large scale.

> Education then took place largely through sermons (which were often faithfully transcribed for wider use, e.g., the sermons of Chrysostom), liturgical hymnography (which contained doctrinal and scriptural themes), Christian art (frescoes, mosaics, and icons which told in imagery the story of salvation), liturgical commemorations (the cycles of feasts and fasts, the sanctoral), liturgical processions, and pilgrimages to holy places and monasteries (especially for confession and spiritual counsel with holy fathers or *startsi*).[14]

While much potential good can surely be seen in such efforts as those noted above, especially the attention paid to the liturgy and its formative and instructional potential, the practice of serious and sustained catechesis for both newer and older believers was largely abandoned.

It was after a prolonged time of relative neglect, then, that this vital area of catechetical ministry received renewed attention from the Reformers. Indeed, it could well be argued that the Reformation itself was a response to centuries of catechetical decline. A largely uninstructed church had been fertile soil for serious error in terms of doctrine, experience, and practice. Luther and his contemporaries fought hard to reform the church in these areas. After efforts to do so from within the structures of the church of Rome had been met with severe opposition, newly emerging evangelical churches became the laboratory for new—or better, renewed—approaches to pastoral and evangelistic ministry and the nourishing of personal faith.

Indeed, it would be doing a great injustice to the Reformers to suggest that they were desirous of being innovators. Theirs was a call to return to the plain teachings and practices of the Scriptures. For Luther, Calvin, and others, this actually meant a return to sound procedures of the ancient fathers of the church. They were persuaded that the church of Rome had long abandoned the ways of their forebears in many vital respects. The medieval church had brought forth countless innovations, but they made for what the Reformers saw as superstitions rather than an understanding of God's Word and ways and of the demands of discipleship. These Reformers were set on rediscovery of the true sources of the Faith.

The Reformation principle of *sola scriptura* needs to be understood in light of this. It was not a rigid plea that "Scripture alone," exegeted directly, should shape the church's faith, without regard for the biblical insights and teachings of the early fathers. Rather, the real sense of the phrase was that Scripture must hold fundamental and inviolable primacy in matters of faith and practice, over and against the often distorted and distorting traditions of the institutional church. The ancient fathers were not always correct, either, and their teachings must also be judged in the light of the Scriptures, as should the teachings of church leaders at all times and in all places. Under that same, sure, and certain light, the Reformers were persuaded that their own teachings had more in common with those of the fathers than did the teachings of the church of Rome at the beginning of the sixteenth century.

Calvin argues this very point in several places, including his introductory remarks to the *Institutes of the Christian Religion* and his written debate with Cardinal Jacobo Sadoleto. Stressing that the Reformers' emphasis was thus on a "return to the sources," David Steinmetz writes:

> The goal of the Reformers was not to supplant a dead or dying church with a new Christianity, as though God had written "Ichabod" over a moribund Christendom and repudiated his covenant. Their goal was a reformed Catholic Church, built upon the foundation of the prophets and apostles, purged of the medieval innovations that had distorted the Gospel, subordinated to the authority of Scripture and the ancient Christian writers, and returned to what was best in the old church. As they saw it, it was this evangelical church, this reformed and chastened church, that was the church catholic. It was the innovators in Rome who could no longer pretend to be genuinely catholic and whose claim to be the custodians of a greater and unbroken tradition was patently false.[15]

For the central figures of the Reformation, a chief concern was a return to the simplicity and power of the biblical Gospel. This, above all, had been obscured due to departure from the principles and practices of the Scriptures and the earliest Christian traditions of church life. The Gospel must be made known and understood as well and as widely as possible. Thus, while Spanish and Portuguese Roman Catholic missionaries of the sixteenth century traveled to distant lands to baptize multitudes who had never before heard of Christ, "the continental reformers, by contrast, confined their efforts to territories in the very heartland of Christendom where universal baptism prevailed, yet where, in Luther's view, while a seamstress might teach her daughter the trade, 'now even the great learned prelates and bishops themselves do not know the Gospel.'"[16]

The Golden Age of the Catechism

Restoring the Gospel would require many things. The Scriptures would need to be available in the vernacular language of the people. The people would need to be educated so that they could read and understand those Scriptures. The liturgy would need to be clear, comprehensible, and in accordance with the Scriptures. God's Word must be preached and taught faithfully and diligently. And catechesis must be returned to a place of prominence in the churches. With this last concern in mind, the Reformers would utilize a relatively new form of technology—the movable type printing press introduced in Germany by Johannes Gutenberg in 1439. The ministry of catechesis would be advanced by the publication and distribution of great numbers of printed catechisms. More than one hundred thousand copies of Martin Luther's *Small Catechism* were printed over the forty years following its first publication.[17]

Luther began to produce sermons and pamphlets centered on instruction in the basic elements of the Christian faith as early as 1516.[18] In 1520, he produced for his own congregation the *Brief Form of the Ten Commandments, of the Creed, and of the Lord's Prayer*. In 1525, he asked two friends to produce a simple catechism for children. But neither this effort nor a subsequent effort undertaken by his friend Philipp Melanchthon in 1528 came to fruition. Finally Luther took the task upon himself. After visiting parishes in Saxony during the fall of 1528, Luther could wait no longer for something to be done. Both Luther's small and large catechisms were published in 1529. He explains all this himself, with typical flourish, in the preface to the *Small Catechism*:

> The deplorable conditions which I recently encountered when I was a visitor constrained me to prepare this brief and simple catechism or statement of Christian teaching. Good God, what wretchedness I beheld! The common people, especially those who live in the country, have no knowledge whatever of Christian teaching, and unfortunately many pastors are quite incompetent and unfitted for teaching. Although the people are supposed to be Christian, are baptized, and receive the holy sacrament, they do not know the Lord's Prayer, the Creed, or the Ten Commandments, they live as if they were pigs and irrational beasts, and now that the Gospel has been restored they have mastered the fine art of abusing liberty.[19]

The aim of the Reformation-era catechisms was, according to the Scottish theologian T. F. Torrance,

> to give a comprehensive exposition of the Gospel of Jesus Christ in the context of the whole Counsel of God and the whole life of the people of God. They sow the seed that germinates in the soil, brings forth living fruit, and provides good grain for use in the next generation. They shape the mind of the historical Church, building up its understanding of the Faith and directing its growth and development so that throughout all its changes from age to age it ever remains the same Household and Habitation of God built upon the foundation of the Apostles and Prophets, Christ Jesus Himself being the chief cornerstone. . . . the Catechism is designed, not for the self-expression and self-culture of a particular Church, but to serve the Communion of Saints, so that all who use it may wor-

ship one God, Father, Son, and Holy Spirit, and be schooled in one Faith in the unity of the whole Church of God past and present.[20]

The Content of the Catechisms

The catechisms of Luther, as indicated by the comments above, were structured around the Ten Commandments, the Apostles' Creed, the Lord's Prayer, and the sacraments—"articles of faith common to all Christians," as Calvin put it.[21] This pattern would mark nearly every major catechism produced by Christians of all camps in the succeeding centuries. It is obvious that Luther by no means understood himself to be an innovator in selecting this content. Rather, he was persuaded that he could not base his own catechesis "better or more plainly than has been done from the beginning of Christendom and retained till now, i.e., in these three parts, the Ten Commandments, the Creed, and the Our Father. These three plainly and briefly contain exactly everything that a Christian needs to know."[22] He says elsewhere, "As for the common people, however, we should be satisfied if they learned the three parts which have been the heritage of Christendom from ancient times, though they were rarely taught and treated correctly, so that all who wish to be Christians in fact as well as in name, both young and old, may be well-trained in them and familiar with them."[23] In the preface to his *Small Catechism*, Luther inveighs against anyone who refused to be catechized in these three summaries:

> If any refuse to receive your instructions, tell them that they deny Christ and are not Christians. They should not be admitted to the sacrament, be accepted as sponsors in Baptism, or be allowed to participate in any Christian privileges. On the contrary, they should be turned over to the pope and his officials, and even to the devil himself. In addition, parents and employers should refuse to furnish them with food and drink and should notify them that the prince is disposed to banish such rude people from his land.

We will consider the wisdom of this pattern of catechetical content more fully in a later chapter. For now, we examine only Luther's claim: that these "three parts"—the Ten Commandments, the Creed, and the Lord's Prayer—represent the central catechetical content inherited from the ancient church. Is the claim a valid one? Let us note that Luther was far from alone in holding this conviction. A quick glance at any of the catechisms that emerged in the era—for example, Calvin's *Geneva Catechism*, the *Heidelberg Catechism* of 1563, and, perhaps surprisingly for some Protestants, the Roman Catechism that emerged from the Counter Reformation work of the Council of Trent—all featured the same elements as their foci. The trend has continued with catechisms ever since. From leading reformers, to English Puritans, to church leaders in colonial America, to recent practice among those churches where catechesis remains central—Lutheran and Reformed, Anglican and Roman

Catholic—we observe the widespread use of the old formularies of the faith. And such use is spoken of as a matter of course. As the twentieth-century Jesuit educator Josef Andreas Jungmann puts it, "Without a doubt, the *old traditional formulation* of Creed, Our Father, Ten Commandments, Sacraments, must determine the plan in some way. It would be a mistake to substitute a scientific schema for this mature, old, and traditional classification."[24]

In fact, as we saw in our survey of the ancient catechumenate, the practice of catechizing in the Creed, the Lord's Prayer, and the sacraments was clearly in place very early in the life of the church. The late first- or early second-century treatise *The Didache of the Apostles* includes instruction in the sacraments and also the command that believers should pray the Lord's Prayer three times daily. Including the Ten Commandments in formal catechesis, on the other hand, was not typical until medieval times. However, the sort of ethical instruction that the Ten Commandments provided in the catechisms of the Reformation era was evident in the earliest of catechetical endeavors. The *Didache*, along with other ancient texts, takes up this ethical concern under the doctrine of the "two ways." It begins with these words: "There are two ways: the way of life and the way of death. And there is a great difference between these two ways."[25] This viewpoint is rooted in the teaching of both Jesus (e.g., Matt. 7:13–14) and the Old Testament (e.g., Ps. 1:6). This is ethical instruction through and through. The way of the Lord, in simplest terms, is the way of loving God and neighbor—the double commandment of love given in Deuteronomy 6:5 and Leviticus 19:18, which, Jesus explained, summarizes all the commandments of God (Mark 12:29–31).

In his fifth-century *Enchiridion*, Augustine argued that every Christian must be instructed in three things—faith, hope, and love. In his manual of instruction on these three "theological virtues" (which form a familiar biblical triad; e.g., 1 Corinthians 13; Colossians 1; 1 Peter 1), Augustine offers expositions of the Creed (this is training in faith), of the Lord's Prayer (training in hope), and of the double commandment of love (training in love). Including the Ten Commandments in the catechism, then, should not be seen as an innovation of either the medieval or Reformation-era churches but simply as an expansion and application of the doctrine of the two ways and of the two great commandments, going right back to the founding of Christianity.

The catechetical pattern that has marked historic catechisms was chosen not only because it was deemed ancient or traditional. It was considered to be a wise and comprehensive primer containing, as Luther put it, "exactly everything that a Christian needs to know." In his shorter preface to the *Large Catechism*, Luther calls these three "the most necessary part of Christian instruction," embodying the ancient fathers' summing up of "the doctrine, life, wisdom, and learning which constitute the Christian's conversation, conduct, and concern."[26] Augustine, as we saw above, regarded these three summaries as essential in cultivating faith, hope, and love in the lives of believers. Such

63

teaching touches humans at the levels of their heads, hearts, and hands—that is, in terms of cognition, affection, and behavior. To say it yet otherwise, the three summaries provide training in doctrine ("truth taken into the mind and heart to live by"), experience ("the conscientious pursuit and conscious enjoyment of fellowship with the Father and the Son"), and practice ("the specific and habitual response of obedience to the doctrinal truth one has received").[27]

A recent document published by the United States Catholic Conference of Bishops describes this comprehensive concern well: "The scope of catechetical content is cognitive, experiential, and behavioral and it requires development in 'the threefold dimension of word, memory, and witness (*doctrine, celebration, and commitment in life*).'"[28] We will consider this comprehensive pattern much more fully in chapter 6.

John Calvin published two catechisms that were also based upon the same general concerns. The first of these, published in the French language in 1537 under the title of *Instruction in Faith*, was an attempt to offer a simplified version of the first edition of the *Institutes*. He recognized that the *Institutes* (though only containing six chapters at that time, there would be eighty chapters in all in the later 1559 edition) was beyond the grasp of children and the majority of laypeople.[29] This first catechism was published in Latin in 1538, but it also turned out to be too lengthy and complex for most children. So in 1541 he produced a second in the French language, which was released in Latin in 1545. This catechism, drafted in the question-and-answer format that Luther had advanced, became known as the *Geneva Catechism*.

Both of Calvin's catechisms chiefly featured expositions of the same three foundational items—the Decalogue, the Creed, the Lord's Prayer—together with teaching about the sacraments. With the second catechism, however, Calvin reversed Luther's order by treating the Commandments after the Creed. This shift reveals an important distinction in the theology of the two great reformers. For Luther, the first and fundamental use of the Law was to reveal to us our sinfulness.[30] The Creed, on the other hand, represented an outline of the Gospel. Thus Luther's preferred catechetical order typifies the Law-Gospel paradigm that has been critical in Lutheran theology to this very day. Calvin shared with Luther in affirming humanity's full depravity and so also believed that the Law therefore functions as a schoolmaster to lead us to Christ (Gal. 3:24). But Calvin also believed that once the Gospel has raised us to new life, we, now indwelt by the Spirit of God, must walk in God's ways, which the negatives of the Decalogue implicitly indicate. The commands of God are thus not only evangelists pointing us to Christ. They are also guides to a God-pleasing Christian life. By placing the Decalogue after the Creed in his second catechism, Calvin revealed his emphasis on the so-called "third use" of the Law.

The *Heidelberg Catechism*, published in 1563, had been commissioned in an effort to help unify Lutheran and Reformed churches of the German

Palatinate. There are several features of the catechism that give evidence of such an effort—including a downplaying of the more distinctively Reformed doctrines of the divine decrees, election and predestination, and an attempt to find common ground on the Lord's Supper. One of the more notable ways in which the ecumenical intention of the catechism can be seen is in its approach to the Decalogue. In what we deem a biblically sound and indeed brilliant stroke, both Luther's evangelistic use of the Law and Calvin's educational use of it are brought together. First, the Law is summarized by means of the double commandment of love and used to help us realize that all of us fall far short of obedience and thus are bound in misery and sin. Next, the Creed is exposited as a Gospel summary of God's great answer to humanity's great need. But then the Law appears once again, this time in the form of command-by-command exposition, as the guide to a life of grateful response.[31]

While the Lutheran churches continued to use Luther's catechisms as their primary teaching tools, the *Heidelberg Catechism* soon supplanted the *Geneva Catechism* as the most popular among Reformed churches. Its popularity continues to this very day in some Reformed churches. In theologically conservative Presbyterian churches in our time its significance is typically second only to that of the *Westminster Shorter Catechism*.

The use of printed catechisms was a staple among the growing communities of the Reformation, including the Anglicans in England and Presbyterians in Scotland. Since 1549 the Anglican Prayer Book has contained a brief but businesslike children's catechism in question-and-answer form, to be mastered by candidates for confirmation (the service at which persons baptized in infancy profess personal acceptance of their baptismal commitment to Christ). It is neatly drafted in five sections: (1) the baptismal covenant; (2) the Creed; (3) the Decalogue and the two Great Commandments; (4) the Lord's Prayer; and (5) the two dominical sacraments (added in 1604). Until the early twentieth century children were regularly required to learn this catechism by heart—unfortunately without it always being adequately explained. As we noted earlier, the use of catechisms was not so strong among Anabaptist groups, but there is evidence of it on occasion there as well.

Rote memorization of catechisms without a lively, interactive relationship of didactic exchange between catechist and catechumens was not of course the Reformers' intent, and warnings against such lapses into the merely mechanical were frequently sounded. Indeed, the Anglican Prayer Book prescribed that children be catechized every week by the clergyman in the parish church at the second Sunday service with their parents looking on. It appears that for the best part of a century this was duly done, but the poor spiritual quality of many clergy plus the obstinate certainty of many parents that learning the Faith with precision was really needless meant that, having briefly waxed in the mid-sixteenth century, catechesis in England was waning again. When the Church of England, outlawed by Parliament in 1645, was reestablished in 1660, this continued to be the story, by and large.

All-age Catechesis: A Short-lived Puritan Experiment

There is, however, a little more to say. The core of the Puritan movement that broke surface in the late sixteenth century was a close-knit community of clergy whose goal was the conversion and discipling of the English nation, primarily through preaching and teaching the life of faith in Jesus Christ. They catechized children very seriously. One of their mid-seventeenth century leaders, Richard Baxter, pastor of Kidderminster parish church from 1641 to 1660 (with a five-year absence as an army chaplain during the Civil War), saw the catechizing of whole families—that is, of everyone in the parish—as a vital ingredient in this pattern of institutionalized parochial evangelism. In *The Reformed Pastor* (1656), which became a bestseller among clergy, Baxter describes how he and his assistant regularly gave an hour's instruction to up to sixteen families each week. They used the *Westminster Shorter Catechism* as a text, interacting with children first, then adults, and ending with exhortation. And, writes Baxter, "Few went away without some seeming Humiliation, Conviction, and Purpose and Promise for a holy life."[32]

The impact of Baxter's catechetical ministry in Kidderminster was by all reasonable measure profound. Reflecting upon this work more than two centuries later, Bishop J. C. Ryle wrote, "When he came to Kidderminster, he found it a dark, ignorant, immoral, irreligious place, containing, perhaps, 3,000 inhabitants. When he left it . . . he had completely turned the parish upside down."[33] Ryle continues his evaluative remarks with Dr. Bates's comments that before Baxter's ministry "the place . . . was like a piece of dry and barren earth; but, by the blessing of heaven upon his labour, the face of Paradise appeared there. The bad were changed to good, and the good to better."[34]

Concerning the renewed observance of the Lord's Day that occurred in that town, "It was said, 'You might have heard an hundred families singing psalms and repeating sermons as you passed through the streets.'"[35] When Baxter had first arrived in Kidderminster, "There was about one family in a street which worshiped God at home. When he went away, there were some streets in which there was not one family on a side that did not do it; and this was the case even with inns and public houses."[36]

So deep was the grounding in the things of God that among the poor common folk were now found those who "understood the whole body of divinity," and "some were so able in prayer that few ministers could match them in order, fullness, apt expressions, holy oratory and fervour."[37]

Baxter himself attributed all this fruit—which represents not a brief episode but rather a ministry that spanned nearly two decades—chiefly to his system of catechizing households.[38] Ryle sees great significance in the fact that in his pastoral work Baxter had focused on things essential and concerned himself with passionate care of souls. "While some divines were wrangling about the divine right of Episcopacy or Presbytery, or splitting hairs about reprobation or free will, Baxter was always visiting from house to house, and beseeching men, for Christ's sake, to be reconciled to God and flee from the wrath to come."[39]

Even in the pulpit, Baxter's preaching was largely catechetical in nature. In his introduction to Baxter's *The Reformed Pastor*, J.I. writes,

> A schoolmaster by instinct, Baxter usually called himself his people's teacher, and teaching was to his mind the minister's main task. In his sermons (one each Sunday and Thursday, lasting an hour) he taught basic Christianity. "The thing which I daily opened to them, and with greatest importunity laboured to imprint upon their minds, was the great fundamental principles of Christianity contained in their baptismal covenant, even a right knowledge, and belief of, and subjection and love to, God the Father, the Son, and the Holy Ghost, and love to all men, and concord with the church and one another."[40]

This commitment to the fundamental principles led Baxter to give special attention to preaching on the Creed, the Lord's Prayer, and the Ten Commandments. Such work, Baxter reckoned, "takes a long time. And when that is done they must be led on . . . but not so as to leave the weak behind; and so as shall still be truly subservient to the great points of faith, hope and love, holiness and unity, which must be still [i.e., always, constantly] inculcated, as the beginning and end of all."[41] Baxter's "main contribution to the development of Puritan ideals for the ministry" was to "upgrade the practice of personal catechizing from a preliminary discipline for children to a permanent ingredient in pastoral care for all ages."[42]

These persistent and passionate labors of Baxter proved to have staying power in the hearts of the catechumens. After his absence of more than five years, he was able to write,

> Though I have now been absent from them about six years, and they have been assaulted with pulpit-calumnies, and slanders, with threatenings and imprisonments, with enticing words, and seducing reasonings, they yet stand fast and keep their integrity; many of them are gone to God, and some are removed, and some now in prison [i.e., for nonconformity], and most still at home; but not one, that I hear of, are fallen off, or forsake their uprightness.[43]

Nearly a century after Baxter's ministry in Kidderminster had ended, George Whitefield, having visited that township in December of 1743, wrote, "I was greatly refreshed to see what a sweet savour of good Mr Baxter's doctrine, works and discipline remain to this day."[44]

Through the impact of *The Reformed Pastor* Baxter's example was widely followed until 1659, when the Restoration process began and "confusion buryed all."[45] Baxter's leadership, and family catechizing with it, were at that point totally eclipsed, and no attempt to revive his catechetical pattern of procedure has ever been made.[46] Throughout the Christian world fresh thought and new beginnings are long overdue.

The Waning of Catechesis

The passion for catechesis that was apparent in the Reformation commitment to publish and distribute catechisms, and in the Puritan echo of that zeal that could be seen in the ministries of men like Baxter, in time would wane. In the introduction we identified some of the reasons for this under the heading *Obstacles*. We noted in particular the impact of, first, the *turn away from external authority* in Western culture, and, second, of the *resistance to authoritative instruction* within the Christian community. In addition to these forces, we would suggest that the following additional factors may have contributed to bringing us to the unhappy state of affairs in which we now find ourselves, in which catechesis is but a little-known and seldom-used strategy in our churches.

1. A Movement from Reformational Piety to Evangelical Pietism

At the time of the Reformation, when catechizing blossomed afresh, and on through the Puritan era an unmistakably theocentric concern held sway, finding expression in both the congregational teaching and the personal piety of the period. The proper question was seen to be, "What has the God of grace revealed that his servants should learn in order to honor him?" In the late seventeenth century, however, the first signs of a cultural shift from God-centeredness to human-centeredness began to appear in churches all over Europe. European pietism, which broke surface in the wake of Puritan piety, borrowing indeed a good deal from Puritanism in both its English and Scottish forms, was shaped by this shift. The German pietism of Spener and Franke, following Arndt; the Dutch pietism of Voetius, Witsius, and à Brakel; the English pietism of the Wesleys and Whitefield; the Norwegian pietism of Hauge; and the Moravian pietism of Zinzendorf, along with parallel developments elsewhere, sought to maintain vital spiritual life in the face of the devotional deadness of state churches.

Within the pietist world of experiential biblicism, however, a world in which life-transforming adult regeneration by the Holy Spirit was well understood and real personal fellowship with the Father and the Son really flourished, three specific shifts gradually occurred. Each went unnoticed at the time but was far reaching in its effects. First, the Reformation tag *sola scriptura*, which had originally meant "no authority *over* the Bible," came to mean "no authority *except* the Bible." Second, the godliness of the individual, rather than the glory of God in the church, became the primary focus of interest. Third, the study of the Bible directly came to be thought of as a much more trustworthy source of truth and wisdom for serving God than any aspect of the church's historical heritage. Slowly but steadily, therefore, the sense of the significance of the church and in particular of the churchly catechetical process evaporated, and the practice itself began to wither on the vine—less perhaps in Presbyterian and Reformed circles than elsewhere, but to some extent everywhere. And in any case, the question now being asked was, "How much (that is, how little!) do I need to know in order to be saved and live for God?"—which made the range of theological themes covered in the older catechetical forms seem excessive and superfluous. We inherit today much of this mindset under the label of "evangelicalism."

2. The Tendency toward Particularism in Catechesis

Historically, catechesis focused on grounding believers in the essentials of the Christian faith. Alongside this there has always been a need to proclaim that faith against the backdrop of competing ideologies. In the ancient church, that usually meant declaring the Christian vision vis-à-vis pagan beliefs and practices. As the church experienced divisions over the centuries, however, it became increasingly common for Christian communities to use catechesis to compete with other Christian communities. Thus catechesis has sometimes degenerated, if we dare to put it thus, into a polemic against other forms of Christianity rather than remaining a primarily positive proclamation of the Gospel and its implications for living. At the time of the Reformation, Protestants and Catholics sometimes used their printed catechisms to disparage each other. As Protestantism further splintered in subsequent generations, catechisms tended to become even more particularized. In many cases, this meant that secondary doctrines were promoted to the status of primary. For many, this made the vision of using a catechism for grounding believers in the Faith far less appealing.

In his *Introduction to the Heidelberg Catechism*, Lee Barrett writes:

> All too often in our history confessional divisions have spawned conflict, bitterness, and even violence. By the late sixteenth century, the proliferation of confessions of faith more often than not sowed seeds of discord rather than concord.[47]

Along these lines, T. F. Torrance quotes Horatius Bonar (1866; regarding distinctions between catechisms of the Reformation and the later Westminster catechisms).

It may be questioned whether the Church gained anything by the exchange of the Reformation standards for those of the seventeenth century. The scholastic mould in which the latter are cast has somewhat trenched upon the ease and breadth which mark the former; and the skilful metaphysics employed at Westminster in giving lawyer-like precision to each statement, have imparted a local and temporary aspect to the new which did not belong to the more ancient standards. Or, enlarging the remark, we may say that there is something about the theology of the Reformation which renders it less likely to become obsolete than the theology of the Covenant. The simpler formulae of the older age are quite as explicit as those of the later; while by the adoption of the biblical in preference to the scholastic mode of expression, they have secured for themselves a buoyancy which will bear them up when the others go down.[48]

3. The Decline of Sound Catechetical Practices

Ironically, the very technological advance that helped to reinvigorate catechesis at the time of the Reformation may well have helped to bring about its demise in the centuries following. The ability to print and widely distribute catechisms was an opportunity that the Reformers (and the Catholic counter-reformers after them) would not and did not miss. But we can see how this could and did have a serious downside. We recall that in the ancient church the basic ingredients of the catechism (that is, the content in which baptismal candidates were instructed) was never to be written down. This meant a full engagement of the mind was essential. It meant too that the relational dynamics between instructor and instructed could not be neglected. The catechist, for example, would declare the articles of the Creed line by line. The candidates in turn would repeat the lines until they were seared into the memory. The process also involved exposition of the lines. There were sponsors as well, members of the faithful with whom candidates could rehearse and discuss what they were learning. Once these things were in printed form it became very easy for the relational and holistic dimensions of catechesis to be lost.

Though the Reformers themselves warned against this, and though later pastors like Baxter worked tirelessly to avoid such problems, in the end it became all too easy in too many places for catechesis to be diminished to a mere memorization of the questions and answers in the printed catechisms. This of course is wholly inadequate for real learning to occur, and it would not be long before serious educators would quite rightly point this out and call loudly and long for something else.

Often, this new educational critique of poor educational practices in the church has been greatly informed by those who are not primarily concerned with a distinctively Christian education. In the twentieth century, for example, the influence of leaders and thinkers like John Dewey upon nearly all aspects of American education has been profound. This influence has made a deep and lasting mark upon evangelical efforts in education.

4. *The Widespread Adoption by the Churches of the Sunday School Model*

Just as there were unintended and unhappy consequences of the printing press upon catechesis, similar things might be said regarding the Sunday school movement. This lay-driven ministry began in 1780 when the Englishman Robert Raikes, at his own expense, gathered some Gloucester children together on Sunday morning to teach them reading and writing, to introduce them to religion, and reform their morals. It was really more of a compassion- and outreach-oriented parachurch endeavor than what we might properly call a Christian education program. But, finally overcoming initial skepticism from members of the clergy, churches on both sides of the Atlantic began adopting the Sunday school model as the chief vehicle for their Christian education efforts. This was the clear trend in North America by the early nineteenth century.

For all the wonderful things God has accomplished through the Sunday school movement, however, there are at least two ways in which this new approach to education in the churches negatively impacted ministries of catechesis. First, because the ministry was from its outset driven by lay members, pastors soon began withdrawing themselves as key players in the teaching ministries of their churches. The gain of having more laymen and laywomen take up the charge of helping to instruct, especially the youngest members of the congregations, was matched, on the negative side, by a diminishing of the vision of the pastor as teacher of the flock, something that was so basic and fundamental to the Reformers and to the Puritans. Grateful as we should always be for the exceptions, the fact is that many pastors have basically handed off their educational duties to others—typically to good-hearted members of the congregation who often have far less theological training or sensitivity than themselves.

A second unintended consequence of the Sunday school movement is linked to the formation of Sunday school unions. These unions were formed to help keep this lay-driven movement sustained and supplied, especially with teacher training and curriculum development. The unions represented ecumenical efforts to advance the Sunday school agenda. Baptists and Presbyterians, Methodists and Episcopalians found themselves working together for a common cause. This of course was praiseworthy in many respects. But this also meant that continued use of catechisms—which had been widely used in early Sunday school endeavors—sometimes became problematic. For example, Question and Answer 74 in the *Heidelberg Catechism* reads as follows:

Q: Are infants also to be baptized?
A: Yes, because they, as well as their parents, are included in the covenant and belong to the people of God.

Obviously such thinking was unacceptable to Baptists and members of certain other denominations (see point 2 above for background here). Partly in order to avoid such doctrinal controversies, the Sunday school unions came to advocate that only the Bible should be used for instruction. This likely sounds like a very reasonable thing to most evangelical Protestant ears. And great efforts were made to introduce a consistency and comprehensiveness in the use of the Bible. But is it really possible to avoid teaching doctrinal controversy by teaching the Bible? In order to come as close as possible to achieving this goal, it was inevitable that the focus of the biblical teaching would shift from doctrinal emphases and would arrive at last at the teaching of Bible stories. While the teaching of Bible stories is surely a good thing, this has often been done in a way that separates the particular stories from the broader story of God's redemptive dealings with humankind. This in turn can easily mean that attention is taken away from the grace of God revealed in Jesus Christ to mere rehearsal of episodic events, often followed by a moral admonition: "We see how Jonah got himself in trouble, so we had better not. . . ." "Mary gave herself wholly to the Lord, and so should we. . . ."

A child who has grown up even recently in an evangelical Sunday school will likely be very familiar with the stories of Noah, Moses, Jonah, and Mary. But that same child will be far less likely to be able to recite the Apostles' Creed or enumerate the Ten Commandments. Here then is yet another great irony. In what was deemed an effort to preserve and promote unity (by removing the historic catechisms from being part of the Sunday school curriculum), attention to those historic summaries of the faith that had previously served as a unifying force among Christians of nearly all traditions was undermined.

5. An Emphasis on "Growing the Church" That Is Often Simplistic and Lacking in Holistic Concern

It seems clear that much of what has occurred in recent decades under the broad heading of "church growth" has been driven largely by the desire to reach as many people as possible for Christ. This noble aim is fed by a biblically appropriate evangelistic passion. But in practice this has often meant that while we are concerned that people *come* to the church, we have not thought deeply enough about what they will *become* in time within the church. And this is complicated further by the very human tendency to look for examples of what seem to be "successful" churches and then to simply copy their behavior. By no means do we mean to imply (for example) that all so-called "megachurches" have sold their souls for the sake of numbers. Rather we are concerned that churches of all sizes and shapes need to take more seriously the fact that our commission is to disciple the nations, not merely to draw large crowds to ourselves. When we focus merely on the latter, we may assume (perhaps mistakenly) that we need to lower the bar of expectations to prove attractive to the masses. A rigorous catechetical experience would surely seem unwise by this standard.[49]

6. *The Impact of the Proliferation of Denominations and of Nondenominational Churches*

The fact is that Protestantism is currently more fractured than ever (there are reportedly more than thirty-nine thousand Christian denominations in the world as of this writing—the overwhelming majority of them Protestant—and the number is rising daily).[50] While many of the denominational splits may have been necessary at the time they occurred (some divisions are inevitable: 1 Cor. 11:19), there can be no doubt that many more have been simply the result of well-meant but wrongheaded and hard-hearted choices. Tragically, we have not taken seriously enough Jesus's commands and prayers for unity (John 13:34–35; 17:23) nor Paul's emphatic pleas for the same (Eph. 4:3). On top of this, there is the proliferation of nondenominational and independent churches. With so much obvious diversity and so little apparent unity, even where catechesis is taken seriously among Protestants it can often seem like a scene from the era of the Judges, when "everyone did what was right in his own eyes" (Judg. 1:25). We who know we really must catechize seem to be constantly reinventing the wheel. This is all the more troublesome in an age when the experience of so many is so transient. As people move freely from town to town, even those evangelicals who underwent some form of catechizing in one church community are very unlikely to find anything significantly similar in whatever new church they may settle into. Against such a backdrop, it should not surprise us that many Protestant pilgrims finally tire of this experience of rootlessness and aimlessness and find themselves attracted—even against their theological convictions—to communities which, by contrast, seem to be havens of stability, such as Roman Catholic or Orthodox churches.[51]

Conclusion

For all the reasons stated above, and doubtless for many others, the idea of a rigorous catechesis has fallen out of favor in most evangelical communities. Nevertheless, the evidence of great need for such instructional and formational ministry in our time is compelling. So too is the evidence that catechetical ministry done wisely and well can be profoundly potent for good. Beginning with the next chapter we therefore turn to proposals for rediscovering or renewing a faithful catechesis in contemporary congregations.

4

Sources and Resources
for Catechetical Ministry

My dear brother, learn Christ and him crucified.[1]

Martin Luther

And beginning with Moses and all the Prophets, [Jesus]
interpreted to them in all the Scriptures the things concerning himself.

Luke 24:27

We now turn our attention to the task of identifying sound catechetical content for application in contemporary congregations. In subsequent chapters, we will address some of the other critical elements that must accompany a good experience of catechesis—developmental and cultural sensitivity, faithful processes in appropriate settings, and the role of vital relationships. For now, though, we consider the makeup of the catechism itself, focusing in on the question: *What* must be taught?[2]

75

Content versus Process?

The first thing to say is that faithful and fruitful catechesis as we conceive it requires sustained attention to issues of both content and process. This is a matter over which it is easy to become one-sided, and many do, both in the church and in all arenas of the wider world in which educational theory is discussed. The exaggerations of cartoonists can, we know, feed prejudice, but they can also clarify issues, and we offer now a cartoon-type version of the modern content-versus-process brouhaha, to help our readers see what is at stake in the debate.

Observe, then, the traditionalists, who argue for rigidity and fidelity in the educational process in terms of *what* we teach. And now observe the progressives, who argue for relevance and effectiveness in the same process in terms of *how* we teach. For the former, content is all; they focus exclusively on the subject matter to be taught. For the latter, however, the focus is entirely on the learners. "I don't teach math," one might say indignantly; "I teach students!" Comeback from the traditionalists: "You teach your students *what*, exactly?" Longing to cultivate critical thinking skills, progressives shrink back from anything that seems like a mere dispensing of information, seeing that as mind-numbing. Traditionalists, for their part, cannot stop wondering just what it is learners will think critically about if they have no adequate knowledge base to start from. But traditionalists reveal a one-sidedness of their own when they concentrate on direct communication of the subject matter to be taught and leave it all to find its own level in the personal outlook of those being instructed. Progressives, championing process, argue in response that mere transmission of content, without evoking interest and thought about it, is precisely not good education; to which the waspish reply is that incomplete and insufficient transmission of content can hardly improve the situation. Say the progressives: "Your method will induce boredom, incomprehension, and apathy." "Your method," retort the traditionalists, "will lead to superficiality, waywardness, and arrogance." So the exchanges go on. Within the church, where the traditionalists are usually conservatives while the progressives are liberals, the two groups regularly manage to speak both past each other and disdainfully about each other at the same time, and all departments of Christian education become battlegrounds. It is a sad scene, and one that leaves the learning process less than fully fruitful across the board.[3]

Against this background of unbalanced, lopsided, and barren feuding, we want simply to say once more that content and process must be objects of equal attention, working together in the communicative transaction, if there is to be faithful and fruitful catechesis. Otherwise, both the teaching and the learning will be defective and deficient. Being really and truly serious, and tenacious, about substantive content must be matched by equal concern and endeavor for sound educational process, the stimulating of critical thought and the formation of discerning powers of judgment. Elevating the task of teaching the given material, in the sense of laying it out in full, must not in any way smother or undercut the reflective exercises of mind that are required for genuinely learning it, in the sense of apprehending and internalizing it. Education is not indoctrination! What confronts us here, then, in this ongoing wrangle are false dichotomies and demeaning suspicions, all of which we reject in no uncertain terms, as we trust that the rest of this book will show.

Our emphasis on sound and substantive catechetical content must be unwavering. But it must be remembered that this is only one part of the task. In the book's final chapter we shall present seven Cs for cultivating faithful and fruitful catechesis in contemporary congregations. Only one of them is primarily concerned with the issue of content. To be diligent at this point but negligent at any of the other six points will likely doom our journey in catechesis to relative failure. But on the other hand to be strong on the other six points and weak on this one will also steer us toward futility.

We turn first, then, to a consideration of *what* it is that we must teach for faithful and fruitful catechesis. At this point our focus, as the title of this chapter suggests, is on discerning sources and resources for catechetical content. In subsequent chapters, we flesh out our proposal for the actual substance of what might with advantage be taught in our churches today.

As a memory aid, we organize our thoughts with this simple numeric pattern in mind: 5–4–3–2–1. These figures represent the following elements:

5—Five founts, or frames, for the catechesis	Triune God → Scripture → the Story → the Gospel → the Faith			
4—Four fixtures of the catechism	Creed	Lord's Prayer	Decalogue	Sacraments
3—Three facets of the Faith	The Truth		The Life	The Way
2—Two fundamentals of the Way	Love of God		Love of neighbor	
1—One focus of the catechetical content	Proclaim Christ			

All of this, of course, requires explanation. The rest of this chapter is devoted to that explanation. After having set forth this proposed outline for the content of our catechesis, the remaining chapters of the book will feature a number of suggestions regarding how to implement these elements in ministries of teaching and formation in evangelical congregations. And not only so—our hope (or should we say our dream?) is to formulate strategies that can be of service wherever the Bible and the Creeds are recognized as the true embodiment and channels of the truth of God's grace as revealed once and for all in and through our Lord Jesus Christ.

5—Five Founts, or Frames, for the Catechesis

To speak of five *founts* is to indicate that we are now identifying sources for all our catechetical content.[4] From these we derive the substance of vital catechesis, and together they form an ever-present backdrop for all catechetical ministry. Although these could certainly be framed or enumerated differently, we here specify the following five as the essential bases of our catechizing:

- *the Triune God*, who alone is God and has revealed himself to us
- *the Scriptures*, the faithful and trustworthy record of God's revelation
- *the Story*, which is unfolded in those Scriptures
- *the Gospel*, which is both apex and summary of the Story
- *the Faith*, which includes the Gospel and its implications

The Five Founts

1. THE TRIUNE GOD, WHO HAS REVEALED HIMSELF TO US

Of course, the ultimate source of all things good is the living God. "For from him and through him and to him are all things. To him be the glory forever. Amen" (Rom. 11:36). The almighty God is immortal, invisible, and incomprehensible. This one true God, according to Christian theology, eternally exists in three persons—Father, Son, and Holy Spirit. This Holy Trinity is an eternal, perfect, loving community. The Triune God, however, would be inaccessible to finite and fallen humans were it not for God's gracious self-revelation. "No one has seen God at any time," writes John, "but God the one and only Son, has revealed him" (John 1:18). To have seen Jesus, the Son, is to have seen the Father (John 14:9). Through the ministry of the Holy Spirit, we are invited into personal knowledge of and vital communion with the living God. That is, we are invited to participate in the life and love, joy and peace, righteousness and holiness that always characterize the Holy Trinity. How do we know these things? We know them because this good God has chosen to reveal them to us in the Scriptures.

2. THE HOLY SCRIPTURES, THE FAITHFUL RECORD OF GOD'S REVELATION

All Scripture, as Paul wrote to Timothy, "is God-breathed, and is useful for teaching, rebuking, correcting, and training in righteousness, that the man of

God may be fully equipped for every good work" (2 Tim. 3:16–17). The Bible is true in all that it teaches us and is the only fully authoritative guide for life and faith. The ministry of catechesis may well employ various traditions as handed down through the history of the church, but these must ultimately be tested and approved by appeal to the teachings of the Bible.

Holy Scripture must always be allowed to have the last word. To put it bluntly, our God is a speaking God who has used particular Hebrew, Aramaic, and Greek words, arranged in sentences and paragraphs in documents of canonical status, to open his mind to us and tell us things—specifically, to tell us of his covenant love for the lost, and to explain to us what he has done, is doing, and will do to re-create and reorder his lapsed world, with ourselves as part of it. This is the revealed truth by which he now calls his believing people, the new humanity, to live.

3. THE REDEMPTIVE STORY, WHICH IS UNFOLDED IN THOSE SCRIPTURES

The Scriptures record for us the marvelous Story of God's redemptive dealings with all that he created, especially with humankind. The Story can be conceived as having various acts or movements. A familiar and very simple outline traces the Story through these four acts: creation, fall, redemption, culmination. There are of course many other ways the Story might be outlined. The vital thing is that God has acted, is acting, and will act in and through Jesus Christ to reconcile all things to himself. In this Story we learn that we, as God's people, have already been reconciled to God through the cross of Christ. And having been reconciled we ourselves have been made ministers of reconciliation.

4. THE GLORIOUS GOSPEL, WHICH IS BOTH THE APEX AND SUMMARY OF THE STORY

The Gospel of Jesus Christ is both the climactic element and the vital summary of this great Story. This Gospel itself can be summarized in three words:

"God Saves Sinners." By this we mean that, *God*—the Triune Jehovah, Father, Son and Spirit; three Persons working together in sovereign wisdom, power and love to achieve the salvation of a chosen people, the Father electing, the Son fulfilling the Father's will by redeeming, the Spirit executing the purpose of Father and Son by renewing; *saves*—does everything, first to last, that is involved in bringing man from death in sin to life in glory: plans, achieves and communicates redemption, calls and keeps, justifies, sanctifies, glorifies; *sinners*—men as God finds them, guilty, vile, helpless, powerless, unable to lift a finger to do God's will or better their spiritual lot.[5]

The good news of the Gospel is not only the apex and summary of the Story; it must also always be the very heart of our catechizing.

5. The Faith, which includes the Gospel and its implications for living

We saw in chapter 2 that the New Testament presents two related but distinct conceptions of faith. There is *our* faith by which we respond to God's revelation of his character, deeds, promises, and will. Such faith is described and illustrated in Hebrews 11. And there is *the* Faith, that is, the good deposit of God's revelation to us through Christ and the apostles. This Faith, once for all delivered to the saints (Jude 3), is to be safeguarded, contended for, obeyed, and passed on from generation to generation. When we speak of catechesis as a process, one of our key goals is to nurture faith in the former sense. When we speak of the content of the catechism, our goal is to properly teach the Faith in the latter sense. Here is a topical outline of what, at a minimum, actually constitutes "the Faith."

1. The glorious Gospel of the blessed God (1 Tim. 1:11), and these further dimensions of the Faith that derive from the Gospel:
2. the sound doctrine that conforms to the Gospel (1 Tim. 1:10);
3. the life-giving benefits that flow from the Gospel (2 Tim. 1:10); and
4. the way of living that expresses and reflects the truth of the Gospel (Titus 2:1).[6]

It is clear from the above that the Gospel is as central to our notion of the Faith as it is to what we have called the Story. Indeed, we could properly call the Faith "the Faith of the Gospel" (a Pauline expression; Phil. 1:27). But whereas the Story presents the vital teachings of Scripture in a narrative framework, the Faith presents them in a historically informed, thematic, and theological framework. Both approaches are biblically affirmed and exemplified, and each has its part to play in a sound ministry of catechesis.

Five Ways of Framing Catechesis

Each of the five founts could be taken up in its own right as the principal source or resource from which to work as we design and implement our catechesis. In other words, each can also provide us with a way of framing, or conceptualizing and organizing, our instruction.

1. A catechesis of the Trinity

Some may choose to build their entire approach to catechesis around the doctrine of the Trinity. Such an approach is suggested by numerous documents regarding catechetical renewal in the Catholic church. In the *National Directory for Catechesis*, for example, we read, "The harmony and coherence of the Christian message require that the different truths of the Faith be organized around a center, the mystery of the Most Holy Trinity: 'the source of all the other mysteries of faith, the light that enlightens them.'"[7] This emphasis on the Triune God is first in what is described as a "hierarchy of truths" within Catholic doctrine.[8] In recent years many evangelical theologians have also shown a keen interest in the Trinity as an organizing principle for displaying the life and ministry of the church. Few, however, have specifically related this to the ministry of catechesis; but for some that will surely be the next step.

From such a way of framing our efforts the goal of catechesis will be that our instruction leads us more deeply into a living communion with the Triune God. James B. Torrance suggests the following definition of Christian worship: "Worship is the gift of participating through the Spirit in the incarnate Son's communion with the Father."[9] We might choose to conceptualize our catechesis as leading us toward a fuller experience of such worship.

Catechetical content, in this framework, can be divided according to the three Persons of the Godhead so that it becomes explicitly a catechesis of the Father, the Son, and the Holy Spirit. As we saw in chapter 3, catechesis has actually had a Trinitarian form from its earliest days. Building upon the baptismal formula of Matthew 28:18–20, "baptizing them in the name of the Father, and of the Son, and of the Holy Spirit," creedal formulations developed in this way. Both the Apostles' Creed and the Nicene Creed have clear Trinitarian structures. These creeds have long been a centerpiece for catechizing, as we have seen already. The renewed emphasis on Trinitarian theology in recent years may make this a particularly appealing framework for today's church leaders, particularly in mainline denominations where liberal incursions have long obscured Trinitarian truth.

2. A Catechesis of the Scriptures

To be sure, all Christian catechesis should be biblically based and Scripture-rich. In some Christian communities, though, cultural sensitivity may require taking this even further. We have already noted the fact that in some church circles there is a strong sentiment that may be, and often is, expressed as follows: "No book but the Bible; no creed but Christ; no law but love." Those seeking to establish or renew sound ministries of catechesis in such communities may find that building their catechetical content primarily upon a biblical framework and employing self-consciously biblical language will reduce resistance from church members. Other church leaders whose members really offer no such protestations but whose congregations, for whatever reason, have not been exposed to regular Bible teaching may well feel that a primarily or exclusively biblical way of framing things is for them the best possible course.

Such a framework may focus on systematically working through the Scriptures, both from the pulpit and in additional settings that are more specifically geared for formal catechesis. Cyril of Jerusalem, we are told, began his own formal catechesis by teaching through "the entire Scriptures," which he managed to do, apparently, in a very brief span of time.[10] More compelling for many in "Bible only" communities will be the example of Jesus instructing the apostles after his resurrection. Jesus said to them, "Everything must be fulfilled that is written about me in the Law of Moses, the Prophets and the Psalms" (Luke 24:44). These three terms represented the threefold division of the Hebrew Bible. Luke explains, "Then he opened their minds so they could understand the Scriptures" (Luke 24:45).

The primary goal of such a "catechesis of the Scriptures" could be well summarized by this text from 2 Timothy:

> From infancy you have known the holy Scriptures, which are able to make you wise for salvation through faith in Christ Jesus. All Scripture is God-breathed and is useful for teaching, rebuking, correcting and training in righteousness, so that the man of God may be thoroughly equipped for every good work. (3:15–17 NIV)

Surveys of the Scriptures, feeding at each point into the realities of biblical faith and living, will always constitute a nourishing diet.

3. A CATECHESIS OF THE STORY

A similar but distinct approach to framing our catechesis would be to take a narrative approach. Here the primary aim will be to help congregants understand God's grand redemptive work so that they may more fully take their appropriate places in that Story. To the disciples on the road to Emmaus Jesus unfolded the biblical testimony that pointed to his own life, suffering, death, and subsequent glorification. "And beginning with Moses and all the Prophets, he interpreted to them in all the Scriptures the things concerning himself" (Luke 24:27). These things were not separate from the Story like hidden objects in a child's puzzle picture but consisted of patterns, performances, and predictions integral to the Story itself. Knowledge of the Story thus was, and remains, necessary for full knowledge of Christ.

Augustine believed that this Story, which he called the *narratio*, was the best place to begin *procatechesis*—that is, the preliminary catechizing of those interested in becoming Christians or at least in learning more about the Faith. To such as these, Augustine wrote, the catechist should tell the Story in a compelling fashion. Rather than surveying all of the Scriptures, emphasis will be placed on a selective "unrolling of the scroll" before the hearers, highlighting the most critical episodes in the drama. For Augustine the *narratio* would extend from creation to the current age of the church.

A Story-based catechesis might be very congenial to many church leaders today, especially where it is perceived that the surrounding culture is largely postmodern in orientation. While a feature of postmodern thought is its dismissal of all forms of a single metanarrative that fits all persons in all cultures, interest in hearing the stories of others is irrepressibly human and often very keen. Thus some evangelistic ministries have moved from more propositional presentations of the Gospel to more narrative-based approaches.[11]

4. A CATECHESIS OF THE GOSPEL

At the heart of the Story, as we have seen, is the Gospel. Using the language of "passing on" what he himself had received, Paul wrote to the Corinthians that "what I received I passed on to you as of first importance: that Christ died for our sins according to the Scriptures, that he was buried, that he was raised on the third day according to the Scriptures, and that he appeared" (1 Cor. 15:3–5). We can see from his language—"of first importance"— that in any faithful approach to catechesis, the Gospel must have a place of priority.

And the Gospel will be not only the starting place for our catechizing; it will guide us from beginning to end. In terms of catechetical aims this approach envisions believers and churches becoming, like the apostle Paul, wholly "set apart for the Gospel of God" (Rom. 1:1). There is recognition that the Gospel alone imparts life and brings immortality to light (2 Tim. 1:10), enabling believers to truly live for the glory of God. In terms of catechetical content, then, the notion is not that we move from the "milk" of the Gospel to the "meat" of something more profound. Rather, we move from the milk of the Gospel to the meat of the Gospel, and, to change the metaphor, to know that we are never able to fully plumb its glorious depths. Neither on earth nor in heaven will Christians ever grow weary of contemplating the truth, faithfulness, justice, and love of the Father and the obedient, self-humbling, self-sacrificing love of the Son, which the Gospel so wonderfully highlights.

5. A CATECHESIS OF THE FAITH

The fifth of our possible frames would be a catechesis built around the concept of *the Faith* once for all delivered to the saints. This is clearly a very ancient form of conceptualizing such ministries. From many of the ancient fathers we hear reference to the Faith, or the "rule of faith," as embodying the proper content in which to catechize others.

While such language was often equated by the fathers with some sort of creedal confession, we believe that the biblical use of the term "the Faith" not only extends to what we believe or should believe, but also addresses how we are to live as well as teaching us where to find the power for such living. In other words, as we saw above, a catechesis in the Faith would include attention to: (1) the Gospel itself; (2) the sound doctrine that conforms to the Gospel; and (3) the life-giving power of the Gospel that enables us to walk in (4) the manner of living that is in line with the Gospel. The goal of such a catechetical framework would be that we more fully believe the Faith and become more obedient to it (see Acts 6:7).

Progressive Fount, Interrelated Framework, Vital Content

There is yet another way to conceive of the above five emphases. Perhaps the reader has already discerned how these can be seen as a progressive fount in the following way. All begins, of course, with the Triune God; from him, through him, and to him are all things. This God has revealed himself to us in the Scriptures. The Scriptures tell us of God's great redemptive Story, the centerpiece of which is the Gospel. The Gospel and its implications constitute the Faith. It is this sort of conception of things that we advocate here. This fivefold relationship could be diagrammed very simply as follows:

the Triune God → the Scriptures → the Story → the Gospel → the Faith

Thinking of the five as being interrelated in this way lends itself to an equally interrelated framework for catechizing. Thus rather than choosing one of our five elements as a primary framework, we would advocate using all of them. Each clearly has something important to contribute to our understanding of the whole. Each has biblical validity. Each has historical precedents. Each, as well, has contemporary practical value and appeal. As the author of Ecclesiastes put it, "For everything there is a season, and a time for every matter under heaven" (Eccles. 3:1). Our approach to catechesis involves a similar conviction about the five elements. There is a time when each of our five features provides just the right emphasis. And there is never a time when any of them should leave our view completely.

Beyond serving as sources for catechizing and/or as ways of framing our catechesis, each of the five elements we have identified can and should be part of its actual content. Certainly catechesis will have much to say about the Triune God—his nature, names, character, decrees, deeds, and more. In a manner of speaking, one might even claim that the God of the Scriptures is the *only* proper subject matter for catechesis. In any case, attention to God must be preeminent in any faithful and fruitful catechetical work. Both the Westminster catechisms begin by establishing an unmistakable God-centeredness and both offer definitions and descriptions of God within their first few questions and answers. In less formal catechesis—such as through our worship, fellowship, and service—God must remain equally central in all our pursuits.

The Scriptures should be read, proclaimed, and explained in all our various settings of preaching and teaching, including those of formal catechesis. The Story, too, is vital content not only for inquirers in the Faith but for all the faithful as well. Annual observance of the church year provides one important opportunity for retelling the Story and reminding us of our places in that Story.

The Gospel is proper content not only for the earliest stages of catechesis but for every phase. Many have argued that every sermon must contain some proclamation of the Gospel. The Gospel is also visually portrayed and proclaimed through the sacraments. In formal catechesis, too, we may move forward *in* the Gospel, but we never move on *from* the Gospel. The Faith, as we have said, includes the Gospel and its implications for life and doctrine. It also constitutes critical content for catechesis, as we shall see.

4—Four Fixtures of the Catechism

- the Apostles' Creed
- the Decalogue
- the Lord's Prayer
- the sacraments

In chapter 3 we observed that the content of the historic catechisms focused on expositions of the Creed, the Commandments, and the Lord's Prayer, together with instruction on the sacraments. Sometimes this content is presented as a fourfold formulation. At other times, it is presented as a threefold pattern to which instructions about the sacraments have been appended. Luther spoke consistently of the "three parts" of the catechism—Commandments, Creed, and Lord's Prayer—as the ancient inheritance of Christendom. But he certainly included in his catechisms instruction on the sacraments. Is it three parts or four then? Perhaps we should think in the language of a Hebrew proverb and say, "There are three parts of the catechism, four that can instruct us."[12] Under the next heading of this chapter—"Three Facets of the Faith"—we will argue for a threefold pattern in catechesis. At present, however, we concern ourselves with our inherited catechisms and their four historic fixtures.

The table below indicates the arrangement of the four fixtures in various catechisms. As we saw in chapter 3, Luther and Calvin were very intentional about the placement of the Ten Commandments relative to the Creed. Calvin's first catechism followed Luther's proposed order, but he changed that order in the *Geneva Catechism*. The *Heidelberg Catechism* aimed at the best of both worlds. Explaining the rest of his ordering choices, Ursinus, author of the *Heidelberg Catechism*, declared that the sacraments follow the Creed because they also help to unfold the Gospel, and the Lord's Prayer follows the Decalogue because both of these parts are concerned with grateful response to God's redeeming work in Christ.

The Westminster catechisms contain no exposition of the Creed (though in printed editions it is often appended at the end, without commentary). Had it been included, though, it would surely have been ordered as in Calvin's *Geneva Catechism.* In place of an exposition of the Creed, the Westminster catechisms contain various theological teachings, including an unfolding of God's redemptive work—a task which others left to the Creed. The earliest Anglican catechism, that of 1549, was very brief and also followed the order of Calvin's second catechism. The most recent of the Catholic catechisms uses an order like that of the *Heidelberg* and a similar rationale is offered.

Luther's catechisms	Decalogue	Creed	Lord's Prayer	Sacraments	Additional teachings
Calvin's first catechism	Decalogue	Creed	Lord's Prayer	Sacraments	Additional teachings
Geneva Catechism	Creed	Decalogue	Lord's Prayer	"Of the Word"	Sacraments
Heidelberg Catechism	Summary of the Law	Creed	Sacraments	Decalogue	Lord's Prayer
Westminster catechisms	Theological foundations	Decalogue	Sacraments	Lord's Prayer	Creed often appended
Anglican catechism[13]	Creed	Decalogue	Lord's Prayer	Sacraments	
Catholic catechism[14]	Creed	Sacraments	Decalogue	Lord's Prayer	

Roman Catholics have perhaps been most explicit in conceiving of the catechism in this fourfold way. From at least the time of Trent—and the catechetical renewal that sprung thence—these four elements have been referred to as "the Four Pillars" of the catechism. The Creed is set forth as having priority of place among the four. The twentieth-century Jesuit catechetical leader Josef Andreas Jungmann writes, "*The Creed should have precedence*—according to the whole of Christian tradition—since, to say no more, the main block of the distinctive teachings of faith are found there."[15]

The priority of the Creed helps us see how these four parts flow naturally from the five founts. The last of our five founts was "the Faith." Such language is, as we saw in chapter 2, very important biblically. This biblical language was taken up by the earliest church fathers who, as we noted above, sometimes used the phrase or a variant—the "rule of faith"—to refer to the emerging creedal formulas of the church. Returning to our five founts, we could say that both the Story and the Faith represent expansions upon the Gospel. The Story expands upon the Gospel in narrative form; the Faith expands in a form that is somewhat more propositional and didactic. Both approaches, we have already argued, are helpful and have important roles to play in catechetical ministry.

The four parts of the catechism represent a sort of distilling of the Faith. We can trace its movements as follows:

There are *five founts, or frames, for catechesis* → the fifth element of which is *the Faith* → which has been traditionally communicated through the *four fixtures of the catechism.*

The rationale for this four-part design of the catechism among both Reformers and Catholic catechists is based upon two primary convictions. The first conviction is that these ingredients of the catechism represent an ancient pattern. We noted this already in chapter 3. The second conviction is that this pattern is wise and comprehensive and addresses all major aspects of the spiritual life for both individuals and congregations. The Creed addresses fundamental Christian beliefs and is thus a sort of primer on theology. The Commandments address Christian behavior and are thus a sort of primer on ethics. The Lord's Prayer helps the believer in his or her communion with God and is thus a sort of primer on prayer. The sacraments also help us in our communion with God, as well as helping us celebrate the Gospel, and are thus a sort of primer on congregational worship.

The following table illustrates how these four components have sometimes been viewed in this comprehensive scheme of things. Note that the sacraments have sometimes been regarded as a separate category in catechisms, but sometimes not. A biblical foundation or precedent for this fourfold content can be seen in the four commitments of Acts 2:42. We have indicated this in the bottom row of the table. The numbers before each item represent the order in which the four elements occur in the various sources.

	Apostles' Creed	Decalogue	Lord's Prayer	Sacraments
Augustine's Enchiridion	1. Faith	2. Love[16]	3. Hope	
Catechism of the Catholic church	1. Profession of faith	3. Life in Christ	4. Christian prayer	2. Celebration of the mystery
Baxter's use of three formulae	1. Doctrine of faith	2. Law of our practice	3. Matter of our desires	
***Growing in Christ* (Packer)[17]**	1. Affirming the essentials: Convictions	4. Design for life: Code of conduct	3. Learning to pray: Communion with God	2. Entering in: Covenanting in baptism: conversion, commitment, and church life
***Anglican Catechism in Outline* (2008)[18]**	1. Faith: new foundation/ the Nicene Creed	3. Love: prepared for good works/ the Decalogue	2. Hope: new identity and calling/the Lord's Prayer	
Acts 2:42[19]	1. The teaching of the apostles	2. The fellowship	3. The prayers	4. The Lord's Supper

In the ancient catechumenate, as we noted in chapter 3, elements such as the Creed and the Lord's Prayer were typically reserved for the final stage of catechetical preparation for baptism. Teaching about the sacraments sometimes preceded the actual celebration of those sacraments. Others, however, preferred new believers to have the tactile and spiritual experience prior to receiving the instruction. While instruction in the Ten Commandments was not a common catechetical practice until medieval times, instruction in the moral behavior that befits Christians was a constant from the earliest efforts to catechize new believers and often included explanation of various biblical commandments.

As we will affirm below, we believe that instruction in these four parts of the catechism is still very profitable today. Luther's catechetical instructions on the sacraments were placed alongside his more basic catechetical materials on the Commandments, the Creed, and the Lord's Prayer. His convictions regarding these "three parts" could well be applied to all four elements. In these, wrote Luther, "everything contained in Scripture is comprehended in short, plain, and simple terms, for the dear fathers or apostles, whoever they were, have thus summed up the doctrine, life, wisdom, and learning which constitute the Christian's conversation, conduct, and concern."[20] Luther's basic conviction has been shared in one degree or another by the majority of Christians through most of the past two millennia. We ought not to be so hasty, then, in dismissing, as though they were no longer relevant, these four parts of the historic catechism in its various forms.

3—Three Facets of the Faith

- The Truth
- The Life
- The Way

As we noted above, the traditional structure of the catechism has sometimes been thought of as having four parts, and sometimes as having three. Thus Augustine's *Enchiridion*—which featured expositions of the Creed, the Lord's Prayer, and the double commandment of love—was constructed on the triad of faith, hope, and love. Luther, as we saw, added instruction about the sacraments, but referred again and again to the "three parts." Jungmann similarly speaks of the three summaries or formulae as forming the heart of the catechism, but continues immediately by suggesting that teaching on the sacraments "can be considered separately."[21]

More recently, in his contemporary catechetical work *Growing in Christ*, J.I. explains that his book is a series of studies on "the three formulae which have always been central in Christian teaching—the Creed, the Lord's Prayer, and the Ten Commandments—plus Christian baptism."[22] The idea of the Hebrew proverb again sounds apt: "three parts, even four." What are we to make of all this?

Here is a suggestion: The four parts of the catechism represent and bear witness to three facets of the Faith. Our journey, then, will look like this:

There are *five founts, or frames, for catechesis* → the fifth element of which is *the Faith* → which has been traditionally communicated through the *four fixtures of the catechism* → which together bear witness to the *three facets of the Faith.*

While the "witnesses" are temporary, the facets of the Faith to which they point are enduring. When faith gives way to sight, we will no longer need a confession of faith, a creed, an "I believe." When we are in God's presence and delivered from all our present sinful proclivities we will no longer need commands to guide our behavior. When the Lord has returned we will no longer need to pray for his kingdom to come or his will to be done on earth. Nor will we need to continue the sacraments that testify to Christ's death and resurrection "until he comes" (1 Cor. 11:26).

Though the Creed is a temporal aid, the truth to which it testifies is enduring. The Triune God in whom we confess our faith is eternal and unchanging. The Decalogue instructs us in the way we should conduct ourselves. That way will still be the way of love and righteousness even when the need for commandments is no more. The life that we receive and celebrate through the Gospel is life abundant and eternal, granting a living relationship with the living God. This covenant relationship, which both sacraments express and celebrate, endures even when the need for ritual remembrance has passed and we no longer need to recite the Lord's Prayer.

We have chosen to call these three facets of the Faith "the Truth," "the Life," and "the Way," making use of the language of Jesus in John 14:6.[23] These were not three words randomly strung together by our Lord. Rather, they represent three critical strands of biblical teaching that are found in both Old and New Testaments.

The Truth refers to all God has revealed concerning himself, especially in Jesus Christ. This is daily shared by and among God's people through preaching, teaching, and living in light of the Gospel (Gal. 2:5; Eph. 1:13) and all the sound doctrine that accompanies it (1 Tim. 1:10). The Truth is to be believed, adhered to, and loved. Many, tragically, reject this Truth and are lost (2 Thess. 2:10–12). Jesus both testified to the Truth (John 18:37) and is himself the Truth incarnate (John 14:6), the totality of God's revelation concerning himself (John 1:1, 14, 18; Col. 1:15; 2:9; Heb. 1:1–3).

The Life, especially in John's writings, bespeaks a vital and eternal relationship with the living God (John 17:3). Jesus offers this Life to others (John 3:16; 4:10; 5:21; 10:10; 11:25–36; 20:31; 1 John 5:11–13) and is himself the Life incarnate. The Life is given through the ministry of the Holy Spirit to all who trust Christ (John 7:37–39; Rom. 8:9). We first experience the Life through the gift of new birth as, wholly by grace, we are made the children of God (John 1:12).

The Way is an expression found throughout the Hebrew Scriptures, typically describing the manner of living that God requires and delights in (Pss. 1:6; 32:8; Isa. 30:21). Sometimes expressed as "the way of the LORD," "the way of the righteous," or "the way of life," it is distinguished from "the way of the world," "the way of the wicked," and "the way of death." Jesus, in the Sermon on the Mount, speaks of two roads, one of which leads to destruction and the other of which leads to life (Matt. 7:13–14). Christians were early known as followers of "the Way" (Acts 9:2; 19:9, 23; 22:4; 24:14, 22). God's way is, in simplest terms, that we live in love of God and neighbor (Mark 12:29–31). As with the Truth and the Life, Jesus incarnated this Way—he, and he only, fully and consistently lived in obedience to these two greatest commandments. Furthermore, by walking in this Way faithfully, he has become for all who believe in him a new and living way into the Holy of Holies (Heb. 10:20). It is through the obedience of this one man (Rom. 5:19), in life and in death (Phil. 2:8), that we are enabled to know the Father and be in right relationship with him (John 14:6–9).

We shall be examining all this in much more detail in chapter 6, so we leave off for the moment and move on to the next item in our 5–4–3–2–1 outline.

2—Two Fundamentals of the Way

- Love the LORD your God
- Love your neighbor as yourself

The third of the three facets of the Faith we explored above concerns our conduct, or manner of life in this world. We have labeled this facet "the Way." Our movement to this point looks like this:

> There are *five founts, or frames, for catechesis* → the fifth element of which is *the Faith* → which has been traditionally communicated through the *four fixtures of the catechism* → which together bear witness to the *three facets of the Faith* → the third of which is *the Way.*

As we saw above, the Way is an important concept in both Testaments of the Bible, as well as in the history of catechesis. In *The Didache of the Apostles* (written sometime in the late first or early second century) the opening words run as follows: "There are two ways, the way of life and the way of death." These two divergent paths have also been known by other pairings, including:

the way of the righteous versus the way of the wicked (Ps. 1:6); the hard way that leads to life versus the easy way that leads to destruction (Matt. 7:13–14); and "the Way vs. not-the-way."[24]

There is a path, or way or manner of living, that has been designed by our loving God. It is a path of blessing, a road that leads to life and *shalom*. Besides those designations we have already noted, it is called in Scripture "the way of the good" (Prov. 2:20), "the way of wisdom" (Prov. 4:11), "the way of holiness" (Isa. 35:8), and "the way of God" (Luke 20:21). Jesus claimed *to be* the Way. His life and death both illustrate the Way and become for us a new and living way to a vital relationship through him with God (Heb. 10:20).

In a world of deep moral confusion, how does one discern the Way and distinguish it from paths that simply are not-the-way? According to the Hebrew Scriptures, the Way is discerned through contemplation upon the Torah. The Hebrew root from which the word *torah* springs means, as we saw earlier, "to shoot" or "to cast" and has the connotation of hitting a target, of pointing or guiding in the right direction. From the same root come words for "parent" and "teacher," as well as a key verb for "teaching." Thus the Torah—in written or embodied form—works to show weary wanderers the Way that they should walk. Isaiah 30:21 puts it like this: "Your ears shall hear a word behind you, saying, 'This is the way, walk in it.'"

A major goal of Christian catechesis is precisely this directive guidance in the Way. Christian teachers are to be models of the manner of living that God requires and desires. And we are to instruct others in the precepts of the Way. The Decalogue, as we have seen, is the primer in the Way historically affirmed by both Jews and Christians. Christian catechesis in this facet has also regularly included instruction from the Sermon on the Mount as well as from a variety of other biblical texts. The biblical book of Proverbs and the letter of James both prominently feature wisdom for walking in God's Way.

In simplest terms, the Way of the LORD is revealed as the way of love. To love is to walk in God's Way. Jesus affirmed more than once that the two greatest of all the commandments were these: "You shall love the LORD your God with all your heart, soul, mind, and strength . . . and you shall love your neighbor as yourself" (Mark 12:29–31; Luke 10:25–37). This double commandment of love is regarded by both Jews and Christians as a summary of the Ten Words and thus a summary of "the whole duty of man" (see Eccles. 12:13).

To love God and to love one's neighbor are the two nonnegotiable fundamentals of the Way. The Way is not a more vital facet of the Faith than either the Truth or the Life. But the Truth and the Life converge to enable us to walk in the Way. We can in fact articulate the goal of all catechetical ministry as follows: *Taught by the Truth and liberated by the Life, we walk in the Way.*

That obedience to God's Way must be our aim is made abundantly clear by a host of biblical teachings. Jesus was especially concerned with obedience (see, for example, Matt. 28:20; Luke 37; John 13:17; 14:15). Any attention to the

Truth and to the Life that does not lead to a sincere desire to walk in the Way profoundly misses the mark and dishonors God. In the ancient catechumenate this emphasis on obedience—on raising up a people who were distinguishable by the fact that they walked in the Way of Jesus—was very clear. At times in church history we have lost sight of this goal. Any serious attempts at catechetical renewal today must once again restore prominence to the life of love to which Christians are called. The two fundamentals of the Way—loving God and loving one's neighbor—must never be allowed to leave our sights.

Even as we point others toward these two fundamentals of the Way, however, we acknowledge that in all of human history there is only One who has fully obeyed and fully walked that Way. It is to Jesus Christ we must turn not only to see the Way lived out but also to receive forgiveness for our own deviance (from the Latin prefix *de* and noun *via*—a departing "from the way") and new power to begin walking in the Way that pleases God. Through Christ alone a "new and living way" has been opened for us to experience fellowship with the Triune God. We shall say more of this later.

1—One Focus of the Catechetical Content

- We Proclaim Christ

We come finally to the one focus of all our catechetical content. It is simply this: We proclaim Christ. This was Paul's stated content in his own ministry of teaching, a ministry which aimed at presenting "everyone mature in Christ" (Col. 1:28). Luther was convinced that what every Christian needs is to "learn Christ."[25] If Christians must *learn Christ* then we who catechize and preach must faithfully and fully *proclaim Christ*.

This Christ-centered approach is evident in all that we have discussed in this chapter. Each element of the fivefold fount points to Christ. The Triune God has revealed himself in Christ. The Scriptures testify to Christ. Christ is the central character in the redemptive Story. The Gospel is the proclamation of what God has done, and does now, in and through Christ. All of this is at the heart of the Faith that we pass on to others.

The four fixtures of the catechism likewise lead to Christ. The Creed focuses on the person and work of Christ. The Decalogue is the grounding, guardian, and guide that leads us as needy sinners to Christ (Gal. 3:24), who alone has completely kept these commands. The Lord's Prayer is the pattern of praise and petition which Christ himself taught; it looks ahead to his coming return and the final establishing of his kingdom. And the sacraments are signs and seals of Christ's saving work in our lives.

By naming the three facets of the Faith as we did—the Way, the Truth, and the Life—we were reminded that in all our teaching it is really Christ himself that we proclaim (Col. 1:28). The two fundamentals of the Way, love of God and love of neighbor, have been fully obeyed by Jesus alone in all of human history. Only from his example, which elucidates his teaching, do we learn what this double love really means. And only through his grace do we find forgiveness for all our wanderings and power to begin walking in the Way of Christian love ourselves.

The content of our catechesis, then, if we may put it so, must always be Christ-obsessed. It must ever be relayed and received as the expression of minds and hearts, the horizon of whose outlook is wholly filled from every angle by the figure—indeed the face—of Jesus Christ in person. We will see also that the best practices of catechesis are those that have been modeled for us by Jesus, the master Catechist. And as we have already seen, the proper aim of our catechetical labors is also all about Jesus Christ. In *Catechesis Tradendae*, his 1979 call to catechetical renewal in the Catholic church, Pope John Paul II explicitly promoted this very sort of Christocentrism:

> At the heart of catechesis we find, in essence, a Person, the Person of Jesus of Nazareth, "the only Son from the Father . . . full of grace and truth," who suffered and died for us and who now, after rising, is living with us forever. It is Jesus who is "the way, and the truth, and the life."
>
> The definitive aim of catechesis is to put people not only in touch but in communion, in intimacy, with Jesus Christ: only He can lead us to the love of the Father in the Spirit and make us share in the life of the Holy Trinity.[26]

Evangelical Protestants, of course, should be just as focused on the pre-eminence of Christ in all that we do, including our ministries of catechesis, as was John Paul II. It is Jesus Christ we must proclaim, and the imparting of true knowledge of him must be our goal. "In him the whole fullness of deity dwells bodily," and we "have been filled in him" (Col. 2:9–10). To know him truly and experientially must be our greatest ambition (Phil. 3:7). Toward this goal, according to "the upward call of God in Christ Jesus," we must ever press on and encourage others to press on with us (Phil. 3:14). May we ever *keep our eyes on the prize as we catechize.* (Pardon our picayune doggerel; it just happened, and will now serve to jog our memories, as perhaps it will jog yours.)

With such a Christocentric focus it is fitting that catechesis also be Gospel-centric. We earlier identified the Gospel as part of the fivefold fount of catechetical content. We saw also that it could serve as a possible overall framework for a faithful ministry of catechesis. In addition to these things we should also see the Gospel as a vital part of the actual content in which we catechize others. Indeed, according to the apostle, the Gospel must have priority of place in such ministry. In the next chapter, we examine this notion more fully.

Concluding Remarks

At the end of our survey of sources for essential content for catechizing, the movement within the 5–4–3–2–1 pattern we have followed looks like this:

> There are *five founts, or frames, for catechesis* → the fifth element of which is *the Faith* → which has been traditionally communicated through the *four fixtures of the catechism* → which together bear witness to the *three facets of the Faith* → the third of which is *the Way* → which has *two fundamentals*: love of God and love of neighbor → which Jesus alone has fully obeyed, and whose grace alone enables us to begin to obey. Therefore Jesus Christ must ever be the *one focus* of all our ministries of catechesis.

How shall we make practical use of these sources and resources for cat-echetical content? Our proposal will be unfolded in the following chapters. In brief, here is the approach we intend to take.

As to the fivefold fount, we acknowledge that all of the five elements are proper sources for catechesis. In practical terms, we utilize the Holy Scriptures as our primary *source* for catechetical material.

As to *framing* our content, we adopt a hybrid approach that includes ele-ments of the Story, the Gospel, and the Faith. These, as we have already suggested, are bound together in many ways. The Gospel is both apex and summary of the Story. The Faith is, in essence, comprised of the Gospel and its various implications for life and teaching. Our frame combines all three of these elements.

As to the actual *content* of instruction, nearly every element that we have identified in the present chapter must be taken up, somehow, in our teaching ministries. Where do we begin? We begin as the apostles did, with "the glori-ous Gospel of the blessed God" (1 Tim. 1:10).

The Gospel as of First Importance

> For I delivered to you as of first importance what I also
> received: that Christ died for our sins in accordance with
> the Scriptures, that he was buried, that he was raised on
> the third day, in accordance with the Scriptures, and that
> he appeared.
>
> 1 Corinthians 15:3–5

Historically, the church has understood that the Gospel of Jesus Christ must be the centerpiece of its *kērygma*. *Kērygma* is typically rendered as "proclamation," "declaration," or "preaching." The word appears eight times in the New Testament in this noun form. The church has long understood that the substance of our proclamation is Christ himself. Paul says precisely this in Colossians 1:28: "We proclaim him." In particular, the *kērygma* concerns certain realities about Christ, namely, the "proclamation of the death, resurrection, and exaltation of Jesus that led to evaluation of his person as both Lord and Christ, confronted man with the necessity of repentance and promised the forgiveness of sins."[1]

It is evident that the apostle Paul saw this Gospel as the sum and substance of his proclamation. He declared to the Corinthians that he had passed on to them, as of first importance, what he had also received (1 Cor. 15:3). He then outlined the Gospel in simple terms: "Christ died for our sins, according to the Scriptures . . . he was buried and on the third day he rose again, according to the Scriptures, and he appeared" (1 Cor. 15:4–6). This, he declares, is the Gospel that he preached to them, which they had received and upon which they had taken their stand (1 Cor. 15:1). Paul's language here is thoroughly catechetical—he has passed on what he himself had received. We can justly say that Paul's catechetical content began with the Gospel. Indeed, during his eighteen months of ministry in Corinth Paul had resolved to know nothing among them "except Jesus Christ and him crucified" (1 Cor. 2:2). In view of such a verse we might conclude that Paul's catechesis not only began with the Gospel; it continued with the Gospel and indeed ended with the Gospel, and set everything within the Gospel as its frame.

Paul described himself as one who had been "set apart for the Gospel" (Rom. 1:1). *In* the Gospel he served God with all his might (Rom. 1:9). *Of* the Gospel he had been "appointed a herald and an apostle and a teacher" (2 Tim. 1:11). "Testifying *to* the Gospel of God's grace" was the task that he raced to complete (Acts 20:24; emphasis added). From verses such as these, it becomes clear that Paul saw the Gospel as more than a onetime-only *kērygma* for unbelievers. Evangelicals have long acted as though the Gospel was the right "medicine" for unbelievers, but that believers need to move beyond the Gospel and go on to other things, a movement from the "milk" to the "meat." But this seems untrue—thoroughly out of step with the biblical witness. We believe, rather, that it is imperative to think of moving on from the "milk" of the Gospel to the "meat" of the Gospel. For in fact the Gospel is more profound and multifaceted than our finite minds can ever grasp. We never move on *from* the Gospel; we move on *in* the Gospel.

Thus we argue that the Gospel, which is the *kērygma* of the church, is also the heart of its *didachē* as well. *Didachē* is the Greek word rendered "teaching" in such New Testament passages as Acts 2:42. We noted earlier this key passage in which we read of the three thousand newly baptized believers who steadfastly devoted themselves to four things: "*the teaching of the apostles, the fellowship, the breaking of the bread and the prayers*" (emphasis added). While *didachē* is a rather general word for teaching derived from the most common of New Testament verbs for teaching—*didaskō*—it, like *kērygma*, has often been seen as also having a technical usage. Some have suggested that these two terms taken together—the *kērygma* and *didachē* of the church—cover the comprehensive content of the church's preaching and teaching ministries, respectively.[2]

We submit, however, that "the glorious Gospel of the blessed God" (1 Tim. 1:11) is the essence of both the New Testament *kērygma* and its *didachē*. Paul's personal interaction with the Gospel demonstrates this. Because the Gospel is the church's *kērygma*, Paul was "appointed a herald." Because it is also our *didachē*, Paul was appointed a teacher of the Gospel as well. He was also, he says in the same verse, appointed an apostle of the Gospel (2 Tim. 1:11). As an apostle Paul took the Gospel to places it had not been before (Rom. 15:20), setting forth this Gospel of Christ as the only sure foundation of faith (1 Cor. 3:10–11) and defending it against any and all perversions, as he does so vigorously, for example, in Galatians 1:6–9. Thus the glorious Gospel of the blessed God we are entrusted with must be proclaimed and taught among us who believe as well as to the waiting world. It is at the center of both our catechetical and our evangelistic work.

Biblical Summaries of the Gospel

The glorious Gospel is immeasurable in its depths and implications, yet it can be quite simply summarized. Here are just a few of the many examples of biblical summaries of the Gospel:[3]

- "He was pierced for our transgressions, he was crushed for our iniquities; the punishment that brought us peace was upon him, and by his wounds we are healed" (Isa. 53:5).[4]
- "For even the Son of Man did not come to be served, but to serve, and to give his life as a ransom for many" (Mark 10:45).
- "God so loved the world that he gave his one and only Son, that whoever believes in him should not perish but have eternal life" (John 3:16).
- "All the prophets testify about him that everyone who believes in him receives forgiveness of sins through his name" (Acts 10:43).
- "Through Jesus the forgiveness of sins is proclaimed to you. Through him everyone who believes is justified from everything you could not be justified from by the Law of Moses" (Acts 13:38–39).
- "He was delivered over to death for our sins and was raised to life for our justification" (Rom. 4:25).
- "But God demonstrates his own love for us in this: while we were still sinners, Christ died for us" (Rom. 5:8).
- "Christ died for our sins, according to the Scriptures . . . he was buried. . . . The third day he rose again from the dead, according to the Scriptures . . . and he appeared" (1 Cor. 15:3–6). Paul writes that this is the Gospel "I preached to you, which you received and on which you have taken your stand. By this Gospel you are saved" (1 Cor. 15:1–2). In outlining it here, Paul asserts that "what I received I passed on to you as of first importance" (1 Cor. 15:3).
- "God was in Christ, reconciling the world to himself, not counting men's trespasses against them" (2 Cor. 5:19).

- "God made him who knew no sin to be sin for us, that we might become the righteousness of God in him" (2 Cor. 5:21).
- "Remember Jesus Christ, raised from the dead, descended from David. This is my Gospel" (2 Tim. 2:8).
- "[He] gave himself for us to redeem us from all wickedness and to purify for himself a people that are his very own, eager to do what is good" (Titus 2:14).
- "Christ was sacrificed once to take away the sins of many people; and he will appear a second time, not to bear sin, but to bring salvation to those who are waiting for him" (Heb. 9:28).
- "He himself bore our sins in his body on the tree, so that we might die to sins and live for righteousness; by his wounds you have been healed" (1 Peter 2:24).
- "Christ died for sins once for all, the righteous for the unrighteous, to bring you to God" (1 Peter 3:18).
- "This is love: not that we loved God, but that he loved us and sent his Son as an atoning sacrifice for our sins" (1 John 4:10).

The above represent just a sampling of the many clear and concise biblical summaries of the Good News. The reader will undoubtedly find numerous other passages springing to mind. In light of such summaries, the essence of the Gospel seems clear: God, in love—love that is as deep as his holiness and as strong as his wrath—has intervened on behalf of fallen humanity to reconcile sinners to himself through his Son Jesus Christ. As we saw earlier, the heart of the Gospel truth presented to us throughout the New Testament can be summarized in three words: God saves sinners.

At the heart of God's reconciling work—as the references above make clear—"is the atoning sacrifice of Christ on the cross and his glorious resurrection from the dead. The Gospel is the *good news* about the God who has acted in history to save us. It answers the very bad news about the fallen state of humanity, our alienation from God and from one another," and the declared wrath of God that we must one day face.[5] Any vision of the Gospel that does not feature at its very center Christ's atoning death *for us* is simply not faithful to the witness of Scripture. There are many aspects of this glorious atonement, to be sure. But the other aspects of the atonement disappear if at its heart it is not a *substitutionary* atonement:

> For Paul, this substitution, Christ bearing our penalty in our place, is the essence of the atonement. Certainly, he celebrates the cross as a victory over the forces of evil on our behalf (Col. 2:15) and as a motivating revelation of the love of God toward us (2 Cor. 5:14–15), but if it had not been an event of penal substitution, it would not for him have been either of these.[6]

And there is more to be said (though never less!). Inseparably linked with the once-for-all event of the atonement, made by Christ on Calvary's cross in approximately AD 30, are the further events of Christ's rising, ascending, and enthroning as the world's present Lord and coming Judge, and his ongoing life—for emphasis, we might say "livingness"—this and every day as the spiritually present Savior, Master, and Friend of all his followers. He is Prophet (teacher), Priest (mediator), and King (master) to all who are his. He is their way, their truth, and their life, all embodied for them in this unique Person, whom now they know in the unique relationship called *faith*.

Faith, in this particular sense, is a usage learned from Jesus's own use of the word in the days of his flesh as he acknowledged the hopeful trust that specific individuals put in him (Luke 7:9, 50). What constitutes faith today? Faith is a frank facing of the above facts concerning Christ that leads to actively adoring, approaching, and accepting him as one's living, present Savior and Lord. By our faith—let us be clear—we not only receive from him pardon for the past; we also enroll ourselves as his disciples, commit ourselves to follow his leading wherever it takes us, and enter upon a new life of permanent union and communion with him and with his Father, who now through him becomes our Father too. (With Christ it is sonship by nature; with us it is a matter of adoption: see Gal. 4:4–7.) In this new life we learn to say in truth with Paul, "I have been crucified with Christ. It is no longer I who live, but Christ who lives in me. And the life I now live in the flesh I live by faith in the Son of God, who loved me and gave himself for me" (Gal. 2:20). Such is the difference that faith makes.

Coming to faith is the most momentous thing that ever happens to us; for faith, as exercised in this habitual action of *believing in* and *into* Jesus Christ (these are the principal New Testament prepositions used to denote the ongoing transaction) has now brought us as close to Christ relationally as were his first-century followers. It has introduced us into a life of radical change as the indwelling Holy Spirit, through whom we first found faith, now works within us to re-form our character in the moral image of our Savior, in liberty from the sins that once enslaved us, in loyalty to God and his truth, and in love to him and to our fellow humans. And it has established in our hearts a peace and a joy that spring from knowing that whatever happens our new relationship with the Father, the Son, and the Holy Spirit is eternal. Such is the transformation of existence to which faithful imparting of the Gospel in its fullness will lead.

The Essence and Implications of the Gospel

Sadly, even tragically, evangelicals have sometimes been guilty of preaching and teaching a Gospel that is not, shall we say, "fully dressed."[7] They may have focused properly on the central features of God's atoning work at the cross,

99

faithfully preached Christ crucified for sinners, celebrated the resurrection as proof that Christ's self-offering for our sins has been accepted, and urged hearers to be reconciled to God. In other words, they have been right about the essence of the Gospel; the key facts have been there in what they have said. But at the same time they have missed some of the critical implications and applications of the Gospel for daily living. They have neglected, perhaps, to explore how the same cross that reconciles us to God reconciles us also to one another in Christ (Eph. 2:11–22). Perhaps they have not duly emphasized that if God has loved us to the point of giving his only Son as an atoning sacrifice for our sins then surely we ought to without limit love one another (1 John 4:10–11). Perhaps they have failed to point out that as God has loved us even while we were his enemies (Rom. 5:8), then we must act with justice and mercy toward all our neighbors and love even our enemies (Matt. 5:43–48). Perhaps they have not exhorted their congregants to work out their salvation in an obedient fear of the saving God who is at work within them (Phil. 2:12–13). Perhaps they have not urged that regular communion with the Father and the Son, good works, and kingdom service are meant to be the outcome of the new birth.

When we fail to conduct ourselves "in step with the truth of the Gospel" (Gal. 2:14), we are in serious error. We are to live in such a way as to make the teaching about God our Savior attractive to our neighbors (Titus 2:10) and to win their respect by responsible and godly living (1 Thess. 4:11–12). Thus our preaching and teaching of the Gospel—that is, our ministries of catechesis—must include teaching the godly manner of living that accords with the sound doctrines of the Gospel (Titus 2:1).

But many Gospel preachers, sad to say, have not seen any of the above as related to authentic Gospel work. Indeed, they often express concern that such preaching and teaching will likely distract us from our real business of "getting people saved." But their understanding of salvation—if they adopt this line of thinking—is too small and their vision of the Gospel is likewise diminished. The Gospel is to be adorned by both sound doctrine and godly living. To set the Gospel before parishioners and public without these is to preach an unclothed Gospel.

Our salvation does not end at new birth. We are taught by Scripture to say not only that we *have been saved* (Eph. 2:8) but also that we *shall be saved* (Rom. 5:9–10; 13:11; 1 Peter 1:5) and even now *are being saved* (Phil. 2:12–13; 1 Peter 1:9). What is the power that saves us? It is the power of the Spirit at work in and through the Gospel (Rom. 1:16) to change lives. We need both a fully orbed doctrine of salvation and a "fully clothed" presentation of the Gospel. But we have often fallen short on both counts.

Reacting against this unhealthy and disjointed view of things, certain leaders in so-called "emerging churches" have been among those championing a full-fledged return to social concern. Toward this end, some of the movement's leaders have been inclined toward novel emphases, among them:

- distinguishing between the "Gospel of the kingdom" and the "Gospel of salvation";
- downplaying Paul in favor of a return to the way of Jesus;
- turning away from overt evangelism toward a wordless "good newsing" —focusing on *being* good news rather than merely *proclaiming* good news.[8]

While such reactions may be understandable, they come with serious risks. If earlier evangelicals were guilty of neglecting critical implications and applications of the Gospel, these newer evangelicals (or "postevangelicals," as some have chosen to call themselves) may well be in danger of substituting the implications and applications of the Gospel for the Gospel itself.

Perhaps what has happened in regard to the thinking of these church leaders is something like this: first, the essence of the Gospel (EG) was accurately but inadequately proclaimed and practiced in evangelical churches. The inadequacy lay primarily in the fact that the implications of the Gospel (IG) were being overlooked, ignored, or even dismissed as being a diversion from the Gospel. Postevangelicals, recognizing these glaring inadequacies and rereading the biblical accounts of Jesus, concluded that EG cannot really in fact be the Gospel. Instead, they turned to IG, declaring this to be the authentic Gospel. As one emerging leader puts it, "The good news is not that [Jesus] died, but that the kingdom has come."[9] Such a statement, of course, puts him directly at odds with Paul's statements in 1 Corinthians 15:1–5.

As a consequence of such thinking the atoning death of Christ on the cross is being pushed, bit by bit, to the margins of the message and ministry of many churches today. This is an example of what J.I. (writing in company with Mark Dever) has called "anti-redemptionism." This current form of "unorthodoxy" involves "sidelining, and in some cases actually denying, the work of Jesus Christ as our redeemer, who did all that had to be done to save us from hell, in favor of Jesus the teacher, model, and pioneer of godliness."[10] The phenomenon is not news. In his commentary on Psalm 85, Charles Spurgeon quotes the well-known remark of "Rabbi" John Duncan to describe the fuzzy vision of the atonement that is put forth whenever Christ's death *for us* on the cross gets sidelined: "Their doctrine of atonement has well been described by Dr. Duncan as the admission 'that the Lord Jesus Christ did something or other, which somehow or other, was in some way or other connected with man's salvation.' This is their substitute for substitution."[11]

We have, as we said, been down this road before. Many will recognize here a trend similar to the divergence between "fundamentalists" and "modernists" in the early twentieth century. Perhaps it is not unlikely that the so-called "postevangelicals" are destined to be the next group of theological liberals. As J.I. has warned elsewhere, "Liberalism keeps reinventing itself and luring evangelicals away from their heritage."[12] In reaction to this diminishing of the essence of the Gospel, theological conservatives may well find themselves decrying the replacement of the "true Gospel" with a more culturally savvy and professedly compassionate "social Gospel." In other words, yet another modernist versus fundamentalist split may loom on the horizon for the church.[13] Indeed, the taking of sides seems already to be well under way.[14]

The Gospel and "the New Perspectives" on Paul

Much of what we have said above could also be applied to another potential threat to the integrity of the Gospel in our day. Often referred to as "the new perspective" (more recently, "perspectives") on Paul, there is here another sort of reactionary movement at work. This movement, in important respects, is quite dissimilar from that of the emerging churches. For example, the emerging church movement is in many respects a sort of "bottom-up" movement. It has been driven at the congregational level and has now begun to influence the curricular shape of seminaries. The new perspectives movement (which we will henceforth refer to by the initials NP) on the other hand has been driven primarily by scholars and is something of a "trickle-down" movement— its influence beginning at seminaries and universities and now reaching into congregations.[15]

The developed use of perspectives (plural) rather than perspective (singular) in labeling the movement reflects the fact that, while the movement has a single fountainhead (E. P. Sanders's very influential explorations of postexilic Judaism, published in the fourth quarter of the twentieth century), scholars have fanned out into a broad spectrum of personal variants on the common theme.

Advocates will certainly claim that it is faithful scholarship that has driven them to read Paul in new ways. In short, these biblical scholars have become persuaded that evangelical Protestants have long misread Paul—especially his letters to the Galatians and to the Romans—because we have been overly influenced by the Reformers' reading of those texts (Luther in particular is targeted here).It is argued that the Reformers misread those Pauline letters partly because they read into Paul's text their own preoccupation with finding peace for troubled consciences and partly because they did not properly understand the Judaism that provided the backdrop for Paul's letters. Concomitant with this, the Reformers imposed their own cultural settings upon the text (something we all tend to do), especially in relation to their struggles with the teachings of the Roman Catholic church. As they battled against what they saw as legalistic perversions of the Gospel in Catholic teaching they imposed a similar view on the Judaism of Paul's day. What we have now come to understand (according to NP proponents), however, is that the Judaism of Paul's day was not really legalistic but truly grace-based. Thus Paul could not have been fighting against the sort of legalism that Luther, Calvin, and others had supposed. The Reformers, battling the medieval notion of meritorious works, simply misread Paul at many key points, and we need to adopt a new perspective on "what St. Paul really said."[16]

At stake here are many critical issues concerning the essence of the Gospel. Evangelicals from the Reformation forward have articulated the heart of the Gospel, in part, by use of the *sola* declarations: *sola scriptura, solus Christus, sola gratia, sola fide, soli Deo gloria*.[17] But the NP calls into question in particular the notion of *sola fide*. Evangelicals have traditionally read Paul's letters as teaching that "we are justified by faith alone." Among some NP advocates one or more of the key words in this familiar articulation have come to be radically queried.

For some the central issue is what Paul means by "justification." Does Paul mean that we are *declared* just in the sight of God in a forensic sense alone or that we are actually *made* righteous in terms of character? Is he saying that the righteousness of Christ is *imputed* to us or that it is actually *imparted* to us, as Roman Catholicism has historically maintained? The old debate, it seems, must be reopened.[18]

For others the primary riddle concerns the meaning of "faith." Is faith to be understood merely as *mental assent* to the Gospel, or is it much more than that? Is not faith in fact an active and working *trust* in God? Is *believing* in Christ not really another way of saying *obeying* Christ? Related to all this is that little word *alone*, originally introduced by Luther to exclude meritorious works and effort. For many the vital question is whether this *sola* has biblical merit at all. If we understand faith to be only cognitive assent, it is argued that "faith alone" is not tenable. If on the other hand faith is taken to be an active, working, and obedient trust in Christ then perhaps we can redefine this Reformational *sola* to mean simply that without faith there is no salvation. But should we thus water its meaning down?

These concerns are vitally important. And as we have noted above there is a wide spectrum of conclusions offered by those who are in some way or another associated with NP teaching. For many NP proponents justification must be understood to involve actual transformation of character, so that the notion of Christ's imputed righteousness is either diminished in importance or rejected outright. And whether or not faith is understood to be an active and obedient trust, the word *alone* is problematic at best when it is applied to the notion of justification by faith.

As we suggested in regard to the critiques arising from some emerging churches, we find here, at least in part, a reaction against what is perceived to be an inadequate articulation and application of the Gospel in evangelical circles. In particular, many are persuaded that evangelicalism has often been guilty of promoting an "easy believism" and a cheap grace. The idea of "once saved, always saved" has often led to apathy and laziness among those who call themselves Christians. The place of good works has not been adequately addressed or properly emphasized in much evangelical preaching and teaching. Problematic also is a perceived layer of anti-Semitism at work when it is suggested that Paul was attacking the Judaism of his day as legalistic. Related to this is concern that the New Testament teaching has been too radically disconnected from its Old Testament roots and thus evangelical believers have often considered the Old Testament to be irrelevant for Christian living today. And the Torah—which has been viewed as life giving by observant Jews—has been reduced to a life-sapping and even death-dealing law by most evangelicals.

We affirm the validity of these concerns. We find here many important issues that really do need to be raised. Evangelicals have in fact often been guilty as charged on all the points noted above. We can be thankful to scholars who have raised these issues to our consciousness. We ought to fight passionately against the anti-Semitism that exists—sometimes implicitly, sometimes explicitly—in some evangelical circles. We ought to be more faithful in our understanding of the beautiful biblical concept of *torah*. We ought to envision true saving faith as manifesting itself always in love and obedience. We ought to return good works to their proper place in our doctrine of salvation (namely as that for which we have been saved; see Eph. 2:10; Titus 2:14). And we must teach the holiness and righteousness of God in a way that leads to a proper and holy fear of the living God who has graciously invited us into an Abba-child relationship with himself.

Nevertheless we find ourselves once again compelled to reject many of the views that have been offered by NP proponents, even while accepting the validity of their concerns and questions. We would judge again that much of the NP teaching nudges its proponents toward a form of anti-redemptionism. In fact, it seems to us that the scholars in question here have been, to some extent, guilty of inappropriately scaling down many key concerns. Among other things we see evidence of tendencies to diminish the following:

- *The complexity of Second Temple Judaism.* If many evangelicals have wrongly assumed that the Judaism of Paul's day was univocally legalistic, it seems that some NP proponents have made the opposite mistake: not adequately acknowledging that pockets of legalism were present in Paul's day (as they have always been present in both Jewish and Christian circles).[19] This naïveté helps nobody.
- *The profound demands of the law of God.* If many evangelicals have been guilty of a sort of antinomianism, it seems to us that many NP proponents underplay the righteous demands of the law when they suggest that it never demanded absolute obedience and that we are justified so long as the general tenor of our lives is marked by "faithfulness."[20] We affirm the "old Gospel," with its insistence on justification by faith alone, in Christ alone, to the glory of God alone. According to this

Gospel God's law demands nothing less than perfect obedience, and we have fallen short at all points. Christ alone has met these demands, in life and in death. It is by faith in him that we now begin to fulfill the demands of God's law, with gratitude, love, and doxology as our new motivation. "Do we, then, nullify the law by this faith? Not at all! Rather, we uphold the law" (Rom. 3:31).

- *The depths of human depravity.* "There is no one righteous, not even one" (Rom. 3:10). As Jesus explained to the pious and wealthy young man, "No one is good except God alone" (Mark 10:18). All the Reformation *solas* make sense because of the reality of *solus Deus*—that is, God alone is good! Humans, by contrast, are not simply sin-sick; they are "dead in . . . transgressions and sins" (Eph. 2:1) and "by nature objects of wrath" (Eph. 2:3). Thus it is not the righteous that are justified—there are simply no such persons. Rather, God "justifies the wicked" (Rom. 4:5) and does so "freely by his grace through the redemption that came by Christ Jesus" (Rom. 3:24), demonstrating through the atoning work of his Son that he alone is "just and the one who justifies those who have faith in Jesus" (Rom. 3:26).

- *The certainty and severity of divine wrath.* The substitutionary work of Christ on the cross is marginalized whenever and wherever a fully orbed doctrine of propitiation is marginalized.[21] And a fully orbed doctrine of propitiation is marginalized when and where God's wrath is not taken seriously. The biblical authors take God's wrath very seriously, and that is clear throughout both Testaments. Paul's argument concerning justification in the book of Romans involves full attention to God's wrath, as is clear in passages like Romans 1:18; 2:1–6, 8, 16; and 5:9. "The wrath of God is as personal, and as potent, as his love; and, just as the blood-shedding of the Lord Jesus was the direct manifesting of his Father's love toward us, so it was the direct averting of his Father's wrath against us."[22]

- *The biblical insights of the Reformers.* We submit that many of the NP scholars really need a new perspective on Luther and Calvin, for it seems that they have not read these Reformers thoroughly or fairly. Were the Reformers' readings of Paul really more culturally biased than our own? Was not their immersion in the biblical drama and their familiarity with the sacred Scriptures far deeper and broader than ours often is? Did they not affirm—at great length and with wonderful insight—the lostness of sinners, the grace of pardon, the duty of godly living, and the necessity of good works in the lives of believers? Which is more thoroughly the case—that the Reformers misread Paul or that NP scholars have misread the Reformers?

- *Their own cultural biases.* One of the unhappy tendencies of some biblical scholars, it seems to us, is to underestimate the significance of their own cultural biases. Many seem to think they should approach the biblical text with detached and impersonal objectivity, with something of a pure, scientific mindset and skill set. But of course the very idea that the Bible should be approached in such fashion reveals just how influenced we moderns have been by Enlightenment culture. Some evangelical Bible teachers seem to display a greater distrust toward the theological implications of biblical history than toward the conclusions of certain contemporary scholars who have often treated the Bible with unbelief or skepticism at best. The New Perspective is then brought in to reinforce this attitude.

- *The centrality of the cross and the atoning work of Christ.* It is not surprising that the cross seems to be pushed to the margins in the works of some NP scholars. But Paul, as we have seen, was able to teach among the Corinthians for eighteen months "resolved to know nothing but Jesus Christ and him crucified." Further, he personally resolved to boast of nothing at all except the cross of Christ (Gal. 6:14). "The cross must be central to all preaching and pastoring."[23] But it is difficult to see how the cross is central in the thinking of some NP advocates.

- *The glory of the Gospel.* The Gospel is seriously diminished when and where it is presented as something like a "ticket to heaven" or a "get-out-of-jail-free card" in Monopoly. We reject visions of the Gospel that reduce it thus just as we reject a vision of salvation that has no place for good works, holiness, and obedience. But on the other hand it is every bit as much a diminishing of the Gospel's glory if we transfer any of the burden of our salvation away from Christ's shoulders and onto our own. And for all the claims of NP proponents that they have retained *sola gratia*, by abandoning the principle of *sola fide* have they not shifted some of the burden for attaining salvation from the Lord to us?

As we have already insisted, we must always consider both the essence of the Gospel and its implications for living. In the next chapter we take up the sound doctrines that conform to the Gospel together with the way of living that conforms to those doctrines. We shall insist that we are called to live in line with the truth of the Gospel (see Gal. 2:14). We have already mentioned some of the implications of all this above, in our response to critiques arising from so-called emerging churches. Much of the same thinking applies as we respond to the challenge of the NP. In both cases we plead for avoidance of two errors. On the one hand we must not confuse the implications of the Gospel with its essence. On the other hand we must not dismiss the implications of the Gospel as unimportant or only minimally significant.

What shall we say then in regard to the Christian's relationship with the law of God? We must reject the antinomianism that characterizes some evangelical teaching and preaching. And we must also reject any reconfigurations of the Gospel that smack of what has been called "neo-nomianism." That is to say, we must reject visions of the Gospel that suggest that the "Good News" is that God enables us by his Spirit to obey his law and will justify us finally on the basis of that Spirit-empowered obedience.

Seeking to avoid erring in either direction we affirm that having believed the Gospel, believers are enabled by the Spirit to *begin* obeying the requirements of the Torah, that is, to love God and neighbor (Rom. 8:1–4; 13:8–10; 1 John 4:10–19). The Gospel gives no license to ignore God's law; rather, it imparts power (the gift of the Holy Spirit) to start obeying it. Believers are obliged to obey God's commands (1 John 5:3) not causally *for* our justification but in good works that flow gratefully *from* our justification, as our only "reasonable act of worship" in response to God's sovereign and free saving mercies (Rom. 12:1). We have been saved apart from any works of our own but we are newly created in Christ in order that we may walk in the good works God has prepared for us (Eph. 2:8–10).

Even our best works, however, are imperfect this side of glory and our obedience is not the basis of our final justification in God's sight. It is only "through the obedience of the one man," Jesus Christ, an obedience "even unto death," that we are made righteous (Rom. 5:19; Phil. 2:8). We are to follow the Lord who redeems and justifies us, and so become people whose lives exhibit a grateful, God-honoring obedience. Having initially obeyed the Gospel itself (2 Thess. 1:8; 1 Peter 4:17) we are called to continue in obedience to God's commands (1 John 5:3), to Christ personally and all that he commanded (Matt. 28:20; Rom. 16:26), and to the Faith (Acts 6:7). But in our ongoing obedience as in our initial obedience to the Gospel we are utterly dependent upon the grace of God, not just for continual power to desire and choose what is right and good, the best option and the least evil, but also for continual pardon as our very endeavors after righteousness open up to us depths of sin still operative in our spiritual system. Our only hope at any and every stage is to look away from ourselves and to look to Christ alone.

> Look to Christ, speak to Christ, cry to Christ, just as you are; confess your sin, your impenitence, your unbelief, and cast yourself on his mercy; ask him to give you a new heart, working in you true repentance and firm faith; ask him to take away your evil heart of unbelief and to write his law within you, that you may never henceforth stray from him.[24]

Pastoral and Formational Applications of the Gospel

We trust that this extended discussion of these two contemporary challenges to the "older Gospel" has actually helped to demonstrate just how vital it is that the Gospel be kept at the heart of our teaching ministries and indeed of all the ministries of the church.

We suggested at the beginning of this chapter that we are mistaken if we suppose that once we are Christians we should move on from the Gospel to other, supposedly more profound or sophisticated things. When Paul wrote to the Romans, whom he had not yet personally met, he spoke of his eagerness to "preach the Gospel also to you who are at Rome" (Rom. 1:15). He is addressing the believers in Rome, who are among those "called to belong to Jesus Christ" (1:5), who are "loved by God and called to be saints" (1:6), whose "faith is being reported all over the world" (1:9). Paul longs to be with them so that he and they "may be mutually encouraged by each other's faith" (1:12). And when, God willing, he is finally with them, what shall he offer them? He will give them the Gospel. Unlike those who would shrink back from the Gospel for fear that others will be offended by this message of apparent weakness and foolishness (1 Cor. 1:18–25), the apostle is "not ashamed of the Gospel," for he knows that it, and it alone, "is the power of God for salvation to everyone who believes" (Rom. 1:16).

The Gospel is God's power to save. And salvation, as we discussed above, involves the entire process of our transformation, reaching from the eternal past and into the eternal future. Christ our crucified and risen Lord "is able to save completely those who come to God through him" (Heb. 7:25). This full and complete salvation is accomplished, Paul would assure us, by means of the mighty Gospel. It is no wonder then that Paul refused to be anything but an apostle, preacher, and teacher of the Gospel. May we be wise enough and bold enough to follow his example in our ministries of catechesis.

A Gospel Alphabet

Pastor Timothy J. Keller of New York's Redeemer Presbyterian Church has been a long-standing and passionate advocate of Gospel-centric preaching and ministry.[25] He has argued on numerous occasions that "the Gospel is not the ABC's of the Christian life; it is the A through Z of the Christian life." In that spirit, we offer the following "Gospel alphabet"—twenty-six pastoral and formational reasons why the Gospel must retain primacy as the content of Christian education.

Why must Christians continually be educated in the Gospel? For reasons of:

A—Alignment

We must continually teach and learn the Gospel because it is to be the "plumb line" for our doctrine and our living.[26] We are to measure all our teaching to ensure that it is in line with—that is, conformed to—the glorious Gospel of God (1 Tim. 1:11). If our teaching about God, humanity, sin, salvation, the church, last things, and whatever other doctrines we may teach do not accord with the Gospel then they must be rejected. Likewise, our way of living must conform to the sound doctrines that flow from the Gospel. If, like Peter and Barnabas, we begin to act in ways that are "not in keeping with the truth of the Gospel" (Gal. 2:14), may God raise up for us a Paul-like brother or sister to confront us and correct us.

B—Belief

We must continually teach and learn the Gospel because even Christians struggle to truly believe God's Good News. The message of the cross is both countercultural and counterintuitive. To the world it is foolishness and weakness. To our flesh it is simply too good to be true. And Satan, the devil—that accuser of the brethren—continually speaks a contradictory word to our hearts. He accuses us before God as surely as he accused Joshua the high priest (Zech. 3:1). Hearing all this we, with full knowledge of our failings, struggle to believe the truth of the Gospel. To believe it at an appropriately deep level, with an appropriate appreciation of all that it presupposes and implies, is a lifelong task. We must hear it again and again and ask God to seal its truth in our hearts.[27] "I do believe; help me overcome my unbelief!" (Mark 9:24).

C—Contextualization

Paul was determined to "become all things to all people" for the sake of the Gospel (1 Cor. 9:19–23). He knew that the Gospel could and should take on different cultural forms in different cultural settings. Yet when we export the Gospel to others, we may be guilty of confusing it with our own cultural trappings. For example, we know that some missionaries have been guilty of imposing their Western cultural forms on those to whom they carried the Gospel. Though this error could be conscious and express cultural imperialism, it is more often unconscious and reflects a lack of discernment about which aspects of our own Christianity are truly Gospel-driven and transcultural, and which are culturally driven and therefore variable. To help us avoid such an error, it is critical that we continually study the heart of the Gospel so that we may better distinguish the treasure we bear from the jars of clay in which we bear it (2 Cor. 4:7).

D—Depth

As we noted earlier, we do not move from the milk of the Gospel to the meat of something else, but from the milk of the Gospel to the meat of the Gospel. Even Paul, concluding his exposition of the Gospel and preparing to move on to its implications for life, closes his argument in awe and wonder: "Oh, the depths of the riches of the wisdom and knowledge of God! How unsearchable his judgments and his paths beyond tracing out!" (Rom. 11:33).

The wonder of how deep and powerful the Gospel is—especially as it works its way into believing hearts—is well articulated in this Puritan prayer:

BLESSED LORD JESUS,
  No human mind could conceive or invent the Gospel.
  Acting in eternal grace, thou art both its messenger and its message,
    lived out on earth through infinite compassion,
  applying thy life to insult, injury, death,
    that I might be redeemed, ransomed, freed.
  Blessed be thou, O Father, for contriving this way,
  Eternal thanks to thee, O Lamb of God, for opening this way,
  Praise to thee, O Holy Spirit,
    for applying this way to my heart.
  Glorious Trinity, impress the Gospel on my soul,
    until its virtue diffuses through every faculty;
  Let it be heard, acknowledged, professed, felt.[28]

E—Evangelism

The Gospel is food for believers. But it is also the only saving medicine for those who have not yet believed. And we are compelled by the love of Christ to declare this Good News to all people. St. Francis of Assisi told his friars not to preach unless they had permission to do so. But, he added, "Let all the brothers, however, preach by their deeds."[29] Francis's words have often been paraphrased along these lines: "Preach the Gospel always; use words when necessary." The fact is that words *are* necessary, every time. We are always witnesses to the Gospel (Acts 1:8) and, as witnesses, we shall be called upon to *testify*. When we are, we must be sure to get the message of the Gospel right for there are many counterfeit "Gospels" in the world.

F—Fidelity

Faithfulness to the true Gospel calls for ongoing study and obedience. It calls as well for watchfulness, lest false Gospels be introduced. The battle against counterfeit Gospels has always been part of church life. Even in the first century Paul battled against such, as did Peter and Jude and John. Like Paul we must be resolved that we will tolerate no other "Gospel," even if it comes from a heavenly angel or springs from our own imperfectly sanctified hearts, and we should expect the same fidelity from those with whom and to whom we minister (Gal. 1:6–9). Only a constant learning and reviewing of the Gospel can ensure that we will be astute enough to separate the chaff from the wheat.

G—Grace

We need to continually learn and teach the Gospel because Gospel-centricity assures and propels us toward grace-centricity. When we swerve from the Gospel we lapse into either antinomianism[30] or legalism. Neither can offer the true beauty or savor of Christ. To be in the presence of individuals or congregations who are not grace-centered is enervating and exasperating. Let us then learn and relearn the glorious Gospel that we may ever stand fast in the true grace of God (1 Peter 5:12) and may indeed "grow in grace and in the knowledge of our Lord and Savior Jesus Christ. To him be glory both now and forevermore. Amen" (2 Peter 3:18).

H—Hope

We focus on the Gospel also because it is the source of our hope. In face of the brokenness that fills the world around us and rises up within our own hearts, what hope do we have? Apart from the Gospel we have none. But in the Gospel is a great and steadfast hope, and from this hope spring forth faith and love sufficient for each day (Col. 1:5). Diminished "Gospels" may promote, on the one hand, easy believism or, on the other hand, may put the burden of salvation back on human shoulders rather than locating and leaving it in the hand of God. These deviations can offer no certain hope. The glorious Gospel is a blessed hope indeed (Titus 2:13), an anchor for the soul (Heb. 6:19). Christ in us is the hope of glory (Col. 1:27). This is the hope held out in the Gospel (Col. 1:23). With such a hope fixed within our hearts—based upon the certainty that God has made us his children and the confidence that we will be with Christ and like him forever—we long for and labor toward becoming more like him even now (1 John 3:1–3).

I—Intimacy

Through the Gospel we are invited into a living relationship with the living God. In the love proclaimed at the heart of the Gospel God has adopted us into his family. "How great is the love the Father has lavished on us that we should be called the children of God, and that is what we are" (1 John 3:1). The Holy Spirit empowers us to believe the Good News and is sent into our hearts, enabling us to cry, "Abba, Father" (Gal. 4:6). Rehearsing the Gospel in our worship, teaching, preaching, fellowship, and service helps us to nurture and celebrate this unfathomably intimate relationship.

J—Jealousy

We learn and teach the Gospel because we are called to be jealous for those we serve. The apostle Paul declared to the Corinthian believers, "I am jealous for you with a godly jealousy. I promised you to one husband, to Christ, so that I might present you as a pure virgin to him" (2 Cor. 11:2). If we think jealousy is unbecoming in the apostle, we should remember that God himself is a jealous God (Exod. 20:5). True love that is covenant based is properly jealous concerning the parties in that covenant. We must keep the true Gospel before the eyes of those whom we teach and serve so that they will avoid what

Paul feared for the Corinthians—that is, that they should "be deceived by the serpent's cunning" and "somehow be led astray from [a] sincere and pure devotion to Christ" (2 Cor. 11:3). Deeper acquaintance with the true Gospel will help believers recognize and reject the preaching of "another Jesus" and "a different Gospel" (2 Cor. 11:4).

K—Knowledge

We continually learn the Gospel, even as believers, because the Gospel is the revelation of the knowledge and wisdom of God. Though the message of Christ crucified seems foolish to many in this age, "to those whom God has called, both Jews and Greeks, Christ [is] the power of God and the wisdom of God" (1 Cor. 1:23–24). The Gospel is "a message of wisdom among the mature" (1 Cor. 2:6), a message that is "God's secret wisdom" that has been hidden for ages (1 Cor. 2:7). But "God has revealed it to us by his Spirit" (1 Cor. 2:10). "'Who has known the mind of the Lord that he would instruct him?' But we have the mind of Christ" (1 Cor. 2:16). Would we grow in the knowledge of God's wisdom? Would we grow in grace and in the knowledge of our Lord Jesus Christ? Then let us remain steadfast in the Gospel.

L—Love

The Gospel is the revelation of God's abounding love: "While we were still sinners, Christ died for us" (Rom. 5:8). We do well to immerse ourselves and the saints we serve in that Good News. The sacrament of the Lord's Supper, for example, is an ongoing, multisensory reminder of Christ crucified (1 Cor. 11:26). God's Gospel love also calls forth love as response. The Lord's Supper both declares God's love and demands that we love one another in turn (1 Cor. 11:27). John, "the beloved apostle," makes these truths very clear. "This is love: not that we loved God, but that he loved us and sent his Son as an atoning sacrifice for our sins. Dear friends, since God so loved us, we also ought to love one another" (1 John 4:10–11). And again he writes, "We love because he first loved us" (1 John 4:19). Would we see love grow in the hearts of God's people and reach to their neighbors—both saints and sinners? Then we must school them continuously in the Gospel of love.

M—Mission

And why must we continually learn and teach the Gospel? We do so that we may not lose sight of the great work that God is doing in our day. God is actively engaged in the wondrous work of reconciling all things to himself. It was for this that the Son of God came forth. "God was in Christ reconciling the world to himself" (2 Cor. 5:19). And this work continues in and through us, the body of Christ, gathered and dispersed throughout the world today.

The very work for which the Father sent the Son, the Son has now sent his church to continue (Matt. 28:18–20; John 20:21). And he promises to be with us always. *Being* in his presence must be taken as seriously as *doing* the work of true mission, for mission can only have power and a cutting edge when Christ is indwelling us and we him.

N—*Narrative*

We must ever study the Gospel because it is the apex and summary of the great narrative of God's redemptive activity in the world. As we saw in chapter 4, it is into this Story that we have been called. In an age when many deny the existence of a single metanarrative that applies to all persons it is more critical than ever that we know the biblical narrative and tell it faithfully to others, asking God to convince hearers as we do so that this is their Story as well.

O—*Obedience*

The Gospel calls forth obedience (Rom. 1:5) in at least three ways. First, we must obey the Gospel by believing and receiving this Good News (John 6:29). Second, the faith that saves works itself out in obedient living by God's empowering grace (Phil. 2:12–13). Third, we are to obey Jesus's command to bring this Gospel to the nations (Matt. 28:18–20). In our ministries of teaching and formation these calls to obey the Gospel must be clear and unequivocal.

P—*Passion*

Passion comes from the Latin *passio*, meaning "suffering." We celebrate each year the passion of our Lord when we attend to the historic remembrance of Holy Week. Likewise, whenever we partake of the Lord's Supper together we "proclaim the Lord's death till he comes." It is given to us not only to believe in Christ the Suffering Servant but also to suffer for him ourselves (Phil. 1:29). Paul saw his own suffering for the Gospel and for the building up of the church as an active participation in the afflictions of Christ (Col. 1:24; Phil. 3:10–11). We must be forthright in teaching our congregants, by word and by example, that this is part of our calling as well.

Q—*Quickening*

Though by nature we were dead in our trespasses and sins and were objects of God's wrath, God quickened us—made us alive with Christ—through his love and grace (Eph. 2:1–5). This God did, and still does, as we believe the Gospel, putting our faith in Jesus Christ. Lutheran theology especially emphasizes the notion that the Gospel is God's quickening word, spoken to us in infinite mercy. We need to hear this word continually for our own sakes and to speak it faithfully to others.

R—Righteousness

In the Gospel "a righteousness from God is revealed, a righteousness that is by faith from first to last" (Rom. 1:17). Paul's argument in the letter to the Romans is deep and complex, but we submit that the Gospel reveals God's righteousness in at least these two ways. First, it is a declaration that *God himself* is just and righteous, for the Gospel teaches that in Christ our sins have been fully propitiated as a basis for his forgiving of us (Rom. 3:24–26; 1 John 1:9; 2:2). Then, second, through the Gospel God declares *us* righteous as we put our faith in Christ Jesus. Thus in the Gospel God demonstrates "his own justice at the present time, so as to be just and the one who justifies those who have faith in Jesus" (Rom. 3:26). It is truly vital beyond words that we faithfully preach and teach this Gospel.

S—Salvation

Intricately related to the above is the whole wonder of salvation. Scripture is quite clear that the Gospel "is the power of God for the salvation of everyone who believes" (Rom. 1:16). As we have already noted, this is not a truth pertaining only to evangelism. The Gospel saves those who believe, from first to last, through and through. It includes all the wondrous doctrines of our great salvation, including election, regeneration, justification, sanctification, glorification, and much more. For this reason alone, the Gospel must remain central in all the ministries of the church.

T—Theology

We saw above that both our doctrines and our manner of living must be in alignment with the Gospel. While errant theological thinking on a variety of issues can lead us to a twisted Gospel it is more to the present point to state that an errant Gospel can unleash a host of heresies. It is worth noting that Satan is a competent theologian with great skill in confusing and misleading with regard to God's truth. We will explore this all further in the next chapter.

U—Unity

A clear Gospel focus in our preaching and teaching has the potential to contribute to the unity of the church. In the latter half of the twentieth century one frequently seen example of this was the evangelistic campaigns of Billy Graham, which typically featured the cooperation of a great diversity of congregations and denominations.[31] At the beginning of this century new movements are afoot for the sake of the Gospel that aim to be both evangelical and ecumenical. We never seem to achieve perfect consensus here because we need to constantly wrestle with variant details of conviction and, of course, with all kinds of intellectual spin-offs of our fallenness. But magnifying the Gospel as our central point of reference can help us keep a variety of lesser concerns in proper perspective (Phil. 1:18).

V—Vision

Keeping our minds focused on the Gospel can help us align our hearts to God's own heart. We so easily fall into pettiness and needless division when we are not prizing the things God prizes. Jesus endured the cross and its shame because of the joy set before him (Heb. 12:2), a joy which we take to refer to the fact that through suffering and death he would bring many children to glory (Heb. 2:10–18). Paul likewise endured all manner of things for the sake of the Gospel and in the furtherance of its saving ministry (1 Cor. 9:23; Phil. 1:12–13; 2 Tim. 1:11–12). A clear vision of the goal imparts great fortitude in struggling toward it and great forbearance in the face of distractions from it.

W—Worship

We must continually teach and learn the Gospel because there is simply nothing else that evokes worship and adoration as the Gospel does. A quick survey of the hymnody of the church through the past twenty centuries makes this clear. The best hymns—ancient and contemporary—which have shown themselves to have staying power have always been Gospel-obsessed. God is glorified, Christ is exalted, and the cross and Christ's atoning work are central. The same is true of the other key elements of Christian worship— our preaching, our confessions, our prayers, our sacraments. Take away the Gospel and Christian worship simply ceases. A sampling from the thousands of Gospel-centered hymns of the church will make the point:

> Not the labor of my hands can fulfill Thy law's demands;
> Could my zeal no respite know, could my tears forever flow,
> All for sin could not atone; Thou must save, and Thou alone.
>
> Nothing in my hand I bring, simply to Thy cross I cling;
> Naked, come to Thee for dress; helpless, look to Thee for grace;
> Foul, I to the fountain fly; wash me, Savior, or I die.[32]

Further comment, we think, is needless. The Gospel as sung in hymns like this moves us endlessly to wonder and adore.

X—Xenophilia

The actual Greek word we have in mind here is *philoxenia*, which literally means "love of strangers, foreigners, aliens." Our coinage, if such it be, means exactly the same.[33] In our English New Testaments, *philoxenia* is rendered as "hospitality" (Rom. 12:13; 1 Peter 4:9) and "to show hospitality to strangers" (Heb. 13:2). Such love of strangers is a required attribute of church leaders (1 Tim. 3:2). In the final judgment Jesus will either commend or condemn based upon whether or not people have welcomed "the least of these" (and thus welcomed Christ himself; Matt. 25:35, 43). Jesus is the great model for *philoxenia*, as is indicated in the Gospel narratives as well as in the whole wonder of his incarnation and passion. Indeed, we were not merely strangers to him; we were God's enemies when he died for us (Rom. 5:8). In declaring such love, the Gospel also calls us to imitate it (1 John 4:10–11).

Y—Yielding

The Gospel must be continually set forth before church members because it is in view of God's mercy that we are provoked to yield our lives fully to God as living sacrifices (Rom. 6:13; 12:1). It is the kindness of God displayed in the Gospel that leads us to repentance (Rom. 2:4) so that we no longer live for ourselves but for him who died for us and was raised again (2 Cor. 5:15).

Z—Zeal

May God stir both our own hearts and the hearts of those we are called to serve with an authentic zeal for the Gospel, and for the Christ of the Gospel. We have seen how fully this marked Paul's life. We could certainly say the same of Jesus, whose first public words were a call to repent and believe the Gospel (Mark 1:15) and whose entire ministry *was* Gospel. All that Jesus said and did and was, in life and in death, was a display of God's Good News for humanity. In all the ways we have addressed throughout this chapter and more, may we and our readers never be lacking in zeal but keep our spiritual fervor as we serve the Lord (Rom. 12:11) in and through this glorious Gospel, the Good News of Christ.

Conclusion

It is clear that we must begin our ministries of catechesis with bold preaching and teaching of the Gospel. In fact, in faithful catechesis we never depart from the sphere of the Gospel any more than we depart from the sphere of the Story or from the sphere of the Faith. In the following chapter we turn our attention to some of the critical implications of the Gospel for faith and for life. As we do so, we return to what we have earlier called the *three facets of the Faith*.

Three Facets of the Faith

Follow thou me: "I Am the way, the truth, and the life."
Without the way, there is no going; without the truth, there
is no knowing; without the life, there is no living. I Am the
way which thou oughtest to follow; the truth which thou
oughtest to trust; the life, which thou oughtest to hope for.
I Am the way inviolable, the truth infallible, the life that
cannot end. I Am the straitest way, the highest truth, the
true life, the blessed life, the life uncreated.[1]

Thomas à Kempis

With the apostle Paul we resolve to proclaim Christ (Col. 1:28). The Lord himself is the essential and basic content of our teaching ministry. In the last chapter we explored the first principle in our Christ-proclamation. We preach and teach the glorious Gospel of God to believers and unbelievers alike. We argued that we should never depart from the Gospel, as if there were more important or more critical content to which we must progress. But as we have seen, the Gospel is multifaceted and deep beyond measure. Its implications and applications are innumerable. In this chapter, we explore some of these other dimensions of our Christ-proclamation.

The Gospel as Our Plumb Line

One way to express what we mean by speaking of various implications and applications of the Gospel is to identify the Gospel as the plumb line for all our thinking, speaking, teaching, and living.[2] A plumb line is a cord or string to which a weight is attached at the end. Plumb lines have been used through the centuries for two main purposes: to measure verticality or perpendicularity and to determine depth. A plumb line might be cast into a well or into a body of water to measure its depth. With the Gospel in mind, Paul marvels at the depths of the love of Christ and prays that by the Spirit's illumination we may come to fathom the unfathomable (Eph. 3:18–19). But no plumb line could be long enough to measure the depths of the glorious Gospel. As a new believer Gary was captivated by the imagery of an old hymn from the very first time he sang it in congregational worship:

> Could we with ink the ocean fill, and were the skies of parchment made,
> Were ev'ry stalk on earth a quill, and ev'ry man a scribe by trade,
> To write the love of God above would drain the ocean dry.
> Nor could the scroll contain the whole, tho' stretched from sky to sky.
> O love of God, how rich and pure, how measureless and strong!
> It shall forevermore endure, the saints' and angels' song.[3]

From those depths of love, mercy, and grace we draw upon the life-giving benefits that invite us into communion with the living God and empower us to walk in his Way. Though no plumb line can fathom the depths of the Gospel, the Gospel itself can be the plumb line by which we measure the depth and quality of our own lives, ministries, and doctrines.

Plumb lines have also been used by builders to help ensure that what they construct is properly vertical, that it is "true to plumb." In the book of Amos God tells the prophet that he has set a plumb line in the midst of his people Israel (Amos 7:7–8). God uses the plumb line to indicate that his people have departed from the Way, that they are not living "true to plumb," and thus have come under his judgment. In similar fashion the Gospel is for us the plumb line by which we measure both our living and our teaching. Paul commanded Timothy to watch both his life and his doctrine, and to persevere in doing so. Thus would Timothy save both himself and his hearers (1 Tim. 4:16).

Paul writes to Timothy further of "the sound doctrine that conforms to the glorious Gospel" (1 Tim. 1:10). Elsewhere he tells Titus that he must "teach what is in accord with sound doctrine" and goes on to detail instructions about the way in which believers are to walk, conduct themselves, and live their lives (Titus 2:1–10). A similar idea is seen in both instances: there is sound doctrine or teaching that properly accords with the Gospel, and there is a manner of living which properly accords with sound doctrine.

The King James Version rendering of Titus 2:1 is an interesting expression of the principle we are presenting. It reads, "But speak thou the things which become sound doctrine." For contemporary Americans this would likely be a confusing use of words. What could Paul mean by speaking of things which *become* sound doctrine? Does he mean to suggest that anything we teach—if we "massage" it enough and repeat it enough—can become sound doctrine over time? As Paul says elsewhere, May it never be! The sense here reflects an older English usage of the word *become*. We still hear it from time to time in expressions such as "That dress really becomes you." This expression implies that the dress enhances the natural beauty of its wearer, that it suits the person very well indeed. Paul's point in Titus 2 is that the church must teach its members to live in such a way that their very lives "make the teaching about God our Savior attractive" (Titus 2:10). Earlier in the letter Paul commanded the teaching of the sound doctrine itself (Titus 1:9). Now in chapter 2 he commands Titus to teach believers to *live accordingly*, to live in a manner *which befits and adorns that doctrine.*[4]

When the church teaches doctrines or permits patterns of living that are out of plumb with reference to the Gospel, much damage occurs. We grieve the Holy Spirit, with whom we have been sealed for the day of redemption (Eph. 4:30) and who is the Spirit of Truth (John 15:26). Doctrines that miss the mark will sow the seeds of heresy or at the very least lead to distortions of the truth. And an unholy lifestyle, rather than making the "teaching about God our Savior attractive," can have quite the opposite effect. By substandard, ungodly living we may drive a wedge between unbelievers and the church's teaching, making it more difficult for them to hear, believe, and receive the message of the Gospel. Citing the prophets, Paul reminded Jewish believers in Rome that when they walk unworthily of their calling "God's name is blasphemed among the Gentiles" as a result (Rom. 2:24; cf. Isa. 52:5; Ezek. 36:22). When Christians fail to walk worthily of the calling we have received (Eph. 4:1), we may likewise cause God's name to be blasphemed by the unbelieving world.

Paul provides us with a concrete example of failure to live according to plumb in reference to the Gospel. He tells the Galatians about his confrontation with Peter, his fellow apostle. Peter had come to Antioch to see what wonders the Gospel had wrought among the Gentiles. He clearly approved what he saw there and had joined gentile believers at meals. Then Jewish Christian observers came to Antioch, having been sent from James and the other leaders of the church in Jerusalem. Peter, we are told, "began to draw back and separate himself from the Gentiles, because he was afraid of those who belonged to the circumcision group" (Gal. 2:12). This "hypocrisy," as Paul bluntly labels it, led astray the other Jewish believers who were present, including "even Barnabas" who had diligently labored with Paul in preaching the Gospel to the Gentiles. Paul confronted Peter and the other offenders about all this, for he "saw that they were not acting in line with the truth of the Gospel" (Gal. 2:14).[5]

Peter himself had articulated vital aspects of the truth that derive from the Gospel when, at the home of the gentile Cornelius, he said, "I now realize how true it is that God does not show favoritism but accepts men from every nation who fear him and do what is right" (Acts 10:34). Later, to those present at the Jerusalem council that was convened to wrestle with the question of the incoming of the Gentiles, Peter stated, "God, who knows the heart, showed that he accepted them by giving the Holy Spirit to them, just as he did to us. He made no distinction between us and them, for he purified their hearts by faith. . . . We believe it is through the grace of our Lord Jesus that we are saved, just as they are" (Acts 15:8–11). But Peter had become guilty of denying by his actions the very doctrines that he had so boldly articulated.

We must not be too harsh toward Peter, for who among us is without similar sins? If we read Paul's writings well we certainly know that *he* made no claim of having attained perfection (Phil. 3:12). Indeed he saw himself forever as the worst of sinners (1 Tim. 1:15). This side of glory, not one of us lives in a manner that fully accords with God's standards. But as Paul and Peter were both obliged to do, we too must make it our aim to walk worthily of our calling, to press on toward the prize of the high calling of God in Christ, to live up to the truth that we have already received (Phil. 3:16).

What are the sound doctrines that accord with the glorious Gospel? There are many, to be sure, and they touch upon all areas of theological concern— what we believe about God, humanity, sin, Christ, salvation, the Spirit, the church, last things, and much more.[6] Surely all the doctrines of grace are in view here, including a sound theology of the atonement, which is so much discussed and debated today. All our teaching in these areas is to be discerned by faithful use of Scripture as we hear, read, and study its meaning "by the power of the Spirit and in the company of the faithful."[7] Careful discernment will lead us to theological conclusions that are fully in line with the glorious Gospel. If they are not, our teaching is out of plumb and we will need to start again.

Likewise, translating sound doctrine into a way of living has innumerable implications and applications. All our behavior toward God and neighbor is to be congruent with and expressive of the truth of the Gospel. When like Peter in Antioch we are guilty of racial discrimination, we are out of plumb. If we show favoritism to the rich and insult the poor—sins which we are warned against in passages such as James 2—we are out of plumb. When we see a brother or sister in need but offer them mere words instead of giving from our plenty to tangibly help them in their want, we are again out of plumb (1 John 3:16–18). The more we meditate upon the Gospel the more we see of its wonders, awesome doctrines of grace, and righteous demands upon our lives.

The essential content of the Faith, then, includes first of all the glorious Gospel of the blessed God, which covers the whole many-sided reality of the divine plan and work of salvation. Secondly, the Faith includes the sound doctrines of the Truth that properly accord with that glorious Gospel. It includes thirdly the Way of living that conforms to those doctrines. And fourthly it includes the experience of all the life-giving benefits that flow from the power of the Gospel and enable us to walk in the Way of the Lord. The last three of these elements may be regarded as three facets or dimensions of the Faith that derive from the Gospel. Having stated these things in principle, we will now consider other historical and biblical ways of articulating and framing these concerns.

The three facets or dimensions of Christian teaching—which we identified in chapter 4 as the Truth, the Life, and the Way—are biblically grounded, psychosocially validated, and historically affirmed by the practices of the Christian church over two millennia. These dimensions of the Faith are inherent in the Gospel. Each of these facets must be further unpacked in its own right though they are never disconnected from the whole. We examine them here in something of an inductive fashion. First we will bring forth "witnesses" testifying to the wisdom of the threefold plan, and then we will offer a summary argument and a proposal. Our witnesses include testimony from various domains—historical, biblical, and psychosocial.[8]

Historical Witnesses

In all its orthodox expressions the church has consistently affirmed that Jesus Christ alone is the answer to the deep needs and longings of the world. But it is not typically noted that the church has also testified to the wisdom of proclaiming Christ in a threefold manner through its teaching ministry. This is most easily overlooked by those communities that have little experience with the ministry of catechesis, for it is in the historic catechisms of the church that we see this threefold witness most obviously.

As we discussed earlier in chapter 3, the Reformation-era catechisms focused primarily on instruction in three great summaries of the Faith—the Apostles' Creed, the Ten Commandments, and the Lord's Prayer.[9] Alongside these three, each also contains some instruction in the sacraments of baptism and the Lord's Supper, though these are not generally afforded quite the same frontline status as the three summaries. We noted as well that the catechisms of the Puritan era for the most part followed the same pattern.

We argued in chapter 3 that Luther and others were in fact essentially correct to say that what they were teaching in their printed catechisms corresponded to what the church had always included in its unprinted catechisms—creedal instruction, ethical instruction based upon God's commands, and instruction in prayer based upon the Lord's Prayer. Having established this we must proceed to ask why the church settled upon these three particular summaries as the basis for catechetical instruction.

It would be difficult to argue that church leaders acted in any officially coordinated way to settle upon the three formulae. In fact it is apparent that they did not. Instead it seems that consensus spontaneously emerged around these three, a consensus that was only later sanctioned by church officials. Why such a consensus occurred becomes clearer when we consider the testimony of the various prefaces and commentaries that have appeared through the centuries relative to the various catechisms that have been published. At least three central arguments appear with frequency.

First, there is an affirmation of the wisdom of historical precedent. This argument may seem least compelling to many evangelical believers today. We are, after all, "Bible people," always demanding in the end, "Where stands it written?" Such concern for biblical fidelity is absolutely essential and praiseworthy. But a flippant dismissal of our own Christian history is not praiseworthy in any respect. It is rather a willful refusal to adopt a biblical spirit. The fact is that we are not the first Christians to wonder about how to make disciples for Jesus. Wisdom and humility demand that we consider what our brothers and sisters through the ages have done by way of catechizing and discipling, and test the merit of these efforts by consideration of the biblical data. We are most unwise to try to continually reinvent the catechetical wheel or to assume that we are more likely than our forebears to be faithful to Scripture.

Our antipathy toward philosophies and practices that emerged throughout church history (particularly with regard to pre-Reformation history) also betrays either a willful ignorance or a profound naïveté about the proper role of the historic church in shaping who we are as Bible people today. Whether we are speaking of the canon of Scripture, what constitutes biblical orthodoxy, what a Judeo-Christian ethic looks like, or why we worship in the ways that we do, there is almost no aspect of what we prize as biblical Christianity that has not been deeply affected by the centuries of church history that have preceded us.[10] Indeed it may well be argued that purposeful inattention to the history of the church makes us far more likely to become unbiblical in some significant way.

In the spirit of Jesus's warning in Matthew 7 we should take care before we presume to judge our forebears about the splinters in their eyes while doing nothing about the planks in our own. Were the ancients or the Reformers affected and shaped, sometimes adversely, by their surrounding cultures? Of course they were. But if we think that we ourselves are free from similar limitations we are deluding ourselves. Let us therefore in a humble spirit listen well to what our predecessors in the Faith may be able to teach us about our tasks.

A second reason the church settled upon the three great summaries of the Faith seems to be the belief that the three summaries are themselves biblically undergirded in specific ways. This is very obviously true with reference to the

Lord's Prayer and the Decalogue. These two summaries are not only inspired Scripture; each actually bears *added* marks of divine origin. The Decalogue (enunciated in its entirety twice—in Exodus 20 and in Deuteronomy 5) was written, we are told, by the very finger of God (Exod. 31:18). These "Ten Words" are referred to many times throughout the Bible, including numerous references in the New Testament (e.g., Mark 10:18–19; Rom. 13:9). What we call "the Lord's Prayer" (to most Catholics, the "Our Father") was articulated by Jesus himself. It is recorded twice in the Gospel accounts (Matt. 6:9–12; Luke 11:2–4) and it seems probable that Jesus taught this prayer on other occasions as well. It is no surprise then that the church accorded special weight to these two formulae.

Regarding the Creed, however, there has not been so uniform an endorsement. The Westminster catechisms do not include expositions of the Apostles' Creed. The Creed itself is often included in printed versions of those catechisms, sometimes as an appendix but without exposition. There is no clear sense of antipathy toward the Creed in this case and churches that use the Westminster catechisms almost always affirm their acceptance of the Creed and its teaching. Still, not including an exposition of it was a departure from the earlier Reformation catechisms.

Some Protestant churches have been far more blatant in their dismissal of the Creed. It is not uncommon, as we have already noted, to see on a church signboard a slogan something like this: "No book but the Bible; no creed but Christ; no law but love." This captures the mindset of many in free church movements. In a sense, however, such pithy slogans are themselves creedal confessions and are part of significant traditions that have been handed down and embraced by others.

We acknowledge that for evangelical Protestants at least neither the Apostles' Creed nor any of the creeds hammered out through the history of the church bear the authoritative weight of sacred Scripture. Nevertheless both Protestant and Catholic Christians from nearly all nations and in nearly all eras have found and proclaimed that the Creed is a faithful and concise witness to basic biblical teaching. For many of the Reformers and their descendants, the Creed is nothing less than a faithful, clear, and concise summary of the most central tenets of our faith.

A third reason why these three great summaries have been at the heart of historic catechetical practice is that they provide introductory instruction in essential biblical concerns and in so doing provide a comprehensive introduction to the Christian faith. The Creed provides basic training in theology. The Decalogue provides a primer in ethics. And the Lord's Prayer introduces the believer to the life of prayer.

These three areas of concern—theology, ethics, and prayer—have been taken up in other ways in the history of the church. In more than one tradition, the same comprehensive triad is denoted by means of the Latin expressions *lex orandi, lex credendi, lex vivendi.* Most commonly, two of these appear together: *lex orandi, lex credendi,* meaning "as we pray (or, as we worship), so we believe."[11] By adding the third expression *lex vivendi* we would be further saying "and as we pray and believe, so shall we live."

What is true of Christian experience was already true in the life of Israel centuries earlier. Abraham Joshua Heschel summed up the Jewish experience of religion in this way: "These three ways correspond in our tradition to the main aspects of religious existence: worship, learning, and action. The three are one, and we must go all three ways to reach the one destination. For this is what Israel discovered: the God of nature is the God of history, and the way to know him is to do His will."[12]

Furthermore, the synagogue has been historically understood as having three central purposes to fulfill. It is a house of assembly, a house of study, and a house of prayer.[13] The purposes of the synagogue also call to mind the rhythm that was built into the life of the Benedictine code and became normative in most expressions of Christian monasticism. A monk's day was typically devoted to three tasks—sacred study, manual labor in service of the community, and most importantly the ministry of prayer, which was the *opus dei*—the "work of God."

In the table below we review at a glance some of the historical examples of this triad of concerns.

The Jewish religious experience	Learning	Worship	Action
Three purposes of the synagogue	House of study	House of prayer	House of assembly
The Christian life experience	*Lex credendi*	*Lex orandi*	*Lex vivendi*
Augustine's *Enchiridion*	Faith (the Creed)	Hope (the Lord's Prayer)	Love (love of God and neighbor)
Benedictine rhythm in monastic life	Sacred study	*Opus dei* (prayer "the work of God")	Labor in service of the community
The Reformation catechisms	Exposition of the Creed	Exposition of the Lord's Prayer	Exposition of the Decalogue

Biblical Witnesses

Our next concern is to consider whether or not the Bible directs us into the comprehensive pattern that we have discovered from the historical witnesses. We have already tipped our hand regarding this question. We do, indeed, believe that the Bible affirms this comprehensive triad of aspects of the Faith as guidance for our teaching and our living. The pattern is not always completely clear, and we will not assert that it is. Nor will we assert that thinking of the comprehensive pattern as threefold is the only way that this comprehensiveness of concern could be organized. But we do believe that there is biblical warrant for concluding that the church has been both pastorally wise and biblically faithful to point believers toward these three aspects of Christian living—what we believe, how we relate to our neighbors, and how we commune with God.

In the great confession of the Jewish faith, the *shema*—as recorded in Deuteronomy 6:4—we find these words. "Hear, O Israel, the LORD our God, the LORD is one." Here is a call to believe and adhere to the most basic of theological truths, that there is one God alone—the LORD. Although Jewish writers through the years have commonly affirmed that Judaism is primarily an ethical rather than a theological religion, it is not disputed that theology matters in Judaism and that this is the central theological tenet of that faith. This most basic Jewish faith confession is immediately followed in Deuteronomy with a command toward the obvious and necessary response: "You shall love the LORD your God with all your heart, and with all your soul, and with all your strength" (Deut. 6:5).

In this foundational biblical text we see at work what might be called two forms of theology—indicative theology and imperative theology. The idea is that to every theological truth we affirm as fact there is a corresponding command attached, implicitly if not explicitly. The same pattern might also be described as the principle of revelation and response. Whatever God has revealed to us about himself, about his mighty deeds or about his will for our lives always requires an appropriate response from us. In the Deuteronomy passage, we can reason as follows: Given that it is true that there is only one God and he is the LORD, then to that One who alone is God we must offer our entire love and devotion.

In several New Testament texts, we find this indicative-imperative, or revelation-response, pattern rather obviously in play. John, for example, writes that "God is love." This indicative theology embraces the imperative to "love one another" (1 John 4:7–8). A few verses later, John expands. "This is love: not that we loved God, but that he loved us and sent his only Son as an atoning sacrifice for our sins. Dear friends, since God so loved us, we also ought to love one another" (1 John 4:10–11). In the same letter, John writes that God is light and exhorts his readers to walk in the light (1:5–7). God is righteous, and thus only those who do what is right can be considered "born of God" (2:29; 3:7). It is clear that as critical as right belief is, it must always be matched by right behavior. This reminds us of our earlier consideration of the Great Commission and Jesus's command that we make disciples for him by "teaching them to obey everything that I have commanded" (Matt. 28:20).

Another witness to the notion of a comprehensiveness of teaching concern in Scripture is the threefold division of the Hebrew Scriptures, of which we wrote in chapter 2 above. In his book *The Creative Word* Walter Brueggemann has made a compelling argument that the threefold division of the Tanakh represents three distinct types of teaching in Israel.[14] The Torah, he argues, represents "the disclosure of binding" to the commands of the LORD. The Prophets represent "the disruption for justice." And the Writings represent "the discernment of order." In building his case Brueggemann appeals to an interesting passage in Jeremiah in which we read the words of evil men who were plotting to kill the prophet: "They said, 'Come, let's make plans against Jeremiah; for the teaching of the law by the priest will not be lost, nor will counsel from the wise, nor the word from the prophets" (Jer. 18:18). While these schemers had only evil in mind, Brueggemann asserts that they quite correctly named the three categories of teachers among the people of Israel—priests, prophets, and sages. These three types of teachers correspond to the three types of teaching represented in the Tanakh.

In the New Testament as well we find a number of passages and ideas that affirm the comprehensiveness of concern we have argued for above. The first letter of the apostle John provides us with a particularly helpful example. John notes that there are several witnesses that testify as to whether or not a person truly knows God, has been born of God, and is a child of God. There is, first, a *theological* test. Those who know God believe that Jesus is the Christ (1 John 2:22), the Son of God (1 John 4:15; 5:5, 10) who has come in the flesh, being sent by the Father to make propitiation for our sins (1 John 4:2, 9–10). There is, second, a *moral* test—only those who do what is right (1 John 3:6–10a), especially by loving fellow believers (1 John 3:10; 4:7–8, 16, 19–21), are born of God. There is also, third, the *witness of the Spirit* within our hearts (1 John 3:24; 4:13), the Spirit who anoints us so that we may discern, hear, and heed the truth (1 John 2:20; 4:6).

We remember also that Paul in his pastoral epistles is especially concerned that Timothy and Titus give proper attention to both sound doctrine and to the lifestyle in which believers must walk. To Timothy he writes, "Watch your life and your teaching. In doing so, you will save both yourself and your hearers" (1 Tim. 4:16). He instructs Titus to teach leaders both to heed "sound doctrine" (Titus 1:9) and to walk in the pattern of life that "is in accord with sound doctrine" (Titus 2:1).

Jesus himself also modeled for us this comprehensiveness of concern in his teaching ministry. He testified to the Truth (John 3:31–32; 18:37) and in his own person and work incarnated the Truth for us, perfectly revealing the invisible God (John 1:14, 18; 14:9). Jesus invited men and women into a vital relationship with the transcendent God and offered Life in and through that relationship (John 5:21; 7:37–38; 10:10; 17:3). And he taught much about the Way of God in which we must walk—the Way of loving both God and neighbor. More than offering instruction at this point, he himself perfectly walked this Way, leaving us an example to follow (Mark 10:45; John 13:15, 34–35). We see in him, in other words, the threefold office of Christ our Prophet, Priest, and King—all evident even in the days of his earthly life.

Finally, we return to the four commitments of the newly baptized believers as mentioned in Acts 2:42. We recall that they had steadfastly devoted themselves to four things: the apostles' teaching, the fellowship, the breaking of the bread, and the prayers. We see here yet another testimony to holistic Christian experience. The apostles' *didachē*, as we have argued, was Gospel-centric through and through. The fellowship was a participation with one another as the body of Christ. The breaking of the bread was a regular sharing of what we call the Lord's Supper, and the prayers were largely communal and liturgical in nature. It is easy to understand how in some faith communities the catechetical commitment would thus have four elements rather than three. Much Roman Catholic catechetical work, for example, is structured under the headings: We Believe, We Celebrate (in the liturgy), We Pray, We Live. As we have seen, the Reformation catechisms also included instruction in the sacraments. But we also noted that even with this fourth category of instruction there has been consistent reference to the "three summaries" or the "three formulae." It has often been pointed out that this catechetical triad provides believers with a creed, a code, and training in *cultus*, that is, corporate worship.[15] All are related to our communion with the living God. While not dismissing the validity of a fourfold approach, we elect to stay with the threefold pattern we have outlined in this chapter and therefore combine attention to worship and prayer together as the substance of *lex orandi*.

There seems, then, to be sufficient biblical warrant for a multifaceted approach to the content of our teaching ministries. If we combine some of these biblical witnesses with some of the historic witnesses we considered above, our table now looks like this:

The Jewish religious experience	Learning	Worship	Action
Three purposes of the synagogue	House of study	House of prayer	House of assembly
The Christian life experience	*Lex credendi*	*Lex orandi*	*Lex vivendi*
Augustine's *Enchiridion*	Faith (the Creed)	Hope (the Lord's Prayer)	Love (love of God and neighbor)
Benedictine rhythm in monastic life	Sacred study	*Opus dei* (prayer, "the work of God")	Labor in service of the community
The Reformation catechisms	Exposition of the Creed	Exposition of the Lord's Prayer	Exposition of the Decalogue
The Tanakh	*Torah*—Torah shapes Israel	*Kethuvim*—Torah contemplated	*Nevi'im*—Torah obeyed
Threefold office of Christ	Prophet, proclaiming truth	Priest, mediating life	King, declaring and enforcing law

John's tests of the believer	Believes the truth about Jesus Christ	Knows God's Spirit witnessing within	Obeys God and loves brothers and sisters
Paul's commands to Timothy	Watch your doctrine	Watch for the kingdom	Watch your life
Paul's commands to Titus	Teach sound doctrine	Look ahead to eternal life	Teach what accords with sound doctrine
Four commitments of Acts 2:42	The apostles' teaching	The breaking of the bread and the prayers	The fellowship
The three theological virtues	Faith	Hope	Love
Proclaiming Christ, who is:	The Truth	The Life	The Way

Psychosocial Witnesses

Finally, we turn to briefly consider what we will call "psychosocial witnesses" to see how the three dimensions of the Faith speak to the deepest needs and longings of the human heart.

That humans possess thirsty souls has been well attested by many notable thinkers, both Christian and non-Christian. In his *Confessions* Augustine articulated the matter with these famous words: "For Thou hast made us for Thyself, and our hearts know no rest until they rest in Thee."[16] Pascal spoke of the futile efforts of people to fill with other things "the infinite abyss" in their souls which, in fact, can be filled "only by God himself."[17] C. S. Lewis used the German word *Sehnsucht*, meaning "longing" or "yearning," to describe this deep longing in our souls. Writing of his childhood, Lewis says,

What the real garden had failed to do, the toy garden did. It made me aware of nature—not, indeed, as a storehouse of forms and colors but as something cool, dewy, fresh, exuberant. I do not think the impression was very important at the moment, but it soon became important in memory. As long as I live my imagination of Paradise will retain something of my brother's toy garden. And every day there were what we called "the Green Hills," that is, the low line of the Castlereagh Hills which we saw from the nursery windows. They were not very far off but they were, to children, quite unattainable. They taught me longing—*Sehnsucht*; made me for good or ill, and before I was six years old, a votary of the Blue Flower.[18]

In her book *Is It a Lost Cause?* Marva Dawn expands upon the notion of *Sehnsucht*. Drawing upon the work of Lewis she describes this phenomenon as a deep, insatiable longing:

This pressing, restless longing for fulfillment that nothing can satisfy more than temporarily. . . . If we have this intense longing and nothing in the world can satisfy it, and nothing in the world can push it under, then we must be made for another world! To recognize that *Sehnsucht* is our God-created longing for our true home in God is to find the roots of the longing itself.[19]

What Lewis and Dawn describe by their use of a single term can also be perceived as having several aspects. John Stott has written of "three quests" that engage all humans in every age and in every culture. These are the quest for significance, the quest for transcendence, and the quest for community.[20] Our *Sehnsucht*, if we follow Stott here, has these three distinct features. We have not only a vague sense of inner hunger; we have specific psychosocial needs as human beings. In God's wisdom and mercy these needs, Stott argues, can be met through the ministry of the church. Through the ministry of teaching the church offers answers to the search for significance. Through the ministry of worship we respond to the quest for transcendence. And the *koinōnia* of the church is God's provision for the human need for community. But tragically, Stott goes on to say, through unfaithfulness and ineptitude local churches too often fail to offer anything that can satisfy searching hearts. Our teaching is too often inadequate, our worship too often inane, and our fellowship too often excludes rather than embraces.

Still other witnesses have testified to this threefold description of our spiritual hunger. Gene Edward Veith, drawing upon the earlier work of Adolph Koeberle, has taken some notions from Luther to speak of three false spiritualities. These he describes as *speculation, mysticism*, and *moralism*.[21] Attempting to fill the great void within us and the quest for significance in which we must engage, some tread a path of intellectual speculation. But this often leads to a situation in which people are "ever learning, but never coming to a knowledge of the truth" (2 Tim. 3:7). Indeed, many have already concluded that truth in any absolute sense does not exist. Thus no destination is ever envisioned for some on this path. They simply join the journey and ask the questions, never waiting for answers.

The second path, that of mysticism, corresponds to Stott's quest for transcendence. Through a landscape of varying "spiritual experiences" one seeks to connect with the divine—whether that divine is perceived as personal or not. This might include forays into various forms of meditation, experimentation with mind-altering drugs, or even the search for ecstatic experiences through sexual exploration.

The third path Veith discusses is moralism. This reminds us of an aspect of Stott's quest for community. In moralism one seeks to do good to his or her neighbor. Enough philanthropic efforts and one may finally find the satisfaction so desperately longed for. But in the end this road, like the path of speculation, proves to be a dead end. It is not uncommon for some "searchers" to try out more than one of these spiritual roadways at various times in their lives. They are like the author of Ecclesiastes who, after seemingly having tried it all, can only conclude, "Meaningless! Meaningless! . . . Utterly meaningless! Everything is meaningless!" (Eccles. 1:2).

The three quests of Stott and the spiritualities Veith renounces bring to mind depictions of human enquiry from earlier times. One of the traditional ways of classifying fields of philosophical study is to use the threefold division of *epistemology, ontology,* and *axiology.* Epistemology is the study of knowing and knowledge. It asks, "What is true, and how do we know it?" Ontology ponders the question, "What is the nature of being?" Axiology asks the question of value: "What is good?"[22] Here we find another searching witness to the threefold pattern that we have been discussing.

Recalling our earlier consideration of the historic witnesses, we find an intriguing correspondence. The human heart seeks significance. The Creed begins to explain to us the momentous Story into which God has brought us. We seek transcendence also. The Lord's Prayer (together with the sacraments) invites us into a life of communion with the living God. We long for community with others. The Decalogue in turn instructs us in how to live well and wisely in relation to both God and our neighbors.

When we take the testimony of these various witnesses together, we see how the glorious Gospel of Christ and the three dimensions of the one Faith speak powerfully to the deepest of our human needs and desires. The old Sunday school joke that no matter what the question is the answer is "Jesus!" surely applies here, but it is no joke. Jesus—the Truth, the Life, and the Way—is truly the answer to our every need, as here to our three profoundest needs. Thus we see fully the wisdom of Paul's resolution: "We proclaim him, admonishing and teaching everyone with all wisdom, so that we may present everyone perfect in Christ" (Col. 1:28).

Naming the Three Facets

We have argued thus far that our proclamation must have a comprehensiveness of concern—that is, it must address individuals and congregations holistically, attending to the various aspects of our humanity. In later chapters we will explore the significance of all this for the *how* of our teaching ministries. In this chapter, however, our focus is on the *what* of our teaching—the content of our catechesis. We have suggested that the one Faith we are called to proclaim has three facets. These facets overlap and interrelate, and we therefore make no overly fine distinction between them. But we do well to name each of the three facets so that we may better understand and apply ourselves more effectively to them.

St. Augustine, as we saw earlier, would label the three dimensions faith, hope, and love, thereby centering attention upon what have been called the three "theological virtues." The wisdom of this approach is heightened by the fact that this triad of terms is found throughout Scripture and has a long history of emphasis in the life and teaching of the church. Through the centuries there have been many authors, Catholic and Protestant alike, who have stressed the foundational importance of these three graces. It is our conviction, however, that these are more fitly seen as the *aims* of our teaching rather than as its content. That is to say, we teach with a view to eliciting faith, hope, and love. By persistent instruction in the three facets of the Faith these responses are cultivated in our hearts.

To name the facets themselves we choose to utilize a different set of biblical terms: the Way, the Truth, and the Life. These are drawn of course from Jesus's words concerning himself in John 14:6. In the passage Jesus tells his apostles that having seen him they have seen the Father. The Son reveals the Father and no one can be in relationship with the Father apart from him. In John's Gospel account Jesus says, "I am the way, and the truth, and the life." These words are so familiar to Christians that we may not often think about what the terms actually communicate. Where did these terms come from? Did Jesus simply pull them out of the air and string them together? Or what?

We will not engage in a full exegesis of John 14:6. Nor do we suggest that Jesus uses the terms in this passage precisely as we employ them in naming the three dimensions of the Faith. But we would make the following points. First, in the larger context of John 14 Jesus is reiterating both his unique personal intimacy with the Father and his claim to be the One through whom we gain access to the Father. Those who know Jesus know the Father (John 14:9; see also John 5:19–27; 17:3). Second, the three expressions that Jesus utilizes—the way, the truth, and the life—speak both to how Jesus incarnates the invisible God and leads us toward relationship with him. Let us now turn to a brief consideration of each term.

The Way

"The way," as seen in the context of John 14:1–5, points us directly to the fact that Jesus alone provides access to the Father. As Jesus says, "No one comes to the Father except through me" (14:6). In this sense "the way" reminds us of his earlier words in John's Gospel: "I am the gate for the sheep" (10:7). And again, "I am the gate; whoever enters through me will be saved. He will come in and go out, and find pasture" (10:9). "The way" reminds us also of Hebrews 10:19–20. There we read that through the shed blood of Christ "a new and living way" has been opened for us into the most holy place, through "the curtain, that is, his body." Paul also refers to the destroying of barriers by the power of the cross, with the result that Jews and Gentiles "both have access to the Father by one Spirit" (Eph. 2:18). "The way" points us to the reality of the atoning death that Jesus was about to die and to the resurrection life, both for him and for us, that was to follow. As Jesus had said earlier concerning the manner in which he was to die, "But I, when I am lifted up from the earth, will draw all people to myself" (John 12:32).

Elsewhere in Scripture, however, "the way" has a different connotation and plays a large role in both the Old and New Testaments. In the Hebrew Scriptures, the expression bespeaks the pattern of one's walk or manner of living in this world.[23] In this respect a contrast is made between "the way of the righteous" and "the way of the wicked" (as in Psalm 1). The way of the righteous is the way of life and of blessing; it is "the way of the LORD." The way of the wicked is the way of death, of cursing; it is the way of this fallen world. Thus a clear choice is consistently set before God's people (as in Deut. 30:11–20). Often, "the way of the righteous" or "the way of the LORD" is simply referred to as "the way" or "the ways of the LORD," "his way," "your ways," and so on (e.g., Ps. 25:4, 7–10). In Jeremiah 6:16 we read of both "the ancient paths" and "the good way" that God's people ought to have walked in—but they refused to do so. In the Old Testament order of things, one discerns the way in which one ought to walk through contemplation upon *torah* (Ps. 119:1–16, 32) and with the aid of wise and godly teachers (Ps. 32:8; Isa. 30:21).

What is "the way of the LORD"? In a word, it is *love*. To walk in God's way is to live a life characterized by love of God and neighbor. Love for God is manifested by obedience to his commands (Deut. 6:4; John 14:15; 1 John 5:3). Chief among the commands we must obey is his command to love our neighbor. Combining Deuteronomy 6:4–5 with Leviticus 19:18 Jesus (and many of his contemporaries) concluded that there are no greater commands than to love the LORD and to love one's neighbor (Mark 12:28–31).

The concept of two ways that stand in stark contrast to each other is taken up by Jesus in Matthew 7 when he refers to two gates with two roads—one leading to life and the other to destruction (Matt. 7:13–14). Those who believed in Jesus came to be called followers of "the Way" early on (Acts 9:2; 19:9, 23; 24:22). In the earliest Christian writings after the New Testament era, teaching about the "two ways" is commonplace. Thus the *Didache of the Apostles*, as we saw above, begins with the words "There are two ways: the way of life and the way of death."

How might we join this large biblical concept of the Way with Jesus's declaration that he is the only way to the Father? We suggest the following line of argument. The way of the LORD is the way of life and blessing. Those who walk in that way by obeying God's commands shall live and prosper before the LORD. As the Torah testifies, "The man who obeys them will live by them" (Lev. 18:5). But as we read in Romans 3:9–18 and elsewhere, there is no one who has fully obeyed God's commands. And the Torah testifies further, "Cursed is the man who does not uphold the words of this law by carrying them out" (Deut. 27:26). The apostle Paul refers to both these Scriptures and argues that (1) no one can be justified on the basis of the law (since none of us fully obey that law); (2) Christ has redeemed us from the curse of the law by becoming a curse for us through his death on the cross; (3) thus we are justified by faith in Christ alone and live by the gift of the Spirit (Gal. 3:6–14). Jesus's full and perfect obedience (Rom. 5:19), even unto death on a cross (Phil. 2:8), overcomes the burden of our disobedience. He has become "our righteousness, holiness, and redemption" (1 Cor. 1:30). In other words, because Jesus is the only one who has fully walked in the way of the LORD he is the only way we can come to the Father for life. From Genesis 3 onward, we had been cut off from "the way to the tree of life" (Gen. 3:24; cf. Heb. 9:8). But through Christ "a new and living way" has been made for us (Heb. 10:19). Believing in him alone we have life in his name (John 20:31).[24]

The Life

This leads us to another of the terms in John 14:6, "the life." To understand this we focus on the Johannine writings where the term is repeatedly used.[25]

- "In him was life, and the life was the light of men" (1:4).
- "That whoever believes in him should not perish but have eternal life" (3:16).
- "The water I give him will become in him a spring of water welling up to eternal life" (4:14).
- "Just as the Father raises the dead and gives them life, even so the Son gives life to whom he is pleased to give it" (5:21).
- "Whoever believes in me, as the Scripture has said, streams of living water will flow from within him" (7:38).
- "I have come that they may have life and have it to the full" (10:10).
- "I am the resurrection and the life" (11:25).
- "This is life eternal, that they may know you, the only true God, and Jesus Christ whom you have sent" (17:3).
- "That you may have life in his name" (20:31).
- "God has given us eternal life and this life is in his Son. He who has the Son has life. He who does not have the Son of God does not have life. I write these things to you who believe in the name of the Son of God that you may know that you have eternal life" (1 John 5:11–13).

A consideration of these references makes it clear that the Life promised in these passages is nothing less than a vital relationship with the living God.

This relationship means that the one who has believed in Jesus has "eternal life and will not be condemned; he has crossed over from death to life" (John 5:24). Thus eternal life is a gift to be enjoyed both now and forever. Those who believe in Jesus possess it already and thereby the hope of glory is truly theirs. This gift of life is clearly linked in John's account to the gift of the Holy Spirit (John 7:38–39). The Spirit's presence ensures and assures us that we are God's children (1 John 4:13), works in us sanctification (2 Thess. 2:13; 1 Peter 1:2), and guarantees our future glorification (Eph. 1:13–14). How do we experience this life? Only in and through a relational embrace of Jesus Christ. Life is in him. He is God's life incarnate.

An intriguing reference to the Life is found in Acts 5. There we read that the angel of the Lord opened the doors of the prison into which the authorities had put the apostles. As he freed them he instructed them to "go and stand in the temple and speak to the people all the words of this life" (Acts 5:20). Some have suggested that "the Life" may thus have been an early identifying name for Christianity, along with "the Way."[26]

The Truth

Finally we focus on the middle term from John 14:6, "the truth," which Jesus also claims to be. All that is true about the invisible God is revealed to us in Christ. Christ is the mystery of God made manifest; in him "are hidden all the treasures of wisdom and knowledge" (Col. 2:2–3). This God to whom the Hebrew prophets faithfully witnessed has disclosed himself fully in his only-begotten Son (Heb. 1:1–3). God's *logos* "was made flesh," writes John. "We have seen his glory, the glory of the One and Only, who came from the Father, full of grace and truth" (John 1:14). To us has been given, writes Paul, "the light of the knowledge of the glory of God in the face of Christ" (2 Cor. 4:6).

We label the three dimensions of the Faith as the Truth, the Life, and the Way. An additional benefit of doing this—as opposed to using terms like faith, hope, and love; or learning, worship, and action; or any other nomenclature—is that we are reminded that it is *Christ himself* we are to proclaim. The One who is set forth in the Gospel is further explicated in our Bibles as the incarnate truth of the unseen God; as the only One who can offer thirsty souls the very life of God; and as the One who both shows us God's way (by the obedience of his earthly life) and has become that way for us (through his full obedience to the Father, even unto death on the cross for us). All this is to be celebrated and reproduced in our catechetical instruction.

We offer below one final summary table of our findings and suggestions to this point. In so doing, we bring together the historical, biblical, and psychosocial witnesses whose testimonies we have considered in this chapter.[27]

The Jewish religious experience	Learning	Worship	Action
Three purposes of the synagogue	House of study	House of prayer	House of assembly
The Christian life experience	*Lex credendi* ("the law of belief")	*Lex orandi* ("the law of prayer")	*Lex vivendi* ("the law of life")
Augustine's *Enchiridion*	Faith (the Creed)	Hope (the Lord's Prayer)	Love (love of God and neighbor)
Benedictine rhythm in monastic life	Sacred study	*Opus dei* (prayer, "the work of God")	Labor in service of the community
The Reformation catechisms	Exposition of the Creed	Exposition of the Lord's Prayer	Exposition of the Decalogue
The Tanakh	*Torah* (Torah shapes Israel)	*Kethuvim* (Torah contemplated)	*Nevi'im* (Torah obeyed)
Threefold office of Christ	Prophet (proclaiming truth)	Priest (mediating life)	King (declaring and enforcing law)
John's tests of the believer	Believes the truth about Jesus Christ	Knows God's Spirit witnessing within	Obeys God and loves brothers and sisters
Paul's commands to Timothy	Watch your doctrine	Watch for the kingdom	Watch your life
Paul's commands to Titus	Teach sound doctrine	Look ahead to eternal life	Teach what accords with sound doctrine
Four commitments of Acts 2:42	The apostles' teaching	The breaking of the bread and the prayers	The fellowship
Three "theological virtues"	Faith	Hope	Love
Our deep longings (Lewis, Dawn)	*Sehnsucht*		
Are expressed in three quests (Stott):	Significance	Transcendence	Community
Which are reflected in philosophy as:	Epistemology	Ontology	Axiology
And issue in false spiritualities (Veith):	Speculation	Mysticism	Moralism
In answer to the above:	"We proclaim Christ" (Col. 1:28)		
By preaching and teaching	The glorious Gospel of the blessed God (1 Tim. 1:11)		
Implications and applications of the Gospel:	Sound doctrine that conforms to the Gospel	The life-giving benefits that flow from the Gospel	The way of living that accords with the sound doctrine
In other words, we proclaim Christ, who is:	The Truth	The Life	The Way

Row section labels (left margin): Historical Witnesses; Biblical Witnesses; Psychosocial Witnesses; Conclusions

135

The Relational Claims of Catechesis

We close this chapter with one more table, this one intended to highlight what we might call the relational claims of catechesis. If the preceding has all seemed too categorical and propositional for the sensibilities of some readers, there is another way we may look at things. Here our focus is on both proclaiming Christ and responding to him. Believing the table to be self-explanatory, we add to it no further remarks.

We Proclaim Christ (Col. 1:28)

Who is (John 14:6):	The Truth	The Life	The Way
And who is our:	Prophet	Priest	King
Each one of us is called to be his:	Disciple	Worshiper	Servant
Together, with all the saints, we are:	The pillar and foundation of the truth (1 Tim. 3:15)	The temple of the living God (Eph. 2:20–22)	The body and bride of Christ (1 Cor. 12:12–27; Eph. 5:22–33)
We are called to live in the light of:	The Faith once for all delivered (Jude 3)	The new and better covenant (Hebrews 7–10)	The kingdom of God (Mark 1:15)
And are called to exercise:	Faith	Hope	Love
Summary of our response to Christ:	Taught by the Truth	and liberated by the Life	we walk in the Way.

Forward in the Faith of the Gospel

The wise are always old, but the old are not always wise.[1]

Ralph Venning

A Biblical Vision for Spiritual Growth

The earliest practices of catechesis, as we observed in chapter 3, envisioned a faith journey that encompassed a life of spiritual progress. Particular individuals passed from being relatively uninterested in the things of God to becoming *inquirers*. Some of these, in turn, devoted themselves to a deliberate and sustained exposure to God's revealed truth by formally becoming *catechumens*. By God's grace, the journey of the catechumen led him or her in time to become one of the *competentes*—that is, candidates qualified for baptism. The newly baptized were now *neophytes* in the church. But this "ending" of the entry process was not an ending of the journey of faith. By God's continued outpouring of grace in their lives these believers would continue to grow and mature as members of *the faithful*.

The Bible consistently affirms a vision for such progress or growth in the spiritual life. Sometimes this is portrayed as being connected to one's natural development from childhood through adulthood. Thus we read that adult members in the faith community are specially charged with teaching the things of God to their children (Deut. 6:1–9; 11:18–21; Ps. 78:1–8; Eph. 6:4). We read as well that children and youth are to be directed toward wisdom and away from folly (Proverbs 1–9). In the New Testament, Paul sometimes crafts his instruction depending upon the ages of those to whom he is writing—one message for parents, and a different message for children (Eph. 6:1–4; Col. 3:20–21).

Christian educators, especially in recent decades, have given a good deal of attention to the matter of natural development, especially owing to the influence of developmental theorists Piaget, Kohlberg, Erikson, Fowler, and others. Such attention is generally a very wise thing, although these theorists need to be read critically and their insights adapted discerningly.[2] Certainly our ministries of teaching should be as sensitive and prudent as possible in enlisting the natural abilities of our learners within the community of faith.

In terms of catechesis, wise application of developmental theory should shape our approach to both content and process. We do well, for example, to seize upon the capacity that most children have to memorize facts, lists, verses, and more. Typically this capacity seems to decrease over time, even as the capacity to engage thought more critically increases. For Spurgeon—who compiled a catechism for use in his own church based upon the *Westminster Shorter Catechism* and some Baptist catechisms—this presented an obvious educational guide in regard to children. Thus he counseled concerning the use of his catechism: "Those who use it in their families or classes must labour to explain the sense; but the words should be carefully learned by heart, for they will be understood better as years pass."[3]

This means that the same essential content could be used throughout one's life but could be engaged through different processes at different stages. The Ten Words or Commandments, for example, could be introduced in a very simple form of do's and don'ts to very young children. When they are a bit older they could be asked to commit the commandments to memory, receiving a rudimentary understanding as they do so. Throughout the long, awkward, sometimes joyful, and frequently painful journey we now call adolescence, catechists can return to these words and engage their meaning and application in ways congruent to deepening cognitive capacities. When the young people become adult learners, the educational experience will likely be more effective as it becomes more collaborative, for adults bring to the educational encounter a host of life experiences to draw upon as they continue learning the implications and applications of the Decalogue.

We have been very unwise when we have swallowed whole the criticisms lodged against having children in the church memorize things by rote. *Mere* memorization of items left to itself is indeed not a sufficient educational or formative experience and can degenerate into mere mumbo jumbo. But is *no* memorization the way forward? Surely it is not. By seizing upon our children's God-ordained ability to commit verses, creeds, hymns, lists, and much more to memory when they are still very young, we are helping them to "fill the cupboard" of their souls. Then, when they are older, they will have resources to draw upon and enjoy.[4] Along these lines, T. F. Torrance wrote:

> Educational theories that insist that teachers must concentrate on drawing out (*educare*) the latent capacities of the child, and help him at every point to form his own judgments, without equal attention to the supply of information, are tragically mistaken. . . . [Catechetical instruction] imparts to a child at an early age long before his mental powers can grasp the meaning of it all, a considerable body of historical and doctrinal matter, and so provides him with something to think about in the years when he is developing his mental and spiritual capacities . . . it so stretches his powers that it helps him to reach beyond his grasp and then grasp beyond his former reach.[5]
>
> You cannot make anything unless you have the tools with which to form and construct it . . . it is important that from the earliest the child should be trained in the rudiments of Christian doctrine, and have these built into his mind and soul, so that he has eyes to see, ears to hear, and a heart to understand the whole message of the Gospel. . . . Give him the tools at an early age, and he will fulfil to the end his discipleship in Christ.[6]

Natural and Spiritual Development

There is not, of course, a one-to-one correspondence between natural growth and spiritual progress. "The wise are always old, but the old are not always wise."[7] That is to say, our growth in grace is not always all that it should be. Simply having been "in Christ" for many years does not guarantee a proportional maturity in Christ. And so it was that the New Testament writers were at times compelled to rebuke believers for their lack of appropriate growth. Paul writes to the Corinthians, "But I, brothers, could not address you as spiritual people, but as people of flesh, as infants in Christ. I fed you with milk, not solid food, for you were not ready for it. And even now you are not ready" (1 Cor. 3:1–2). The writer to the Hebrews similarly rebukes his readers in this regard: "For though by this time you ought to be teachers, you need someone to teach you again the basic principles of the oracles of God. You need milk, not solid food" (Heb. 5:12).

It is no surprise then that the Scriptures most often speak of spiritual progress without suggesting a link to one's natural age or development. The emphasis rather is upon the fact that all believers ought to grow up in their experience of salvation. When John addresses some of his readers as "children" or "little children," others as "fathers," and still others as "young men," it is virtually certain that his terms refer to spiritual, rather than natural, levels of maturity (1 John 2:12–14).[8]

The following references represent but a brief sampling of the biblical concern for ongoing spiritual growth in the lives of believers:

- "Until we all attain to the unity of the faith and of the knowledge of the Son of God, to mature manhood, to the measure of the stature of the fullness of Christ, so that we may no longer be children, tossed to and fro by the waves" (Eph. 4:13–14).
- "And it is my prayer that your love may abound more and more, with knowledge and all discernment, so that you may approve what is excellent, and so be pure and blameless for the day of Christ, filled with the fruit of righteousness that comes through Jesus Christ, to the glory and praise of God" (Phil. 1:9–11).
- "I know that I will remain and continue with you all, for your progress and joy in the faith" (Phil. 1:25).
- "Not that I have already obtained this or am already perfect, but I press on to make it my own, because Christ Jesus has made me his own. . . . I press on toward the goal for the prize of the upward call of God in Christ Jesus. Let those of us who are mature think this way" (Phil. 3:12, 15).
- "Therefore, as you received Christ Jesus the Lord, so walk in him, rooted and built up in him and established in the faith, just as you were taught, abounding in thanksgiving" (Col. 2:6–7).
- "Train yourself for godliness" (1 Tim. 4:7).
- "Let us leave the elementary doctrine of Christ and go on to maturity" (Heb. 6:1).
- "Like newborn infants, long for the pure spiritual milk, that by it you may grow up into salvation" (1 Peter 2:2).
- "Make every effort to supplement your faith with virtue, and virtue with knowledge" (2 Peter 1:5).
- "But grow in grace and in the knowledge of our Lord and Savior Jesus Christ" (2 Peter 3:18).

Progress within the True Gospel

It is not just any appearance of spiritual progress that is praiseworthy. True Christian growth must—and actually only can—occur within *the Faith of the Gospel*. It is only the one who has fixed in his heart the assurance of God's saving love and who possesses the hope of being with Christ and like Christ forever—a hope supplied by the Gospel alone—who grows in godliness and purity of heart (1 John 3:1–3).

Writing to the churches of Galatia, Paul focuses his indignation on how believers there were departing from the Faith of the Gospel. The trajectory of their progress, in other words, was all wrong. If they were in fact to abandon the true Gospel for a pseudo-gospel, they would surely come under the spell of unsound doctrines. Apart from the true Gospel there would be no experience of the Spirit's life-giving power. Thus there would be no capacity to faithfully walk in the Way of the Lord. Knowing all this, Paul is unsparing in his reproofs. Here is a sampling:

- "I am astonished that you are so quickly deserting him who called you in the grace of Christ and turning to a different Gospel—not that there is another one, but there are some who trouble you and want to distort the Gospel of Christ. But even if we or an angel from heaven should preach to you a Gospel contrary to the one we preached to you, let him be accursed" (1:6–8).
- "O foolish Galatians! Who has bewitched you? It was before your eyes that Jesus Christ was publicly portrayed as crucified. Let me ask you only this: Did you receive the Spirit by works of the law or by hearing with faith? Are you so foolish? Having begun by the Spirit, are you now being perfected by the flesh?" (3:1–3).
- "Formerly, when you did not know God, you were enslaved to those that by nature are not gods. But now that you have come to know God, or rather to be known by God, how can you turn back again to the weak and worthless elementary principles of the world . . . ? I am afraid I have labored over you in vain" (4:8–10).
- "My little children, for whom I am again in the anguish of childbirth until Christ is formed in you! I wish I could be present with you now and change my tone, for I am perplexed about you" (4:19–20).
- "You were running well. Who hindered you from obeying the truth?" (5:7).
- "If we live by the Spirit, let us also walk by the Spirit" (5:25).

To the Colossians Paul expresses similar concerns in more positive terms. He writes, "Therefore, as you received Christ Jesus the Lord, so walk in him, rooted and built up in him and established in the faith, just as you were taught, abounding in thanksgiving" (Col. 2:6–7). He moves on immediately to warn them against being taken "captive by philosophy and empty deceit . . . and not according to Christ" (Col. 2:8).

Having begun our journey in the Gospel we must move on, and indeed *can* move on, only in that same Gospel. The righteousness that is from heaven is empowered only by the saving power of the Gospel and is by faith from first to last (Rom. 1:16–17; Phil. 3:9). Paul reminds the Philippians of the beginning of their exposure to the Gospel—"Moreover, as you Philippians know, in the early days of your acquaintance with the Gospel . . ." (Phil. 4:14 NIV). But they had soon become full partners in the Gospel (Phil. 1:5). And for the sake of "the faith of the Gospel" Paul urged them toward living in a manner worthy of the Gospel of Christ (Phil. 1:27).

Spiritual growth is to be expected in healthy Christians just as natural growth may be expected in all healthy humans. Where such growth in grace is lacking, loving admonition is both appropriate and necessary. True and healthy spiritual progress, for both individual believers and communities of the faithful, must take place within the Faith of the Gospel. For the Gospel alone leads to sound teaching of the Truth, imparts life-giving power through the Spirit, and thereby enables us to walk in the Way of the Lord. Therefore any movement toward a self-generated and self-absorbed vision of spiritual development is an exercise in futility and represents a deadly deviance from the glorious Gospel.

Ancient Model, Contemporary Applications

With these things in our mind we are now ready to ask questions about *when*, *where*, and *how* to teach *what*. In the course of the preceding chapters we identified a number of areas of essential Christian teaching. These included the great redemptive Story, the glorious Gospel that is both apex and summary of that Story, and three facets of the Faith that derive from the Gospel. We also explored how this teaching was historically introduced via catechetical instruction in the Creed, the Lord's Prayer, the Decalogue, and the Gospel sacraments. We have suggested as well that the Faith of the Gospel represents the appropriate frame for Christian teaching throughout our lives. But how do we approach issues of catechetical content in light of the insights we have just been considering about Christian growth?

In the ancient catechumenate that developed between the second and fifth centuries we observe a process that typically involved multiple stages, or phases, in the journey of faith toward, into, and in Christ. Although this varied from setting to setting and the models changed somewhat over time, we suggested a possible trajectory of the journey based on the catechumenate as it came to take shape under the ministry of Augustine. In the table below we remind the reader of this model (discussed in chapter 3), focusing now especially upon the relationship between the stage of catechetical development and the primary content.

Phases of a Catechetical Journey under the Ministry of Augustine		Content Emphasis
Inquirers	Those expressing interest in the Faith	The *narratio* (the great redemptive Story) told in compelling fashion
Catechumens	Those newly submitted to instruction in the Faith	A long, sustained exposure, mostly in the setting of congregational worship, to biblical instruction that was both moral and doctrinal

Phases of a Catechetical Journey under the Ministry of Augustine		Content Emphasis
Competentes	Those enrolled as candidates for baptism	An intense time of preparation that included prayers, fasting, moral admonition, and instruction in the Creed and the Lord's Prayer
Neophytes	Those who have just been baptized	A first experience of the Eucharist, with instruction about the meaning and mystery of the sacraments
The faithful	Those who have been baptized believers for some time	Regular retelling of the redemptive Story, ongoing instruction in the Scriptures, primarily in the context of assembled worship

The Rite of Christian Initiation of Adults (RCIA)

It is typical among those who champion the idea of catechetical renewal in our day to follow in some fashion or other the ancient pattern of catechizing in successive stages or phases. We offer three examples of this before proposing in the following chapters our own vision of how the best parts of the biblically based and historically informed catechetical vision might be implemented in contemporary evangelical churches.

The first example is the Rite of Christian Initiation of Adults (RCIA) as practiced in the Roman Catholic church. The RCIA has grown out of the *Order of Christian Initiation of Adults*, which was established by order of Pope John Paul II in response to calls from the Second Vatican Council for a revival of the ancient catechumenate. Since 1988, the RCIA has been mandatory among Catholic churches in the United States. The RCIA is actually a series of steps marking stages of a journey toward faith in Christ and into the full life of the Catholic church. Preceding and succeeding each step is a period of instruction. The process, as prescribed in 1988, is outlined as follows:

Outline for Christian Initiation of Adults (from the RCIA)[9]

- *Period of evangelization and pre-catechumenate.* This is a time, of no fixed duration or structure, for inquiry and introduction to Gospel values, an opportunity for the beginnings of faith.
- *First step: Acceptance into the order of catechumens.* This is the liturgical rite, usually celebrated on some annual date or dates, marking the beginning of the catechumenate proper, as the candidates express and the church accepts their intention to respond to God's call to follow the way of Christ.
- *Period of the catechumenate.* This is a time, in duration corresponding to the progress of the individual, for the nurturing and growth of the

catechumens' faith and conversion to God; celebrations of the Word and prayers of exorcism and blessing are meant to assist the process.

- *Second step: Election or enrollment of names.* This is the liturgical rite, usually celebrated on the first Sunday of Lent, by which the church formally ratifies the catechumens' readiness for the sacraments of initiation and the catechumens, now the elect, express the will to receive these sacraments.

- *Period of purification and enlightenment.* This is the time immediately preceding the elect's initiation, usually the Lenten season preceding the celebration of this initiation at the Easter Vigil; it is a time of reflection, intensely centered on conversion, marked by celebration of specific scrutinies and presentations and of the preparation rites on Holy Saturday.

- *Third step: Celebration of the sacraments of initiation.* This is the liturgical rite, usually integrated into the Easter Vigil, by which the elect are initiated through baptism, confirmation, and the Eucharist.

- *Period of post-baptismal catechesis or mystagogy.* This is the time, usually the Easter season, following the celebration of initiation, during which the newly initiated experience being fully a part of the Christian community by means of pertinent catechesis and particularly by participation with all the faithful in the Sunday eucharistic celebration.

Each step is marked by a liturgical rite celebrated in the community of faith. The various rites each are designed with prayers, songs, symbols, and ritual speech. Here is one brief example, taken from the Rite of Acceptance into the Order of Catechumens:

Celebrant—This is eternal life: to know the one true God and Jesus Christ, whom he has sent. Christ has been raised from the dead and appointed by God as the Lord of life and ruler of all things, seen and unseen.

If then, you wish to become disciples and members of his church, you must be guided to the fullness of the truth that he has revealed to us. You must learn to make the mind of Christ Jesus your own. You must strive to pattern your life on the teachings of the Gospel and so to love the Lord your God and your neighbor. For this was Christ's command and he was its perfect example.

Is each of you ready to accept these teachings of the Gospel?

Candidate—I am.

Celebrant turns to the sponsors and the assembly and asks them in these or similar words—Sponsors, you now present these candidates to us; are you, and all who are gathered with us, ready to help these candidates find and follow Christ?

All—We are.

With hands joined, the celebrant says—Father of mercy, we thank you for these your servants. You have sought and summoned them in many ways and they have turned to seek you. You have called them today and they have answered in our presence: we praise you, Lord, and we bless you.

All sing or say—We praise you, Lord, and we bless you.

Next, the cross is traced on the forehead of the candidates. . . . The celebrant says _____, receive the cross on your forehead. It is Christ himself who now strengthens you with this sign of his love. Learn to know him and follow him.

All sing or say the following or another suitable acclamation—Glory and praise to you, Lord Jesus Christ!

Journey to Jesus

Another proposal that merits attention is laid out in a book called *Journey to Jesus*.[10] Developed by evangelical worship theologian Robert Webber, this model is likewise based chiefly upon the pattern of the ancient catechumenate. Here is Webber's proposal in outline:

Stage	Spiritual Goal	Content	Passage Rite
Seeker	Conversion	The Gospel	Rite of Conversion
Hearer	Discipleship	Disciplined in what it means to be the church; what it means to worship; and how to read and pray Scripture	Rite of Covenant
Kneeler	Equipping	Equipping for spiritual warfare with prayer (the Lord's Prayer) and faith (the Apostles' Creed)	Rite of Baptism
Faithful	Incorporation	Incorporated into the full life of the church to discern and use gifts, steward creation, and become a witness	Eucharist as the continuing rite of nourishment

Webber refers to his model as being built upon the ancient pattern of evangelism. His book offers a helpful description of the ancient practices of catechesis, though he avoids use of the actual term itself. As the outline above indicates, he envisions four stages of instruction with various rites of passage marking the journey. Webber also produced a series of booklets to serve as resources for each stage of instruction.[11]

Commitments for a Congregational Curriculum

A third model, recently proposed by Gary in a book coauthored with Steve Kang, is built around seven commitments that are intended to always be part of a congregation's ministries of teaching and formation. The first five of these commitments may be viewed as stages, or processes, through which congregants pass while the final two are more concerned with the ethos of the church. The commitments are set forth by use of a miniature acrostic

145

	Grounding	Growing	Giving	Going
A—Access to the glorious Gospel	An Alpha-type experience for inquirers. Ideally in homes, hosted by lay members. Focus on the Story and the Gospel.			
B—Baptism		Formal catechetical experience in preparation for baptism, featuring instruction in the "three summaries." Open to candidates for baptism and confirmation, and to those who are already members. Taught by pastoral staff and mature lay members. Baptism and confirmation are joyously celebrated by the church.		
C—Commitment to the covenant community		An intensive course of instruction in preparation for becoming members of the church (or additional elements of instruction prior to baptism). Taught by pastoral staff and mature lay members. Further instruction in the Gospel, in the three "great streams" of the Truth, the Life, and the Way. Instruction in the distinctives of the church and its denomination or other affiliation. Instruction in the privileges and responsibilities of membership. Beginning steps are taken in vocational understanding and involvement.		
D—Deepening and developing in the Gospel		Members submit to the discipline and instruction of the church, participating regularly in the four commitments of Acts 2:42. In addition to participating in the liturgy and in formal learning experiences, growth occurs in a wide variety of informal settings. Along with continued growth in the Truth, the Life, and the Way, emphasis is placed on ongoing training in the Word, sharing life in community, and on growing in vocational understanding. Small groups and Bible studies may be "labeled" to help members understand intended sequence or priority (e.g., grounding, growing, giving, going). Members are trained in and involved in both ekklēsia (when the church assembles) ministry and diaspora (when the church disperses) ministries.		
E—Engagement in the ministry of reconciliation			Those who have become members (and others who are interested in joining them, when this is appropriate) engage in a wide variety of ministries (both ekklēsia and diaspora). There is an emphasis on vocational training via ministry opportunities, service projects, mission trips, or seminars regarding Christianity in the workplace. Ongoing leadership training raises up and sustains leaders (who must be members) for the various ministries of the church.	
F—Follow-up	Those who have walked through the "A–E" process outlined above have not "arrived." They are still sheep who must be lovingly tended by the shepherds of the flock—pastoral staff, elders, mature believers—who are ever watchful, prayerful, and careful for the well-being of the flock.			
G—Grace cultivation	Lest the processes outlined above fall victim to legalistic abuse, grace must be central in the preaching, teaching, hymnody, fellowship, and every ministry of the church. This must be intentionally cultivated by the leadership of the body and prayerfully guarded by all members.			

This table originally appears in Gary A. Parrett and S. Steve Kang, *Teaching the Faith, Forming the Faithful: A Biblical Vision for Education in the Church* (Downers Grove, IL: IVP Academic, 2009), chap. 13. Used by permission of InterVarsity Press, P.O. Box 1400, Downers Grove, IL 60615, www.ivpress.com.

featuring the letters A–G. On the facing page is their chart that provides an overview of the model.

The A–E commitments, again, represent something like phases through which believers move forward in the Faith of the Gospel. *Access* envisions use of a ministry such as Alpha or Christianity Explored.[12] The *Baptism* commitment represents a formal catechetical experience to prepare candidates for baptism. The same, or similar, process can also be used for the confirmation of those baptized in infancy. Those who are established as members of the faithful are also invited to participate in this phase of instruction, from time to time, for refreshment or recollection. *Commitment* is a further stage of formal instruction that focuses on taking one's part as a fully functioning member of the local church. In the *Deepening* commitment, a wide variety of ongoing experiences along the lines of the four commitments of Acts 2:42 is envisioned. *Engagement* focuses on preparing and engaging the maturing believers in various ministries of reconciliation. The final two commitments—*Follow-up* and *Grace cultivation*—are chiefly concerned with ethos. The former reminds of the continual need for pastoral care of all congregants, regardless of where they may be on their own journeys. The latter is an encouragement to set all of this in an atmosphere of grace rather than in a culture of legalism.

Conclusion

Each of these three visions for helping people move forward in the Faith, it seems to us, seeks to take seriously the thoroughly biblical notion of spiritual development. Attention to this is a vital component in catechetical ministries. In the next chapter we turn attention to two more ingredients we deem necessary for faithful and fruitful catechesis.

Drawing Lines and Choosing Sides

> In things essential, unity; in non-essentials, liberty; in all
> things, charity.[1]

In this chapter, we highlight two additional features of faithful and fruitful catechesis, which we will call "drawing lines" and "choosing sides." By *drawing lines*, we mean, first, that good catechesis helps believers distinguish primary doctrines from those that may be considered secondary or tertiary. Not all things that the church teaches are equally important. Simply making this point is, in and of itself, a potent act of teaching. A second sort of line drawing that catechists engage in is pointing out that what we believe at each level of importance—primary, secondary, and tertiary—needs to be distinguished from what others have taught. We believe *this* as opposed to *that*. Hence, our line drawing also involves *choosing sides*. These aspects of catechesis can be seen throughout the history of catechetical work and, we will argue, continue to be of vital importance for our own efforts at catechetical renewal today.

First Things First

With our earlier sketch of "the Faith" and related terms, we have already argued that some areas of catechetical content are more important than others. If we take biblical testimony seriously, there are some things which *must* be taught by the church in all times and places. But this does not apply to all matters. Some things, furthermore, must be taught before others can or should be. Some doctrines, in other words, are simply "weightier" in importance than others, and basic to others.

The apostle Paul, for example, plainly saw the Gospel as primary in his own catechetical work. When he outlines his message of the Gospel he writes to the Corinthians, "For I delivered to you as of first importance what I also received" (1 Cor. 15:3). First things, Paul insists, must come first. He laid the foundation of the Gospel. Its message, as we argued earlier, is the cornerstone of all other aspects of the Faith.

In our vision of catechetical content we must begin the work of catechesis by introducing those doctrines that are of primary concern. In catechesis we help learners grasp the relative weightiness of certain doctrines by drawing lines between these primary concerns and other teachings. The use of terms like *primary*, *secondary*, and *tertiary*, however, might well be too loaded for the liking of some believers. While such language may be potentially very helpful we recognize that others may be put off by it. This is also true with regard to the familiar language of "essentials" versus "non-essentials," made famous in the saying "In essentials, unity; in non-essentials, liberty; in all things, charity" (see note 1). It may be difficult to persuade a Baptist, for example, to see the doctrine of "believer's baptism" that is central to his own denominational identity as a non-essential or secondary matter. Pentecostal believers may well have similar problems with regard to distinctive teachings about the baptism and gifts of the Spirit, and so on with reference to other faith communities.

We are persuaded that faithful catechesis must sooner or later underline the point that what makes us part of the one body of Christ is finally more important than what makes us, say, Presbyterian or Anglican. But perhaps there is other language that can be used to help us toward this sort of drawing lines, language that will not prove a stumbling block to quite as many people. In such hope we propose a different set of terms or, better, a different way of framing matters. We suggest thinking of catechetical content as having four layers, which we label: (1) Christian Consensus; (2) Evangelical Essentials; (3) Denominational Distinctives; and (4) Congregational Commitments.[2]

Here is a fuller description of what we mean by each of these expressions. We examine how these might be worked out in a catechetical strategy later, in chapter 9.

1. Christian Consensus

That which has been believed everywhere, always, and by all (in other words, the fundamentals of "the Faith")

The Faith, as we have argued throughout, is the proper content of catechesis. This Faith may be taught in many ways—topically, thematically, within a narrative framework, or in some combination of the above. Few Christians would argue against the idea of teaching the Faith, even if they never actually get around to doing so. For those who do take such a teaching task seriously, though, there is often disagreement about what constitutes the Faith, as we have already seen. What we intend by "the Faith" here includes that which others have labeled *mere Christianity*, and still others have called *the Great Tradition*.[3]

We see much that is commendable in these terms. Still, we would give preference to the more commonly used biblical language of "the Faith." In our proposal for catechetical content we have suggested that teaching the Faith requires primary attention to the following components:

- *The Gospel* in its simplicity and depth (which must be taught "as of first importance"—that is, it must always be viewed as primary and foundational)
- *The Story* of redemption, of which the Gospel is the apex and summary (the sacraments provide a means of continually retelling the Story)
- *The Truth*, that is, the doctrines that conform to the Gospel (the Creed provides the historic primer on the Truth)
- *The Life*, that is, the life-giving power that flows from our relationship with God (the Lord's Prayer provides the historic primer on the Life)
- *The Way*, that is, the manner of living in this world that conforms to the Truth of the Gospel (the Decalogue provides the historic primer on the Way)

We have no illusions that all believers who would concur with the basic elements of such an outline will agree on its details. For example, Catholics hold that there are seven sacraments, Protestants have historically affirmed only two, and Orthodox believers have tended to avoid any dogmatic numbering of the sacraments. More critically, our unpacking of the Gospel will surely differ in critical detail between these various groups. Still we are convinced that there is much to be gained by beginning our catechetical efforts, in whichever of the historic Christian communities we may belong to, with emphasis on those things which have been held in common by the vast majority of Christians through the ages. Utilizing the four fixtures of the catechism—the Creed, the Decalogue, the Lord's Prayer, and the sacraments—is a very practical and tangible way to affirm a non-compromising, irenic, and properly ecumenical approach that takes seriously the prayer of Jesus for the unity of believers in John 17:20–23 and the apostle Paul's emphatic plea for unity in passages such as Ephesians 4:3 and 4:13.

2. Evangelical Essentials

> Those things which mark us off as evangelical Protestants
> vis-à-vis Catholic and Orthodox believers

Admittedly, the word "evangelical" is problematic in our day. Some would argue that the term has simply lost its usefulness because it has come to mean wildly different things to many different groups. For some the term is identified with right-leaning politics. For others the term is synonymous with "fundamentalist." Some groups that have very little in common with orthodox, historic Christianity now seek to lay claim to the label of "evangelical." The problems are complex indeed. Some have perhaps concluded that we would do best to dismiss the term altogether in favor of some other designation.

Troublesome though the term can be, however, there is still much to commend its usage to us. It has biblical roots, being built from the Greek term *euangelion*, meaning "good news." It thus reminds us of the importance of Gospel-centricity in the lives and ministries of our churches. Furthermore the term is historically important. It was the self-designation of many of the Reformers (who came to be called "Lutherans" or "Protestants" by others). In many parts of Europe, this is evident in the fact that Protestant churches are called simply "evangelical churches" to this day.

Aside from the confusion that can pop into the minds of many upon hearing the word "evangelical," a case can be made that a broad and deep evangelical consensus around central doctrines does in fact exist even now. Drawing upon numerous statements and declarations that have been generated by a wide variety of evangelical organizations from the mid-twentieth century to the beginning of the twenty-first, J.I., together with Thomas Oden, offered a summary outline of that consensus in the book *One Faith*.[4] Their summary argues compellingly for evangelical consensus in the following areas:[5]

1. The Good News: the heart of the Gospel
2. The Bible: the authority of Holy Scripture
3. The One True God: Father, Son, and Holy Spirit
4. Human life under God: creation fallen into sin
5. Jesus Christ: his person and work
6. Christ's reconciling work on the cross: his penal substitution for our sins
7. The exalted Lord: his resurrection, ascension, and session
8. Justification by grace through faith: the acquittal
9. The meaning of salvation: God saves sinners
10. The sending of the Holy Spirit: uniting the faithful to Christ
11. The holy life: sanctifying grace
12. Unity in the truth of the Gospel: the unity of all believers
13. The church: the people of God

14. Religious pluralism and the uniqueness of Christ: salvation in Christ alone
15. Christian social responsibility: the integration of words and deeds
16. The future: the last things

While the title of J.I. and Oden's book is *One Faith*, they are not claiming that their outline represents what we have called "the Faith" as it is affirmed by believers in all the major historic communities—Orthodox, Catholic, and Protestant. Their focus instead is unity of conviction among evangelical Protestants.

Another possible way of framing what should constitute evangelical essentials for purposes of contemporary catechesis would be to turn to the Reformation *solas*: *solus Christus* ("Christ alone"), *sola gratia* ("grace alone"), *sola fide* ("faith alone"), *sola scriptura* ("Scripture alone"), and *soli deo gloria* ("glory be to God alone"). Many evangelical believers will still find these emphases very useful for the second phase or layer of catechesis that we are here proposing.[6]

3. Denominational Distinctives

> Those doctrines that distinguish various Protestant groups (denominations or other affiliations) from one another (Baptist from Presbyterian, Pentecostal from Methodist, etc.)

Evangelical Protestants may well agree on a good number of doctrines and emphases, but there can be no doubt that there are many teachings and practices that keep us from fully experiencing our unity with one another. How divided are we? We have already mentioned the nearly forty thousand denominations that exist today. Beyond the official denominations, there are countless ad hoc affiliations and associations of churches as well. Some of these divisions are doubtless the product and legacy of sinful and selfish and stubborn human hearts. We certainly have not paid due heed to the prayer of Jesus and the pleas of Paul that we mentioned above. These divisions weaken our witness and credibility in the eyes of our nonbelieving neighbors just as Jesus implied would be the case (see John 13:34–35; 17:23). The divisions that exist among ourselves as evangelical Protestants also make it exceedingly difficult for us to have meaningful dialogue with Catholic and Orthodox Christians. Were we to envisage anything approximating a truly ecumenical council of the church today, for example, how would we go about choosing representatives from an evangelical world so diverse and unorganized?

On the other hand, not all divisions are sinful or inappropriate. Paul decried the Corinthian divisions that were based on social standing, spiritual giftedness, and improper attention to human leaders. But he also noted that some divisions within the body of Christ are unavoidable and serve to show who is moving and ministering in ways that are pleasing to God (1 Cor. 11:19). Some divisions are born not merely of sinful proclivities but from genuine convictions about matters theological, ethical, ecclesial, and liturgical. Furthermore, by what must be regarded as a happy irony, such divisions can actually provide opportunities for profound displays of unity. When Christians work together toward common ends of evangelism, service, and mission in spite of their theological diversity, they offer a picture of an authentic and critical aspect of biblical unity. Unity in the Bible—which derives ultimately from the Christian doctrine of the Holy Trinity—is not a *uniformity* void of diversity. It is rather a *unity* in and through diversity.[7]

Catechesis, however, requires that we draw lines between our doctrines in such a way as to demonstrate their relative importance. Teaching that helps believers understand, for example, that the doctrine of the Trinity is actually more important than our particular doctrine of ecclesiastical polity is a God-honoring ecumenical act in its own right. This is not to say that concerns such as the latter are unimportant. In fact, these are critical issues that need to be understood and addressed by the congregation's teaching ministry. When there are significantly divergent convictions about the meaning of the Lord's Supper, it will prove difficult for believers to worship together on a week-by-week basis. But when in spite of our differences regarding the sacraments (or ordinances—the choice of language itself points to our differing convictions) or polity or the end times we find ways to concretely express our love and respect for one another as fellow believers in Jesus Christ, we are doing something truly beautiful.

4. Congregational Commitments

> The vision, values, and practices that are perceived as
> unique commitments of this particular church

Even within a given denominational context, each particular congregation will have certain commitments that are distinctly its own. These may be the function of the unique sense of call or burden that the congregation had when formed or toward which it has more recently felt directed by God's Spirit. They may also be shaped by the particular cultural setting in which the church lives, including matters of ethnicity, socioeconomic realities, geography, nationality, or a general sense of the times in which the church has been chosen, by God's sovereign appointment, to live and minister.

Wise church leaders will want their members to be well educated in the distinctive commitments of the congregation. But here again what it means to be a member of, say, "First Church" must be placed in proper perspective relative to all the other sorts of belonging that apply—belonging to a certain

154

denomination or affiliation, belonging to the Protestant evangelical community, and belonging to the "one, holy, catholic, and apostolic church" of Jesus Christ.[8]

Clarity in Our Courses

One way we might draw lines for our people is in regard to those teaching ministries that are ongoing in the life of the congregation. For example, a given church may offer adult Sunday school classes throughout the year. Some churches that formerly featured a vibrant Sunday school have moved away from this particular format, replacing it with small groups that meet throughout the week, a midweek gathering, or perhaps with monthly or quarterly seminars. Regardless of the particular format, we need to consider whether we are drawing lines for our members that can help them recognize the relative importance of the issues being taught and discussed.

Suppose, for example, that a certain church offers four small group or Sunday school options for adult learners each week. The offerings may be determined simply by the fact that four members of the church have volunteered to teach on subjects of interest to themselves. One has decided to offer a class on parenting young children. Another leads a discussion on a recent book by a popular Christian author. A third offers a study through the book of, for instance, Philippians using a published Bible study guide. The fourth class turns out to be an introduction to what Christians believe.

In such a scenario there are many problems at work that really need to be addressed. First of all the scheme for teaching is ad hoc and haphazard. One year will thus look very different from the next and there is no apparent coherence or cohesion in the curriculum. Secondly the teachers may be inappropriate for the task. Have they simply volunteered themselves? Are they biblically qualified teachers? Do they have adequate training? Are they mature believers? There is much we could say about these problems and many more that are implicit in this little sketch. But the problem we want to point out just now is simply that there are no lines drawn for the learners. All four courses are effectively offered as electives. There is nothing to suggest to anyone that one of these courses may be more basic for Christian learning than the other choices.

A very practical way to improve upon such a situation is to have offerings that are divided into at least two categories. The first might be called something like "Basics," "Foundations of the Faith," "Faith Essentials," and so on. One church with which Gary consulted about these matters chose several courses to comprise what they began to call the "Cornerstone" series. The second category could be described with words like "enrichment" or "development" or simply "electives." After drawing lines in this manner, we can then make it clear that our intention is that church members begin their learning with classes in the first category.[9] Once we have established five or six such classes we should offer them on an ongoing basis. We might then urge that learners finish all of these before jumping into offerings from the second category. Alternatively we could suggest that learners vary their selections throughout the year—a class from the first category one quarter, and from the second category the next quarter—until they have finished all the "Basics" classes. Offerings in the second category are more open-ended and new courses may well become available each year. For those who have been in the church and in this schooling aspect of its ministry for many years, there will be the option of taking one of the new courses offered each year or of refreshing oneself in some of those things that are considered essentials. Of course some of the longtime members will themselves become teachers in this ministry. The crucial move will be to establish the expectation that all members will take courses regularly, as part of their church commitment.

We can now see that there are at least two related but different ways in which we must draw lines as we catechize. First we draw them between doctrines based on relative importance. Second we draw them wherever and whenever we must between the various families of faith within the Christian world. This latter aspect of drawing lines should sadden us because we long for a fuller experience of the true unity of the body of Christ. But honesty requires us to draw the lines where they in fact exist. May God help us to do so with as charitable, fair, and irenic a spirit as possible.

Choosing Sides

Because of the second aspect of line drawing—that is, distinguishing our doctrines and practices from those of others—the work of catechesis also involves what we are calling "choosing sides." At some appropriate place in our catechizing we must acknowledge that there are significant differences of conviction and opinion among evangelical Protestants. As we address these various points of divergence we are effectively drawing lines and choosing sides. We must seek to honestly explain the differences on the given doctrine or practice and then articulate why it is that our denomination or congregation believes or practices as it does: "Here we have a sort of line between us and other believers. We stand on this side of the line, and here's why. . . ." Our teaching must communicate love and respect toward our fellow believers but we should not be shy to acknowledge honest differences. Done properly, confessing our diversity on secondary matters can actually be an act of acknowledging our fundamental unity with fellow believers.

We trust that for many, if not most, contemporary evangelicals it will not prove difficult to take such an approach to our differences with other evangelicals. But distinguishing our positions as evangelical Protestants from those of

Catholic and of Orthodox churches, on the other hand, will prove a greater challenge. In fact, there are many evangelicals who simply do not regard Catholics or Orthodox as true Christians. Or at the very least they imagine that while it may be possible for a Catholic or Orthodox to be a "real Christian," that would be a very rare thing. Catholics and Orthodox, for their part, are likely to find more affinity with one another than with Protestants. Some in both of these communities will actually regard their church as the only true church, which of course is what is officially claimed. When Catholics say "the Church" they are typically referring to the Roman Catholic church. When Orthodox Christians say "the Church" they are typically referring to the various expressions of the Orthodox church. When evangelicals say "the Church"—with a capital "C"—they are typically referring to the so-called "invisible Church," the church, that is, as God sees it (though man cannot), which is comprised of all genuine believers in Jesus Christ. This, in the eyes of many evangelicals, would include all or most evangelicals and perhaps also some Catholics and Orthodox. Sadly, when many evangelicals say "the church" they do not think in terms of a capital "C" at all. The only church they have in mind is their own congregation. But we need a more generous view of things.

Years ago my wife and I (Gary) accompanied my sister and brother-in-law to a Lenten service in the local Catholic church where they regularly worshiped. My wife and I were deeply impressed by the amount of Scripture read during the service, including a good deal of biblical language in the liturgy. Afterward we confessed to my sister and brother-in-law that neither of us had ever heard so much Scripture in a service before. In reply my brother-in-law, a lifelong Catholic, offered a lament along these lines: "Most of those people had no idea what it all meant." The Scriptures were read and recited but apparently things were done by rote for many. There was little biblical exposition or teaching in the service and most of those in attendance were far removed from their childhood interactions with a catechism—an experience which may or may not have been a positive one.

I had a second strong impression from the service. When the Mass was celebrated my wife and I knew we would not go forward to partake of the Lord's Supper, and had already discussed this with my sister and brother-in-law. Because of different understandings of the meaning and mystery of the sacrament we felt that we could not participate. Remaining in my seat I began to peruse the missal (which provided detailed guidance in the liturgy, together with some readings and songs) located in the back of the pew in front of me. On the inside front cover was a word of welcome and some instructions regarding participation in the Mass. The instructions were offered under four heads: "For Catholics," "For Other Christians," "For Those Not Receiving Communion," and "For Non-Christians." I knew the heading "For Other Christians" was intended for my wife and me, and for others like us. That section contained two paragraphs. The first read:

We welcome our fellow Christians to this celebration of the Eucharist as our brothers and sisters. We pray that our common baptism and the action of the Holy Spirit in this Eucharist will draw us closer to one another and begin to dispel the sad divisions which separate us. We pray that these will lessen and finally disappear, in keeping with Christ's prayer for us "that they may all be one" (John 17:21).

The second paragraph began with these words: "Because Catholics believe that the celebration of the Eucharist is a sign of the reality of the oneness of faith, life, and worship, members of those churches with whom we are not yet fully united are ordinarily not admitted to Holy Communion."[10]

I had several thoughts about what I was reading. On the one hand, while the prayer of Jesus was referred to—a prayer to which I fully join my heart—there was nothing in the statement to suggest that the Catholic church was anticipating movement on their part toward my Reformed understanding of the sacrament anytime soon! My strong sense was that the statement's prayer that our "sad divisions which separate us . . . will lessen and finally disappear" was envisioning a day when all the wayward sheep would come "home to Rome."

But on the other hand the irenic language of the statement struck me. My wife and I along with our fellow Protestants were being addressed as "fellow Christians" and as "our brothers and sisters." This language left my heart feeling strangely warmed. I wondered if my own congregation—which at the time was an independent evangelical church—would dare to use such language toward Catholic believers who might come to our congregation for one of our quarterly (yes, it was only quarterly) celebrations of the Lord's Supper. In fact I felt fairly confident that many of our members would have strongly opposed addressing Catholics as "fellow Christians" and "brothers and sisters."

In the evangelical church of which I am now a member, many years later, I am bold to believe that far more of us would be inclined to offer this sort of gracious language. There are several factors that may contribute to this. First, our church is part of a denomination and so our members have a better sense that "the church" is far bigger than just our own congregation. Second, our particular denomination takes very seriously the idea of "majoring on majors" and thus would be more likely to extend grace regarding our differences with Catholics. And third, the age in which we now live lends itself to tolerance of difference (far too easily, it must be said). A fourth factor that has influenced at least some of our members is that we actually do engage in a limited, formal catechetical ministry in our church. All who are preparing for baptism or confirmation go through a period of instruction in which our convictions are taught, including this denominational commitment to "major on the majors." And in our ongoing catechetical ministries—preaching, worship, teaching, small groups—these values are strongly reinforced. Our town is heavily Roman Catholic, and this too has had the effect of increasing our sensitivity toward our Catholic neighbors.

Disagreeing . . . with Gentleness and Respect

In an even more rigorous and intentional ministry of catechesis, we would work hard to emphasize what we as evangelicals hold in common with Catholics and Orthodox Christians. We would also draw lines and choose sides where necessary, endeavoring always to do so in love as befits the people of God. There are in fact significant points of divergence between Catholics, Orthodox, and evangelical Protestants. Among these are different understandings of biblical authority, the nature of the church and its sacraments, and the Gospel and the saving work of Christ. Such things must be addressed directly, as is currently being done by the group called Evangelicals and Catholics Together, of which J.I. is a member. This group's long-term aim is to map the continuing differences, so as to see both what would have to happen for consensus to be achieved, and also how far, if at all, pastoral cooperation is possible while consensus is lacking. Whether any form of common catechesis is yet possible is a question that for this group hangs in the air. In the Reformation era, however, this was not anyone's question; both sides saw the catechetical task as one of making clear the differences themselves.

To see this, one need only browse through the various catechisms that emerged first from the labors of the Reformers and then from the Counter Reformation work of the Church of Rome. It was inevitable that the Reformers would need to draw lines and choose sides in their published catechisms. They were newly emerging from the oversight of the papacy and had to explain where and why they differed on critical points of doctrine. Most notably differences regarding the number and meaning of the sacraments and regarding the nature of justification and justifying faith were regularly cited by the Protestant catechisms. Increasingly, as the Catholics answered back with catechisms of their own, the tone sharpened, and often grew severe.

In response to harsh language—including declaration of anathemas—found in the Roman catechisms regarding the Protestant teachings on the Lord's Supper, Elector Frederick III insisted that an additional question and answer be included in the *Heidelberg Catechism* (published originally in 1563) to fire back. Question 80 addresses the differences between "the Lord's Supper and the Papal Mass." The answer provided closes with these words: "Therefore the Mass is fundamentally a complete denial of the once for all sacrifice and passion of Jesus Christ (and as such an idolatry to be condemned)." The addition was unfortunate for two reasons. First, it is completely out of character with the overriding tenor and purpose of the catechism as a whole. The *Heidelberg Catechism* is particularly irenic in tone and was actually commissioned, in part at least, out of a longing to see greater unity between the Lutheran and Reformed churches of the German Palatinate. Secondly, the language in the answer to Question 80 does not seem a fair estimate of the Catholic position.

In recent years some Protestant bodies that have long made use of the *Heidelberg Catechism* have acknowledged that Question 80 and its answer are problematic to say the least. Some Reformed churches now publish the original language of the answer in italics and/or add comments indicating what is perceived to be a more accurate portrayal of Roman Catholic views.[11]

As we saw earlier in chapter 3, a tendency toward particularization and the uncharitable exchanges between various Christian bodies that accompanied this trend must bear part of the blame for the decline of catechesis in recent history. While we should not duck away from our differences we do no favors to ourselves by exaggerating them either, or by articulating them in ways that are unkind and likely to generate mutual hostility. Recent documents from the Catholic church regarding catechizing in our day likewise emphasize charity and fairness in representing the views of other Christian groups. For example, we find these instructions in the *National Directory for Catechesis*:

> Catechesis seeks to present the teachings of other churches, ecclesial communities, and religions correctly and honestly. It explains "the divisions that do exist [between and among Christians] and the steps that are being taken to overcome them." It avoids words, judgments and actions that misrepresent other Christians. This will help Catholics deepen their understanding of their own faith and develop genuine respect for the teachings of other ecclesial communities while also bearing witness to the Church's commitment to seek the unity of all Christians.[12]

"You Have Heard That It Was Said . . . but I Say to You"

The preceding remarks provide a word of introduction to our next major point. We have spoken above about drawing lines at the third and second layers, or phases, of catechetical work. In fact, however, we would argue that such efforts are primarily appropriate not for initial catechesis but for subsequent teaching of a congregation's maturing believers. The focus of initial catechesis—such as that in preparation for baptism or confirmation—should be instead on those doctrines and practices we have referred to above as the Christian Consensus. Or perhaps we could envision such catechesis as *primarily* concerned with matters of Christian Consensus supplemented by some attention to Evangelical Essentials and far less attention to Denominational Distinctives and Congregational Commitments. *Catechesis proper* is primarily concerned with grounding believers in the fundamentals of the Faith. Those doctrines and practices which distinguish groups of Christians from one another belong more properly to the work of *ongoing catechesis*. Therefore, in other words, the primary line drawing in formal, initial catechesis in our age should be between the Christian worldview and competing, non-Christian worldviews.

There has always been an impulse in sound catechetical work toward something like the language of Jesus from the Sermon on the Mount. In that passage Jesus distinguishes his teaching from that which was popular in the surrounding Jewish culture of the time. Thus we hear him say several times, "You have heard that it was said . . . but I say to you" (Matt. 5:21–22, 27–28, 31–32, 33–34, 38–39, 43–44). Jesus summarized some of the teachings of the religious authorities of the day and then countered those teachings with his own. He was, to use our language, drawing lines and calling his hearers to choose sides. This sort of practice had ancient precedents. It is evident throughout the Old Testament as the people of Israel were warned through the preaching and teaching ministries of everyone from Moses to Malachi against the idolatry and immorality of their surrounding nations. It is also apparent in the various New Testament letters written to churches in specific contexts, as well as in the book of Revelation.

Such an approach has been a constant throughout the history of serious catechetical work. In the ancient church we see this sort of thing at work in the various ecumenical councils of the church. Truth was expounded at the expense of heresy. Careful catechists introduced those becoming Christian into the new world of the Bible and Christian reality in part by contrasting this new world with the old world from which they were turning. Typically, attention was especially given to those competing truth and morality claims that were predominant and most likely to affect and challenge the new believers. Context was obviously critical. Thus we see Cyril of Jerusalem pointing up Christian teaching vis-à-vis "the Jews"—that is, the unbelieving Jews who dominated the landscape of Jerusalem. The hostility between non-Christian Jewish authorities and the Christian church—largely gentile by this time, but including Jewish believers as well—was often fierce.

The Reformers had an obvious opponent as they catechized. They had recently broken from the rule of Rome and necessarily needed to distinguish their beliefs and practices from those of the Catholic church. This sort of practice is evident in some Orthodox catechisms as well. In one such contemporary catechism, for example, following nearly every key teaching is an explicit contrast with the Roman Catholics, Anglicans, Protestants, and several other groups.[13]

The majority of recent catechetical documents that have been developed by the Roman Catholic church have continued this sort of "vis-à-vis" approach. It may surprise some evangelical Protestants to know, however, that the usual target is no longer Protestantism. Rather the target is more often the amorphous New Age spirituality that dominates much of the North American scene today. Here is one example:

Catechesis in relation to these New Age movements should accurately describe the beliefs and practices of adherents to these movements and carefully contrast them with Catholic beliefs and practices. It should help the Catholic faithful deepen their knowledge of Sacred Scripture, awaken a vibrant experience of prayer in them, to understand the teachings of the Church thoroughly, and articulate those teachings clearly. It should educate them to accept responsibility for the Catholic faith and to defend it vigorously against error and misunderstanding.[14]

Competing Catechisms of the Culture

Evangelicals who would catechize today need to properly identify the appropriate "vis-à-vis" for their own catechetical ministries. In other words, when we say, in effect, "You have heard that it was said . . . but the Scriptures say to you" we need to be clear about the influences that have been speaking into the lives of our congregants. Catechesis must always be attentive to the counter-catechesis at work in our lives. Earlier we dealt with the causes and consequences of the uncatechized church. In reality, however, all our members actually *have* been catechized—thoroughly so—in competing worldviews.

The venues and processes for this cultural catechesis are many and varied. A young person growing up in North America today has their worldview and values powerfully shaped by forces from all fronts. There is the constant influence of all sorts of media, the values inculcation that the schools and educational leaders have devoted themselves to, the political forces that legislate and enforce ever-shifting understandings of morality, the relentless worldview shaping that is driven by forces of advertising and marketing, and much more. The potency of such formative forces is enhanced by the fact that catechumens live among peers who are shaped continually by, and are often deeply committed to, these same things.

What can stand against the power of such influences? When families are fractured and churches are catechetically ineffective and inattentive, will the children in our own churches grow up to have faith in the living God? Survey data for some time now suggests overwhelmingly that among North American youth there is very little difference in values or lifestyle between teens who self-identify as evangelicals and those who profess no religious belief. The evidence overwhelmingly points, on the one hand, to unformed and poorly articulated beliefs. And those beliefs professed, on the other hand, seem to have little or no bearing on how the teen actually chooses to live.[15]

It is not only for the sake of those coming into the Faith from the outside but also for those growing up on the inside of our church communities that we must return to holistic, intentional, biblically faithful, and culturally sensitive ministries of catechesis. The counter-catechisms of our surrounding culture offer contrasting instructions regarding nearly every point of biblical catechesis. We would speak the Truth but our hearers have been schooled in numerous false *-isms* of the age. We witness to the Life that comes from a living relationship with the living God; our hearers have long been trained in the worship of assorted idols within the culture. We point toward and strive to lead in the Way; the culture has catechized our congregants toward a very different way—toward perverse practices and habits that are plainly not-the-way. We tell God's redemptive Story; the culture propagates countless other narratives. We proclaim the Gospel, but pseudo-gospels have been trying to lead us astray for many years.

The wise Christian catechist must discern the competing catechisms at work in controlling the heads, hearts, and hands of our congregants. We then draw lines and choose sides. With Joshua we are bold to name competing gods and call for decision. Will it be "the gods that your fathers served in the region beyond the River, or the gods of the Amorites in whose land you now dwell" or will it be the One, the true God, the LORD? We ourselves must lead in the declaration, "As for me and my house, we will serve the LORD" (Josh. 24:15).

Evangelical Protestants in North America must carefully discern the counterpoint to their catechetical work. What in fact are the competing catechisms fighting for the minds and devotion of our members? Perhaps in some instances it will still be the case that our primary focus in this regard would be some other Christian community. In a heavily Latino community where the majority of our members have grown up with a Catholic culture and worldview we probably will have to deal seriously with the tenets of Catholicism. In a Russian or Greek community where the majority has previously known only the Orthodox vision of the Faith we will have to address that vision candidly. If we are receiving new members who have come from fundamentalist Protestant backgrounds, "health and wealth" spiritualities, or theologically liberal mainline backgrounds—or whatever the case may be—we must keep the background clearly in mind as we teach.

Given the cultural realities in which we live as twenty-first-century North Americans, however, most of us will likely find ourselves confronting different primary competitors. The *-isms* that must be confronted by the truth of Christ include materialism, naturalism, relativism, and the like. The idols that must be cast down are possessions, pleasure, passion, power, and many more. The perverse practices of the day have the flavor of "Me first," "It just feels right," "Whatever it takes to get ahead," and so on. When we are concerned with the most basic level of catechesis—of grounding people in the fundamentals of the Faith once for all delivered to the saints—with its implications for what we believe, how we live, and how we come to know God, we ought not to waste our precious energies denigrating other Christian communities who share so much in common with us about the most important realities.

As we have already seen, evangelicals share with observant Catholic and Orthodox Christians belief in the One, Triune God; the Scriptures as God's sacred revelation; the full deity and full humanity of Jesus Christ; the redemption for sins accomplished through Christ's death; the bodily resurrection of Christ and his ascension to heaven; and the glorious return of Christ to rule and reign forever. We share, furthermore, deep convictions about a wide range of ethical issues. We believe together that persons come to know the living God through the mediation of Jesus Christ.

There is certainly a time and place for drawing lines and choosing sides relative to other Christian communities. Such work, however, should not be the focus of our primary, foundational catechesis. In the first phase, or layer, of catechesis we identify the most basic realities of the Christian worldview. We outline the Gospel, expand on the redemptive Story, and articulate the basic elements of the Truth, the Life, and the Way. As we do so we cannot help but offer our unique perspective on these matters since we speak as evangelical Protestants. This will surely affect our presentation of the Gospel, for example. In many, if not most, instances the presentation of the Gospel from the lips of an evangelical Protestant will be different in some significant ways from the presentation by a Catholic or an Orthodox Christian. Such differences will be inevitable *within* evangelical circles as well. Reformed teaching about the Gospel will at points be different from Arminian teaching or Lutheran teaching on the same subject.

We need not be shy about these differences. But we should not go out of our way, on the other hand, to magnify these differences at the earliest stages of our catechetical work. Our focus instead should be on how the message of the Gospel is so very different from all the false gospels of the culture that surrounds us. This will mean that we also distinguish the Christian vision from the message of other major religions. This is especially vital in the Western world today when people from so many religious and cultural backgrounds live side by side in our cities. All this teaching we seek to conduct with gentleness and respect (1 Peter 3:15; 2 Tim. 2:24–26) but we are clear that the call of Christ is radically different relative to the myriad competing visions of reality that surround us.

Concluding Remarks

In this chapter we considered the ideas of drawing lines and choosing sides in our ministries of catechesis. In faithful and fruitful catechesis we must make a distinction between primary, secondary, and tertiary teachings. In the most basic of catechetical work we must especially labor to distinguish the teachings of the Christian faith vis-à-vis other philosophies, practices, and worldviews of the surrounding cultures in which we minister and live. Having drawn these sorts of lines we are honest and clear as to when and where we must choose sides. But we are to do all these things in a biblical spirit of gentleness and respect.

Moving In and Moving On

Christ came chiefly for this reason: that we might learn
how much God loves us, and might learn this to the end
that we begin to glow with love of him by whom we were
first loved, and so might love our neighbor at the bidding
and after the example of him who made himself our neighbor by loving us.[1]

St. Augustine

In this chapter we outline a model for configuring and implementing ministries of catechesis in evangelical churches today. The proposal seeks to
draw together issues we have been talking about throughout the course of
the book. In the first place we concern ourselves with the matter of content
that was the focus of chapters 4–6. Next we aim to be attentive to the issues of
spiritual development and cultural sensitivity we addressed in chapters 7 and
8. In addition to these central concerns we bring into this proposal insights
concerning educational processes and practices.

The following table presents our proposal in overview. The reader can see
at a glance the 3 × 3 × 3 structure we intend: three facets of the Faith, three
phases of the journey, and three forms of education. We unpack all of this in
the succeeding pages.

	The Truth	The Life	The Way	
Procatechesis: First glimpses of the Gospel	Unfolding the Story in compelling fashion, perhaps utilizing programs such as Alpha or Christianity Explored			*Formal*
	Hearing the Word taught and proclaimed	Appropriate observation/ participation in worship gatherings	Appropriate observation/ participation in community, outreach	*Non-formal*
	Cultivating an ethos of hospitality and *xenophilia*[2]			*Informal (and implicit)*
Catechesis proper: Formal grounding in the Gospel	Exposition of the Creed; further training in the Truth	Exposition of Lord's Prayer; further training in the Life	Exposition of Decalogue, Sermon on the Mount; further training in the Way	*Formal*
	Continually hearing the Word taught and proclaimed	Deepening participation in prayer and worship	Deepening participation in community, justice, mercy, vocation	*Non-formal*
	Cultivating an ethos of solemnity and celebration			*Informal (and implicit)*
Ongoing catechesis: Further growth in the Gospel	Continual study of the Scriptures and sound doctrine	Continual training in prayer, worship, and evangelism	Continual training in ethics, service, vocation	*Formal*
	Continually hearing the Word taught and proclaimed; personal study	Deepening participation in prayer, worship, evangelism	Deepening participation in community, justice, mercy, vocation	*Non-formal*
	Cultivating an ethos of humility and teachability			*Informal (and implicit)*

Three Facets and Three Phases

The three facets of the Faith (highlighted in the top row of the table above) we have labeled "the Truth," "the Life," and "the Way." We explored these facets at length in chapter 6. These three dimensions of catechetical content, we argued, all derive from the Gospel, and we may therefore aptly speak of "the Faith of the Gospel." *The Truth* concerns the sound doctrine that accords with the Gospel. *The Way* concerns that manner of conduct in the world that conforms to the sound doctrine. *The Life* concerns the life-giving power inherent in the Gospel that liberates us from our bondage to sin and enables us to begin walking in the Way.

To teach with these three dimensions as our content is to instruct God's people in the Gospel itself. Since the Gospel is the apex and summary of the great Story of God's redemptive dealings with humankind, these three facets also represent ongoing education in and training for our participation in that Story. And all of this is really and truly a faithful form of proclaiming Christ himself—the Truth, the Life, and the Way—the central figure of the Faith, of the Gospel, and of the Story.

In the left-hand column of our table we indicate the idea of movement, or progress, in the journey of faith. Broadly speaking we envision three phases of catechesis. The first we label *procatechesis*. This employs the language of the ancients in describing a vision of pre-Christian fellow-travelling toward discipleship. In this phase we offer first glimpses of the Gospel to those whom the ancients might have called *inquirers* and whom many contemporary churches might call *seekers*. The second phase is concerned with *catechesis proper*, or with a formal grounding in the Gospel. Later we will subdivide this phase into two steps. Phase three envisions an open-ended commitment to *ongoing catechesis* wherein believers experience further growth in the Gospel.

Three Types of Education, Three Types of Curricula

For the past half century or so Christian educators have been working out and articulating distinctions between three forms of education which have come to be called *formal, non-formal*, and *informal*.[3] The impetus behind such distinctions was chiefly the concern that too much of what was done in the name of Christian education involved the "schooling model." Here we see perhaps another unintended outcome of the Sunday school movement and its adoption as the major setup for teaching and learning in many of our churches. While some form of a serious schooling in the Faith and in the Scriptures is always necessary, it is unwise to view such teaching/learning experiences as the only sort of education we should engage in. We teach (and learn) the things of God in many ways. As the saying goes, much of what we really learn is better *caught* than *taught* (in the formal sense of the word).

While the lines between these three forms of education are not always clear, for our purposes we use these terms as follows. *Formal* education refers to our efforts to teach explicitly and intentionally in structured, designated educational settings such as a Sunday school class, a Bible study, a gathering of catechumens for instruction, and so on. By *non-formal* education we intend those experiences which are intentionally planned and designed, and are clearly formative but are not explicitly identified as educational. Such experiences might include, for example, worship gatherings, service opportunities inside or outside the church, gatherings for prayer, fellowship, and so on. *Informal* education, finally, we take to refer to the whole range of interactions and experiences we have that may be unplanned and unstructured yet are still very formative. Much of this has to do with matters of ethos and forces of socialization or acculturation that occur with or without our knowledge or intention.

A similar and related insight from the world of education is that we who teach need to always remember that there are also three types of curricula: the *explicit curriculum*, the *implicit* (or *hidden*) *curriculum*, and the *null curriculum*.[4] This is only one of many approaches to thinking about curricula that have been put forth by educational theorists and leaders, but we find this curricular triad particularly helpful. For our purposes we mean by explicit curriculum (sometimes called the *overt* curriculum) that which we actually intend to teach others—the formal content of our instruction. The implicit curriculum (the same idea is sometimes called the *hidden curriculum* or the *covert curriculum*) refers to that which is taught by the ways in which the teaching occurs—structures, practices, processes, that which teachers model or communicate by their actions, words, or attitudes, and so on. It is often the case that there is a serious disconnect between what we think we are teaching and what is in fact being learned by others. This is similar to the notion that our formal educational programs can be undercut by what happens in our non-formal gatherings or informal interactions.

The null curriculum speaks of that which we fail to teach. Like our implicit curriculum, this could be by design or could be unconscious and unintentional. Either way it is a powerful teacher in its own right. In the context of preaching or Christian education the idea of the null curriculum would come into play with reference to those passages of Scripture we never exposit, those doctrines and imperatives we never bring before our people, and so on. When we fail to address passages and themes, our failure to do so also teaches. In any given church there are doubtless many congregants who have little or no idea that the Bible addresses certain aspects of their lives that, in fact, desperately need addressing. On the other hand our failure to name and confront the *-isms*, idols, and perverse practices of the culture may be teaching congregants that God has nothing to say about those matters.

In our proposal we have tried to give attention primarily to matters of formal and non-formal educational settings and practices. Our content proposals focus on the explicit curriculum but we urge church leaders to try to be thoughtful, conscious, and self-critical about the null curriculum of the church and to commit themselves, by God's grace, to declare the whole counsel of God. Finally, because we acknowledge the formative power of the implicit curriculum and know that all our informal interactions are influential, we encourage church leaders to prayerfully labor to cultivate the sort of ethos that will help ensure that these forces tend more toward good than ill.

With this supporting information before us we now turn to a brief consideration of each of the three phases of catechesis we propose.

Phase One—Procatechesis: First Glimpses of the Gospel

In this first phase of catechetical work, we are concerned with faithfully providing first glimpses of the Gospel to our neighbors. The evangelistic commitments of a church can and should take many forms. These could include particular evangelistic efforts or programs in which church members reach out to their neighbors. They should surely include as well the commitment to cultivate in church members the sense that they are always called to "be my witnesses" (Acts 1:8). Such a realization will mean that wherever they may be over the course of a given day or week they really do represent Jesus Christ as his appointed ambassadors (2 Cor. 5:20). Through their hard work, godly living, and ethical commitments they "win the respect of outsiders" (1 Thess. 4:12 NIV), "make the teaching about God our Savior attractive" (Titus 2:10 NIV), and let their "light shine before others, so that they may see your good works and give glory to your Father who is in heaven" (Matt. 5:16). It will not be a wordless witnessing, however. As witnesses we must also verbally testify to Christ, proclaiming his Gospel to others as God grants opportunity (Mark 16:15; Luke 4:18).

Our commitment to evangelizing should take another form as well. Not only are we to take the Gospel to those outside the church, we are to declare it inside the church community also, and to do so clearly, compellingly, and consistently. As we observed earlier, this was clearly an unwavering commitment of the apostle Paul (Rom. 1:15; 1 Cor. 1:23; 2:2; Gal. 3:1). In the gatherings of the church community for worship, for example, it is the Gospel that we preach and teach. By the grace of God this Good News will not only fall regularly upon the ears of the believers who gather each week but will also engage nonbelieving friends, relatives, and neighbors whom God sends our way. We should fully pray and expect that nonbelieving visitors will regularly be among us on Sunday mornings. And when they come, we should be ready for them. How so? By being sure that the Gospel is always our central concern and by cultivating a culture of hospitality, an ethos that communicates "come and you will see"—the very sort of invitation that Christ himself extended to others (as in John 1:39).

On the level of formal education, we may offer first glimpses of the Gospel to our neighbors through implementing ministry strategies like Alpha or Christianity Explored. Such programs, which we introduced earlier in this book, have been widely used and often found to be wonderfully fruitful. The focus of these ministries is on introducing the Faith to those who have expressed interest in learning more about the Bible, Jesus, or the church. Typically the instruction is set in the homes of church members. A meal is served, teaching is offered (in some cases, by means of video presentation), and discussion follows. While the setting is intended to be inviting and informal, this is an explicit teaching effort and we categorize it as formal education in our design.

Such formal efforts as this can be supported non-formally by inviting persons to regularly attend our worship services and to observe us, or even to join us at times, in our efforts to serve others. With concern for matters of informal education and the implicit curriculum we commit ourselves to cultivate an ethos of hospitality and *xenophilia*. We seek to be a community that intentionally and wholeheartedly welcomes the stranger (Matt. 25:35), whoever he or she may be. It is, in other words, a matter of obedience to one of the fundamentals of the Way: namely, that we love our neighbors as ourselves.

Phase Two—Catechesis Proper: Formal Grounding in the Gospel

The second catechetical phase is *catechesis proper*. In some church communities catechesis is used solely to refer to this phase of formal preparations for baptism or confirmation. Our focus now is on a formal grounding in the Gospel. As we suggested above, we are dividing this phase further into two steps as sketched out on the table below.

Step	Content Emphasis
1. Preparing for baptism or confirmation	Christian Consensus Evangelical Essentials
2. Preparing for official membership in, or leadership within, the local congregation	Christian Consensus Evangelical Essentials Denominational Distinctives Congregational Commitments

Step 1 of this phase is preparing candidates for baptism or confirmation. Clearly this is the piece of the catechetical puzzle that most closely corresponds to the historic practices. The length of this phase can vary from setting to setting. It is incumbent upon church leaders to make wise choices in this matter, basing their decisions upon a number of factors, including a sense of the culture in which the church lives. How near to or far from the biblical vision of the Truth, the Life, and the Way, they must ask themselves, are those who have been formed in this alien cultural context?

We recall that in the ancient catechumenate the final intense preparations for baptism were conducted through the six weeks of the Lenten season. But we also recall that before one even became a candidate for baptism one may already have been a catechumen for many months, or even several years. As leaders wrestle with the question of how much instruction candidates will need in their own context before baptism, we would stress how important it is that they honestly and openly evaluate cultural realities where they live, and seek the Lord's wisdom about how best to proceed. Corners must not be cut here.

For the sake of argument we will propose that a six-week, intensive period of time represents an appropriate minimum for such preparations. Within these parameters we would further urge that wherever possible, and without compromising conviction or conscience, efforts be made to follow principles and practices evident in the ancient pattern. By doing this we remind congregants that they are being baptized into that innumerable throng that is the "one, holy, catholic and apostolic church," an assembly that spans the globe and reaches through the ages (Heb. 12:22–24; Rev. 7:9–10).

Formal catechesis in this step will focus upon the three historic summaries of the Faith—the Creed, the Lord's Prayer, and the Decalogue—together with instruction on the sacraments of baptism and the Lord's Supper. It may be very useful to utilize at this point one of the Reformation catechisms such as the *Heidelberg Catechism*.[5] As they do so, however, catechists will need to demonstrate wisdom. They will do well to use the questions and answers contained in the catechism as starting points for their instructions, rather than as ending points. Ideally, those questions and answers—written originally in the sixteenth century—will give rise to many more questions that reflect life situations in the twenty-first century contexts in which we live. The aims in our instruction must include clarity of understanding, cultural congruence in application of the truths we are interacting with, and above all, pointing candidates to Christ and the Gospel.

During the period of preparation for baptism or confirmation candidates should also be engaged in a host of non-formal catechetical experiences, including regular attendance at the worship services of the church. They should be urged to begin developing their own disciplines of prayer, Bible study, devotional reading, and more. They should be invited to continue participation in the various ministries and fellowship gatherings of the church, and they are to be prayed for and exhorted on a daily basis by church leaders and by sponsors who are chosen to walk alongside them—especially in this critical leg of their journey.

The church seeks to cultivate an ethos of solemnity and celebration to support these formal and non-formal commitments. Becoming Christ's disciple and a new creature in him is a somber, mysterious, and mighty thing being undertaken and experienced. It is at the same time an occasion for joyous celebration. A discerning embrace of some of the ancient practices associated with baptism that we described in chapter 3 will go a long way to reminding us of these realities.

In step 2 of this phase of grounding in the Gospel, those who have been baptized or confirmed are to be prepared for active membership in the local church. In many church contexts this will appear as a strange idea, since baptism or confirmation will be seen as having already settled the matter of membership. However, the vision of every member being involved in ministry may not yet have taken hold. Such a vision is firmly anchored in the New Testament, and in the church, as elsewhere, everybody is, or can be, a leader to somebody. It is very fitting that (for instance) step 2 catechumens be paired off with persons coming along in the process behind them to provide them with informal help and encouragement—which will be their first taste of leadership ministry. In some cases, perhaps it will be appropriate to actually envision three steps in which individuals are prepared for (1) baptism or confirmation; (2) official membership in the local congregation; and (3) a recognized leadership role within the congregation. For now, however, we will envision only a second additional step of a formal catechizing for service which occurs after one's baptism.

Once again, it is incumbent upon church leaders to determine how long a period of instruction will be required for this membership (or leadership) training. Let us suppose once again a minimum of six weeks is dedicated to this experience. What will the focus of the content be? Generally speaking, we would advocate the following: first, a rehearsal of the most fundamental points of the Gospel, the Story, and the Faith; second, a foundational focus on the biblical doctrine of the church, especially with a view to explaining the relationship between membership in the "one, holy, catholic, and apostolic church" and one's local congregation; third, attention to what we earlier termed "Evangelical Essentials" to provide some rudimentary understanding of where evangelicalism fits into the larger church; fourth, attention to Denominational Distinctives (or another affiliation that may better help situate this particular congregation); fifth, attention to Congregational Commitments, that is, the burdens and tasks that are unique to this local church. All throughout there will be an accompanying concern to explain the meaning, privileges, expectations, and service responsibilities of official membership in the church.

Our formal instruction in these things then will include further instruction in those aspects of the Truth, the Life, and the Way that have been distinctively emphasized by evangelicals within our own denomination or in our own particular congregation. For example, we can introduce the Reformation *solas*. We can instruct our members in our denominational understandings regarding the sacramental ordinances, or spiritual gifts, or ecclesial polity. And we can explain the unique sense in which we as a congregation feel called to live out God's way in the community to which God has called us.

The formal education that occurs in these sessions is supplemented and supported by continued and deepening participation in the worship gatherings, fellowship meetings, and service and outreach opportunities that are regularly part of the church.

Alongside the periods of instruction that are central to this grounding-in-the-Gospel phase of catechesis proper, we would suggest that a discerning use of some historically affirmed rites of passage be employed. Webber's work, which we referenced in the previous chapter, can prove very helpful here. If the word *rite* is off-putting to some we can simply use a more familiar term such as *service*, as follows:

- A service of *enrollment* for those who are now to begin their baptismal preparation
- A service of *holy baptism* (or confirmation) after the baptismal preparation is completed; as part of this service, the newly baptized partake of, for the very first time, the Lord's Supper[6]
- A service of *membership* in which those who have completed membership training are formally welcomed as official members of the church
- A service of *commissioning* in which those who have completed leadership training are commissioned (or installed, or ordained) for recognized service in the church

We would be wise with regard to such things to reject the knee-jerk tendency of many evangelicals to simply dismiss anything that smacks of ritual. Empty ritualism is certainly unhelpful and even dangerous. But our rituals need not be empty. They can be biblically informed and kept full of meaning through regular words of reminder and instruction. The fact is we all have our rituals. Most of the time we are simply not conscious of them. Further, ritual is a common feature in Scripture. In the Old Testament we find ritual central to the celebration of the holy festivals God ordained as well as to heartfelt episodes of remembrance for God's gracious acts of intervening on behalf of his people. Joshua had the people place twelve stones in the Jordan river to remember how God faithfully and graciously led his people into the land of promise (Josh. 4:1–7). Samuel set up a stone, calling it Ebenezer ("stone of help") as a perpetual reminder of God's waging war against the Philistines on behalf of Israel (1 Sam. 7:12). In the New Testament too ritual is actually commanded by the Lord, most notably in the sacramental ordinances of baptism (Matt. 28:18–20) and the Lord's Supper (1 Cor. 11:23–26).

By adhering to even the simple, brief procedures of catechesis proper that we have outlined above as Phase Two, church leaders can have some sense that they have actually grounded their people in the basics of the Faith of the Gospel. No one will become a leader in the church who is not a member. No one will become a member without having passed through formal training for membership. No one will be eligible to begin membership training who has not been baptized or confirmed. No one will be baptized or confirmed who has not been prepared for this through a period of catechesis. By such steps some grounding in the Gospel for all is assured. A system is put in place that has some "teeth" in it; that is, there is a compelling component to the catechesis.

Ordinarily, of course, pastors will inherit a certain number of leaders and members when they assume a position in the church. Many of these who have already been baptized or confirmed will not have participated in the catechetical journey we are envisioning. What is to be done in such instances? Undoubtedly as we begin to put in place a new vision for catechesis we will have to "grandfather" some in, in light of church by-laws and the history of the local congregation. We probably must say therefore that to fully implement the ideas we have been proposing in this book will probably be possible only with a generation-long ministry, or a new church plant. In the latter case these commitments to catechize can become part of the cultural fabric of the congregation from the outset. In established congregations, the process will take longer.

Nevertheless even existing cultures can be changed, at least to some extent, with serious efforts. As Andy Crouch has argued, we do not change a culture by analyzing it, critiquing it, withdrawing from it, or simply setting up alternatives to it. We change culture when we create new culture.[7] When we commit to creating a new culture of catechesis in our congregations we can—over time, with sustained efforts, and by God's grace—begin to change the culture of these churches. As something emerges that is self-evidently biblical and life giving, many of those who have not experienced it in the past will find it compelling and will want to join in. This has often proved to be the case in churches that have adopted Christianity Explored or Alpha. These programs, though designed for those who are not yet believers, have often attracted the participation of large numbers of church members and regular attenders. These believers come to recognize that they themselves have not been adequately catechized and they long to experience the very good thing that they hear others are experiencing.

Furthermore, we can offer our pastoral pleas that even though existing members will not be stripped of their membership, they ought to take advantage of the new opportunities for learning and formation that are afforded by our new commitment to catechesis. In the ancient church the final stages of catechesis were reserved for the baptismal candidates. "Ordinary catechumens" were not to join these sessions. But the doors were open to members of the faithful who were invited, and even encouraged, to participate alongside those who were preparing to be baptized. We can and should warmly welcome all our baptized members to a time of refreshing and remembrance by encouraging them to join baptismal candidates during their experiences of catechesis proper.

Phase Three—Ongoing Catechesis: Further Growth in the Gospel

From the time of the Reformation, as we saw, "higher" catechisms began to be published alongside the introductory catechisms of the day. Such were

Luther's *Large Catechism*, Nowell's catechism, and the *Westminster Larger Catechism*. The goal of such catechisms was to furnish both clergy and mature laypeople with a clear, accessible summary of the Scriptures and of the Faith. In addition to this, many wrote commentaries to accompany the shorter or smaller catechisms, expanding upon those brief epitomes of the Faith. Here again help for clergy and mature laypeople was in view.[8]

In our own day it is far more common for professional theologians to devote their time and energy to writing theology for the academy rather than for the church. Often this means that they write theology for other theologians. The result of course is that what they write can often be relatively difficult for the average layperson to access. Indeed, their work can seem inaccessible to all but the most highly trained and highly motivated pastors. Is it any wonder that for many "ordinary Christians" there seems to be so little capacity for theological depth? Can we blame our church members if they seem only to be able to handle bumper-sticker or T-shirt-sized "sound bites" of theology? Must we who have been appointed by God to provide theological and spiritual leadership of the church not bear much of the blame in these matters? Have we forgotten that the best fruit needs to be found on the lower branches of the tree if our people are to have benefit of it? Have we imposed unreasonably low expectations on our people and then lamented when they *lived down* to our expectations?

In the spirit of Augustine, Luther, Calvin, Baxter, Owen, Spurgeon, and many others, we urge a renewed commitment to making the deeper things of theology and of the Christian life accessible to the whole church community. Of course, we must meet people where they are. And where they are may not be where we wish they were. But if we will take action with a biblically lofty vision of where we ought to be and a commitment to lovingly lead others, we can—by God's great grace—move forward. Like Paul we all actually long to know Christ better, to know him so well that we become conformed to his likeness, both in resurrection power and in sacrificial suffering (Phil. 3:7–11). Through the Holy Spirit we can actually press on toward the prize of the high call of God in Christ Jesus. All who are mature will take such a view of things (Phil. 3:12–16). For "if anyone imagines that he knows something, he does not yet know as he ought to know" (1 Cor. 8:2). In fact, all of us "know in part" (1 Cor. 13:9).

Phase Three envisions such commitments to a perpetual, persistent, and passionate pursuit of the knowledge of God and his ways. Those who have become members of the church are encouraged to keep on growing, to never stop learning. We strive to cultivate in the church a culture of humility and teachability. Teachability, Calvin argued, is at the heart of Christian piety. We work toward such an ethos when the pastors and teachers of the church prove to be role models of such a spirit.

This spirit also pervades our ongoing participation in worship, prayer, small groups, fellowship, and service. Aside from this matter of ethos and our non-formal experiences of ongoing catechesis, we also need to put in place formal structures for further training. Among these must be some structure designated for serious and sustained teaching and learning of the truth. If the Sunday school setting is viable for such a task, then it can be used for it. If the small group structure does the job, then that's fine. Perhaps the church, evaluating its culture, determines that another time during the week would work better, or perhaps that a weekend seminar format is best. Whatever the case may be, church leaders must determine their venues and make unapologetic and unceasing use of them. Such a commitment should be made across the age span. Our children and youth, in particular, can and must also be taken ever deeper into the things of God.

Alongside such instructional opportunities for groups of learners, churches should provide more personal instruction in smaller, and even in one-on-one, settings. In this case leaders will be seeking out and servicing individuals who seem to have a unique call upon their lives, as manifested by an unusual hunger and thirst to go deeper in their study of God's Word and God's ways. This is a wise and necessary supplement to larger congregational commitments.

As we envision this further, ongoing training in the Faith we recall that not all our setups ought to be of the schooling variety in the traditional sense. We can learn the Truth in wonderful ways as God's Word is read and exposited at our gatherings for worship. We will best learn the Life through our experiences in prayer, worship, and evangelistic outreach. We best learn the Way by participating in fellowship and in service of others. But we will still need venues that permit sustained presentation of and significant interaction with the various dimensions of the Faith.

Doctrinal Frameworks for Our Ongoing Catechesis

In order to help with conceiving and designing courses for our ongoing training in the Truth, the Life, and the Way, we offer some possibilities for a doctrinal framework for such instruction. On the following pages, we present three potential configurations.

Framework One

As J.I. writes elsewhere, the key truths in which we must catechize seem to be as follows:

In the Bible, the Gospel is the entire saving plan of God revolving around the Person, place, and power of our Savior Jesus Christ, the incarnate, crucified, risen, reigning, returning Lord. Preaching and teaching the Gospel requires us to show how Jesus Christ relates to every part of God's plan and how every part of that plan relates to us who are savingly related to the living Christ through faith.[9] This means dealing with six main topics.

1. *The truth about God.* The one God who made and rules everything is revealed as three coequal, coeternal persons in and through his plan of salvation. The Father, the Son, and the Holy Spirit who love each other also love us and work together to save us from sin and make us holy. Jesus Christ, the Son of God now and forever incarnate, is at this time Lord over all the powers of evil as he is over every other created reality and is at work through the Holy Spirit building his church by drawing sinners to himself. Any other view of God would be idolatry.

2. *The truth about ourselves.* We were made for God, to bear his image and be like him in moral character. But sin now controls and spoils us, leading us to defy and deny God so that we need to be brought back to God to be forgiven and remade. Jesus Christ, who brings us back, is himself the model of true godliness. Any other view of him or of us would be deception.

3. *The story of God's kingdom.* Step by step, as Scripture tells, God has been working since humanity first went astray to exercise his kingship by establishing his kingdom of redemption in this fallen world. Jesus Christ is now the King and our lives are to be his kingdom at its heart. King Jesus is also appointed to be the world's Judge, and those who have not bowed to his kingship here will not share his joy hereafter. Trusting, loving, and honoring Jesus and serving others for his sake is the core and center of true godliness. Any other form of religion would be error.

4. *The way of salvation.* Jesus Christ, our sin bearer on the cross, now from his throne reaches out to rescue us who are lost in the guilt and shame of sin. He calls for faith (trust in him as Savior) and repentance (turning to him as Master). He sends his Holy Spirit to change us so that we hear his call, addressed to us personally, and respond to it wholeheartedly. We are forgiven and accepted (justified), received as God's children (adopted), moved to rejoice at our peace with him (assurance), and made to realize that now we are living a new life of co-resurrection *with* Christ *in* Christ (regeneration). Any lesser view of salvation would be deficient.

5. *The life of fellowship.* Christians belong in the church, the family of God, sharing its worship, work, witness, and spiritual warfare, and enjoying its worldwide fellowship in Christ. Any lesser view of the Christian calling would be sectarian.

6. *Walking home to heaven.* Helped by the ministry in the church of word and sacrament, prayer and pastoral care, spiritual gifts and loving support, Christians live in our constantly hostile world as travelers heading

for a glorious destination. Praise and worship, personal and corporate, directed to both their heavenly Father and Jesus Christ their heavenly Friend, strengthen them to live in obedience to the divine commands and to endure whatever happens under the divine providence, in undying hope of good things to come. Led and inspired by their Savior through the Holy Spirit, they seek to do all the good they can as they go, and to battle all forms of evil they meet. Any lesser view of the Christian life would be worldly.

Framework Two

Another way of arranging the material is as follows:

1. *The authority of Scripture*, our true, trustworthy, God-given and God-interpreted source of knowledge about God in relation to his world and to ourselves as part of it
2. *The sovereignty of God* in creation, providence, and grace undergirding the reality of our own free and responsible decisions
3. *The truth of the Trinity* in which all three persons work as a team for our salvation, while yet God is one and remains one; he is they, and they are he
4. *The sinfulness of sin*, total egocentric perversity of heart leading to total inability to respond to God from the heart, and total unacceptability in God's sight by reason of the sins to which our sinful hearts have led us
5. *The centrality of Jesus Christ*, God incarnate, our Mediator and penal substitute, our Prophet, Priest, and King, crucified, risen, reigning, returning; Savior, Lord, and Friend to all who turn to him; our Companion through life, both here and eternally hereafter
6. *The graciousness of salvation* which is the gift of a new status (reconciliation, justification, adoption) and a new state (regeneration, sanctification, resurrection, and perfection to come), both of which are bestowed by Christ through the Holy Spirit, embraced by faith and repentance, and expressed in a life of worship, prayer, and obedience
7. *The power of the Holy Spirit* through whom alone faith, repentance, good works, Christian hope, Christian assurance, and Christian love and fellowship become reality
8. *The circuitry of communion* whereby, through the means of grace, Scripture, prayer, the Lord's Supper, and the interchanges of Christian fellowship, Christ and the Father come to us in our personal awareness, and the Holy Spirit spurs us to respond to them in devotion, doxology, and permanent practice of the divine Presence in faith, love, hope, and service

9. *The mission of the church*, which is the international company of Christians who congregate together in local units to worship and work for God. Being the church—that is, doing what the church does—means praise and prayer, preaching and teaching, celebrating the sacraments, practicing discipleship and discipline, spreading the faith worldwide, warring against all forms of evil and unbelief, watching for Christ's return, and looking forward to the life everlasting in heaven. It also means spending and being spent in outreach—making disciples, founding congregations, impacting communities for Christ, vindicating Christian truth, and opposing public sin and all that dehumanizes.

10. *The glory of God*, in the twofold sense of the praiseworthiness of God revealed to us in the plan of redemption and the praise we give to God for that revelation, thus beginning to glorify him here as we shall be doing eternally hereafter

Framework Three

Here is a third possible layout:

1. *God.* (a) God is known through his self-testimony in the canonical Scriptures, which the Holy Spirit interprets to the church. (b) God is the Holy Trinity, the Father, the Son, and the Holy Spirit in unity together (the "they" who are "he"). God is three persons, but tritheism is false. God is one being, but Unitarianism is false. (c) God is the Creator. The created order is distinct from him but dependent on him. Created rational beings are self-determined but providentially overruled. God in sovereignty governs all he has made according to his own will. (d) God is the Restorer. Facing the guilt and alienation of sinful humankind, and cosmic disorder thence resulting, God the Father sent God the Son to take on humanness within his divine identity; to die for human sins, thus making peace; to rise from death to live and reign as our Savior-Lord; and to return to judge the world, perfect his own people, and renew all creation. The Father and the Son now send the Holy Spirit to impart and sustain the life of restored fellowship with God.

2. *Humanity.* (a) Humans are creatures, made for loving fellowship with and grateful service to their Maker. (b) Humans are sinners, rebels against God and now guilty, defiled, degenerate, and helpless in self-centeredness. (c) Humans are saved through personal repentance toward God, personal trust in Jesus Christ as one's Savior and Lord, and continuance of both thereafter.

3. *Salvation.* (a) Salvation is rescue—from sin and Satan. (b) Its tenses are: past—rescue from sin's guilt and condemnation; present—rescue from sin's down-dragging power; future—rescue from sin's presence and

perversions. (c) It is a guarantee: God's promise, warranting, obliging, creating hope.

4. *The Christian church.* (a) The church is the family of the Father (children and heirs); the body of Christ (ministering units); the fellowship of the Holy Spirit (all alive to God); the community of the (new) covenant (with sacramental signs and seals displaying union with Christ). (b) The calling of the church is worship, work, witness, and spiritual warfare.

5. *The Christian life.* (a) Its character consists of obeying God (holiness and righteousness; virtue and law-keeping); pleasing God (devotion, adoration, love); and exalting God (thanksgiving, doxology, celebration). (b) Its ethical expression consists of sanctity (consecration, avoiding sin); stewardship (using possessions for God's cause, and privileges and position for God's kingdom); the use of powers (creativity in all forms) for God's glory; and service (in family, church, and state). (c) Love of God (gratitude and admiration) and of neighbor (compassion and desire to help) are the motivations God requires and the Holy Spirit evokes.

Concluding Remarks

These three formulations of the syllabus for the ongoing teaching of sound doctrine are simply offered as examples. No doubt there are many other ways in which this material could be arranged, and all teachers should have liberty to fulfill what is indeed their responsibility, namely to arrange their material in what for them is the most effective way. But in teaching this syllabus, however one presents it, there are three things that must always be kept in view. The presentation must be *God-centered*, with God as the subject and humanity and ourselves as, so to speak, the predicate throughout. It must be *doxological*, showing how each action by God reveals his praiseworthiness, and calls for actual praise as well as formal acknowledgment. And it must be *practical*, bringing out the response God requires to each truth that we teach. All Christian instruction should have this threefold quality. In other words, we must couple to our teaching of the Truth instruction concerning what we have called the Life and the Way. We catechize, then, with concern for doctrine, devotion, and duty. And all is done that our delight in the Lord may grow ever deeper.

10

Championing Catechesis in Contemporary Congregations

[The Reformation catechisms aim] to give a comprehensive exposition of the Gospel of Jesus Christ in the context of the whole Counsel of God and the whole life of the people of God. They sow the seed that germinates in the soil, brings forth living fruit, and provides good grain for use in the next generation. They shape the mind of the historical Church, building up its understanding of the Faith and directing its growth and development so that throughout all its changes from age to age it ever remains the same Household and Habitation of God built upon the foundation of the Apostles and Prophets, Christ Jesus Himself being the chief cornerstone.[1]

T. F. Torrance

It is our sincere hope, and indeed prayer, that we have succeeded thus far in encouraging readers to look more seriously into this biblical business of catechesis. Even more, we pray that some will take up the cause in their congregations, becoming champions for such efforts. Pastors, parents, elders, deacons, devout congregants—whoever may find their hearts stirred by what they have read in this book—can help make some of the things we have explored become reality in their own settings. To help advance this cause further we offer in this chapter essential concerns for would-be champions of catechetical ministries. For those church leaders who want to take serious steps toward renewing this ancient practice, we believe the following are seven vital elements in faithful, effective, and sustained ministries of congregational catechesis.

Much of what follows is a restatement and confirmation of what we have considered earlier in the book; on such items, our comments here are relatively brief. Some of what we say here is new material at this point, and on those elements we have somewhat more to say. From the title of this chapter it should be apparent that C is to be our featured letter. Each of the essentials we list below is thus set "in the key of C." In the spirit of the reformation catechisms we take up each of the seven items below by means of a series of questions and answers.

1. Clarity of Concept
2. Conviction regarding Content
3. Comprehensiveness of Concern
4. Confrontation of Counterfeits
5. A Compelling Continuity
6. Cultivation of Catechists
7. Commitment to the Cause

Clarity of Concept

1. Are Congregants Clear about the Nature of Christian Catechesis?

In order for a ministry of catechesis to truly take hold in a congregation and have staying power, members of the church need to be clear about its nature. It is incumbent upon pastors and other ministry leaders to make sure that people have such clarity. Steps toward achieving this might include written documents available either in print or online (or both), and made available to newcomers and old-timers alike. Those who are engaged in any phase of the catechetical journey should regularly be reminded of just what it is they are engaged in. Concerning the ministry of catechesis, pastors should both advocate and educate, both from the pulpit and in pastoral visits with congregants.

Our working definition of catechesis in this book has been as follows: *Catechesis is the church's ministry of grounding and growing God's people in the Gospel and its implications for doctrine, devotion, duty, and delight.* This simple description helps us tie together our rationale and our aims. It is, in other words, a brief summation of our overall concept of the task of catechesis. We noted also in chapter 1 that some may commit themselves to the work of catechesis without ever calling it by that name. We reaffirm that what matters most to us is to see the work advanced, even if it is called by some other name. It does matter, however, that congregants have clarity and consistency in their understandings.

A further unpacking of our definition may be helpful at this point. We call this "the church's ministry" to remind us that this is a task to which the whole congregation must attend. It is not the task merely of pastors, priests, or parents. If there is not a commitment on behalf of the congregation as a whole, a ministry of catechesis cannot be as fruitful as it needs to be. Nor can it thrive over the long term. All members must come to prize this process of building believers and to take their appropriate places in the endeavor.

"Grounding believers" refers in particular to what we have called catechesis proper. Because this is so critical for the overall health of both individual Christians and of the whole congregation, we put in place a structure that ensures that all inquirers, baptismal candidates, potential members, and leaders be catechized in an orderly, intentional manner. "Growing believers" reminds us that catechesis is a lifelong process. We never really "arrive" this side of glory. And so we must press on.

Those we direct this ministry toward are *God's* people. They are not *our* people, as though we were aiming to grow our own congregation and thereby make a name for ourselves as the builders of Babel sought to do so long ago (Gen. 11:4). We do not make disciples for ourselves, but only and always for the Lord. The calling of God's people also envisions ongoing labor among those who may not yet be believers, so far as we can tell, but who have expressed an interest in the things of God and have been brought by God into the range of the church's ministry. The Lord told an apparently fearful apostle Paul to keep testifying among the Corinthians even in the face of serious hostility. "I have many in this city who are my people," he told Paul (Acts 18:10). Over the next year and a half as Paul proclaimed Christ crucified among the Corinthians, those who belonged to the Lord became evident.

We ground and grow God's people *in the Gospel*, for it is, as we have argued from the outset of the book, *the* content for catechetical ministry. We may preach it, teach it, and unpack it in a variety of ways, but it is the Faith of the Gospel that is ever our content. We move on *in* the Gospel, but never *from* the Gospel. At the heart of the Gospel is the cross of Jesus Christ. At the heart of the message of the cross is the fact that Jesus died *for us* as the one and only, full and final, substitutionary sacrifice of atonement for our sins.

As we move on in the Gospel we have much to teach about the implications of that Gospel for doctrine, devotion, and duty. These three words correspond to what we summarized elsewhere as the Truth, the Life, and the Way. All this reminds us that the call to catechize is comprehensive in coverage. We preach the whole counsel of God that testifies to the whole position, person, and work of Christ, and we do so until everyone shall be presented complete in Christ (Col. 1:28).

To the triad of doctrine, devotion, and duty we add the word *delight*. This reminds us that all this instruction is really an invitation to experience more fully the abundant life Jesus came to bring (John 10:10). Learning the sound doctrine that conforms to the glorious Gospel; walking in the way of the Lord; demonstrating devotion to the one true and only living God—all of this is an invitation to "delight yourself in the LORD, and he will give you the desires of your heart" (Ps. 37:4). The *Westminster Larger Catechism* surely got it right: "The chief end of man is to glorify God and fully to enjoy Him forever." God help us to always remember this promise of joy and delight as we seek to introduce and implement catechesis in our congregations.

2. Is It Clear to All Why This Ministry Is So Vital?

Congregants must know not only what catechesis is but also why the church considers this to be a vital ministry. Here we are offering a rationale for catechesis. On this point we have little need to say more. The entire book has been devoted to probing this very matter. We need only to reiterate our central conclusions thus far. We catechize because we must. For catechesis is both a very biblical idea and a faithful practice of the church through the ages. Where wise catechesis has flourished, the church has flourished. Where it has been neglected, the church has floundered. We catechize in obedience to the Great Commission of our Lord Jesus Christ and in imitation of the Lord's own ministry when he walked among us. He has charged the church to make disciples from all people groups of the earth. This discipling requires a rigorous ministry of teaching obedience to all that Jesus commanded. Catechesis is precisely such a ministry.

3. Are the Ends for Which We Catechize Also Clear?

It is also necessary that congregants have clarity about the goals or aims of our ministries of catechesis. In other words, to what end do we catechize? Is the aim biblical literacy? Is the aim to grow the congregation numerically? Do we do this simply because this is what churches have done? We have been dealing with the matter of catechetical aims throughout this book, at least by implication. What we have implied earlier, however, we now seek to make explicit. There are many ways we might discuss the goals of catechesis. For the sake of simplicity, we do so now under three heads, and describe the principal aims of catechesis as *confession, conversion*, and *conformity*.[2]

CONFESSION

Through faithful and effective catechesis we aim first of all at unity in our confession of the Faith. This is historically attested to by the development of the baptismal creeds and confessions, the emerging rule of Faith, and finally the fuller creeds and confessional statements that were adopted as part of the Christian Consensus to which we have made reference. The apostle Paul argued that achieving unity in the Faith was one of the proper goals of the church's equipping ministries for which we have been gifted by the Holy Spirit (Eph. 4:13). While we are already one in the Spirit (Eph. 4:3), such unity "in the faith" is not a given. So long as there are false teachers to trouble us from without or from within, and so long as there are apathetic or rebellious sheep in our flocks, diligent attention to teaching the Faith will be essential. This aim reminds us of the historic language of *lex credendi* (the law of belief), of the theological concern for orthodoxy, and of training in what we earlier labeled *the Truth*.

CONVERSION

A second aim of our catechesis is that all of us, the teacher and the taught, together should wholeheartedly turn to the Lord. This involves ongoing realignment of our wayward affections and ongoing repentance for our rambling lifestyles. *Conversion* is a rich and multilayered word that captures these concerns and much more. Many Christians equate the word simply with being "born again." Conversion includes this, to be sure, but it goes beyond this to incorporate lifelong goals of growing in godliness and sanctification. We aim at an ever-increasing and intimate "knowledge of the Son of God" (Eph. 4:13; Phil. 3:7–16). This aim corresponds to *lex orandi* (the law of worship, of prayer), to the concept of *orthopatheia* (that is, right affections), and to training in what we have called *the Life*.

CONFORMITY

Finally, we catechize to fulfill the goal of growing in conformity to the likeness of Jesus Christ. This is God's stated goal for all those he has foreknown (Rom. 8:29) and it was Paul's goal in his own ministry as an apostle, herald, and teacher of the Gospel (Gal. 4:19). The goal is realized over time as we are transformed from glory to glory by the power of the Spirit (2 Cor. 3:17–18) and through the renewing of our minds as part of that process (Rom. 12:2). Our aim, in other words, is to grow as disciples of Jesus, as people who learn from him and follow him. To be like Jesus Christ is to love God with all one's heart, soul, mind, and strength, and one's neighbor as oneself (Mark 12:29–31). Both individual believers and the congregations of which they are a part are thus to "become mature, attaining to the whole measure of the fullness of Christ" (Eph. 4:13 NIV). Such an aim corresponds to what has been called *lex vivendi* ("the law of life"), to what could be called *orthopraxy*, and to training in the Way of the Lord.

Conviction Regarding Content

4. What Do We as a Church Community Consider to Be Essential Content?

In chapters 4–6 we outlined and expanded upon our own proposals for essential catechetical content.[3] The outline we offered may have had some original features but the content itself was really in keeping with historic precedents in catechesis. As we said earlier, when it comes to catechetical content novelty is the last thing we should strive for. Rather a faithful catechist will say, "what I received I passed on to you" (1 Cor. 15:3).

We have no illusions, however, that all church leaders will resolve to follow the pattern we have set forth here. There certainly are other ways to identify and frame the content for catechesis that can be faithful and effective in *grounding and growing God's people in the essentials of the Gospel and its implications for doctrine, devotion, duty, and delight.* What matters is that church leaders have seriously considered how they would answer the question, "What do we consider essential teaching for our members?" If not the proposals set forth in the historic catechisms or the somewhat modified visions of that pattern we have suggested, then what will the church use as a basis for instructing its congregants? Church leaders should study and discuss the matter until consensus emerges.

5. How Many of Our Congregants Seem to Be Well Acquainted with This Content?

Once agreement has been reached about what constitutes essential content for the church's ministry of catechesis, leaders should next estimate how many of those regularly involved in the church have actually received instruction in these areas. Our guess is that this question will prove discouraging for many. Research in the North American scene, for example, has long been testifying to just how little church-attending Christians seem to know about the Bible and the Faith.[4] When we have agreed upon our outline of essential teaching there is obviously much more that needs to be done: the teaching task that faces us is huge.

6. What Means Do We Presently Employ in Delivering This Content to Congregants?

If the answers to the previous question discourage, a likely culprit in the problem is our method of delivering such teaching. We may have adequately identified our essential teaching and yet not have identified effective ways of ensuring that this instruction reaches those whom God has entrusted to our care. We may have been relying upon a Sunday school program that formally engaged a majority of congregants but now attracts relatively few members.

In chapter 8 we considered the problems that arise from failing to "draw lines" in our Sunday school classes in order to distinguish things essential from important, but secondary and tertiary, concerns. We may be relying upon the new small group focus of the church only to discover that this has proven to be a structural pattern better suited for mutual encouragement than to sustained teaching of the Faith. Perhaps the pastor has assumed that others in leadership would work out this matter of essential teaching, while those others have been anticipating pastoral leadership in this area.

7. How Can the Situation Be Improved Upon?

If our answers to any or all of the previous three questions have proven disheartening, we should look to the Lord for wisdom in order that we may improve the situation. Throughout this book, especially in chapter 9, we have put forward proposals for moving the ball forward in this critical area of catechesis. We have also tried to point toward other resources which we hope will prove beneficial to readers and the churches they represent.[5] In any event, we would urge church leaders not to be content with mediocrity or with a half-hearted approach to such vital matters. Let us seek rather to honor our Lord and serve his sheep by giving our best biblically informed, Spirit-empowered efforts to renewing the teaching ministries of our congregations.

8. How Can We Better Connect Ourselves to the "One, Holy, Catholic, and Apostolic Church" in Terms of Our Catechetical Content?

We leave the issue of catechetical content with one more plea to consider how we might better connect members of our particular local church with the grand and beautiful church of Jesus Christ that our confessions have identified as "one, holy, catholic, and apostolic." In the spirit of unity and humility we urge local church leaders to remember that they are neither the first to attempt disciple making for Jesus nor the only ones doing so today. If we can connect to the larger church of which we are inextricably a part by prudent use of historic creeds, hymns, prayers, sacraments, catechisms, and practices, then let us do so. Not only can we advance by looking back in these ways, we can also learn much by looking around at what God is doing among his people scattered throughout the earth today. Some two billion name the name of Jesus nowadays. Jesus taught his disciples and prayed for them with a view to the unity of the church (e.g., John 13:34–35; 17:21–23). Paul commanded that we should make every effort to preserve the unity of the church (Eph. 4:3). But we have fallen tragically short of God's heart in this regard. Here, then, is another area where we have much work to do if we would walk in step with the truth of the Gospel.

Comprehensiveness of Concern

9. How Are We Engaging the Heads, Hearts, and Hands of Our Congregants?

To achieve the catechetical ends we labeled above as confession, conversion, and conformity, it is necessary that both our content and our educational processes be comprehensive in scope. We seek to nurture faith, hope, and love toward Christ who is the Truth, the Life, and the Way. We long, in other words, to be a people who are taught by the Truth, liberated by the Life and, with increasing faithfulness, walking in the Way. In our ministries of catechesis, we must continually resist the temptation to reduce what must be whole-person engagement to something more narrow. If we fixate exclusively on stimulating the mind, or on simply warming the heart, or on busily engaging the hands, we shall miss the mark. All three concerns must be kept in view always as we labor to make disciples for Jesus. In the previous chapter we offered a number of suggestions that had in view such a holistic educational goal.

We recall that during the long period of "hearing the word" in the ancient catechumenate, the catechumens were engaged in a holistic journey throughout. They listened to God's Word read and proclaimed, and became serious students of the Scriptures. As regular participants in all aspects of the liturgy except the service of the table, they heard the prayers of the faithful and joined in the hymns of the saints. And all along they were to be engaged in good works of love and service as they allowed the Lord to remake their patterns of living.

In the final phase of catechesis too the concern was comprehensive. They received daily instruction in the Scriptures, and committed to memory and heard exposited the Creed and the Lord's Prayer. They sang and prayed, and had hands laid upon them every day as church leaders prayed for them. They continued their commitment to good deeds and participated in various spiritual disciplines, such as fasting, that helped train their bodies for service.

Jesus of course had trained the Twelve in a whole-person fashion. Their minds were challenged by his powerful and authoritative teaching. Their hearts were shaped as they joined him in prayer and worship and were deeply moved by his words and deeds. Surely this was the case when, for example, Jesus rebuked their posturing for position and power by having a young child stand in their midst (Matt. 18:1–6) or by stooping to wash their soiled feet (John 13:1–17). Of course, their hands and feet were continually employed as they followed their Master who had come to do the works of his Father (John 4:34) and now invited them to join him in doing the same (John 9:4).

All of this speaks wisdom to us regarding our own ministries of catechesis. It is not only by engaging the mind that we must proceed. Formal instruction in the sound doctrines of the Faith is critically important. But so is leadership in prayer and in song, in spiritual disciplines, and in taking aim at the affections of disciples, not merely at their intellects. And we must challenge and help redirect patterns of behavior, urging that (for instance) "the thief no longer steal, but rather let him labor, doing honest work with his own hands" (Eph. 4:28). We must urge all in the community not to let their anger lead to sin, not to permit corrupt speech to leave their lips, and in all ways to live lives of love in imitation of God himself (Eph. 4:29–5:1). Earlier we argued that much of the New Testament is in fact catechetical instruction. A quick review of the various letters immediately reveals this apostolic attention to every aspect of the lives of believers. No part of our being is to be left untouched by the Spirit of God's application of the Word of God. For we are commanded to love the Lord our God with all that is within us—heart and soul and mind and strength, and to love our neighbors as ourselves (Mark 12:29–31).

There is one particular catechetical strategy that has the potential to deeply engage our minds, hearts, and bodies at the same time in a unique way—the singing of well chosen hymns of the Faith. Such singing was often a key feature in the history of catechesis. Ambrose of Milan wrote congregational hymns to catechize, and said of their usage in his church, "All therefore have been made teachers, who before were scarcely able to be learners."[6] Among those who were present singing the Faith under Ambrose's ministry was Augustine himself. In his catechetical renewal efforts Martin Luther restored congregational singing to a significant place and wrote hymns such as "A Mighty Fortress Is Our God" for this use. Luther explained his rationale thus: "Our plan is to follow the example of the prophets and the ancient fathers of the church, and to compose psalms for the people in the vernacular, that is, spiritual songs, so that the word of God may be among the people also in the form of music."[7] Later hymnists such as Watts and the Wesleys gave great energy to instructing through their hymns. Some may protest that our songs of worship are to be sung to God alone. But Paul wrote that even while we sing and make melody in our hearts to the Lord, our singing is also a form of "speaking to one another in psalms, hymns, and spiritual songs" (Eph. 5:19). To the Colossians he said that such congregational singing was a critical element in ensuring that the word of Christ would dwell richly in our hearts (Col. 3:16).

We do well to ask about the catechetical value of our songs of worship. What vision of God do they convey? Do they serve well the proclamation of the biblical Gospel? Are the doctrines they exposit or imply sound doctrines that conform to the Gospel? Are our songs biblically based, and clearly so? Have we humbled ourselves to learn from the saints who have gone before us by singing the best of the songs from of old? Or do we limit ourselves to only the newest of the new songs? How can we do a better job of seizing upon the catechetical nature and formative power of our past and present hymnody?[8]

It is in the context of a holistic vision for shaping the whole person in the midst of the whole community of the church that all our formal efforts to catechize must proceed.

10. How Should Our Formal Instruction in These Critical Matters Proceed?

A time-honored tag among schoolteachers is, "no *im*pression without *ex*pression," and this is as true when we teach the Gospel to persons of any age as it is of teaching anything else. Expression takes at least four forms: answering questions on what has been presented; working out logically its implications and applications; positioning oneself by personal commitment to act on the truth one now sees; and actually obeying that truth by forming habits of thought and behavior that reflect it. Response to the Gospel message, whether spelled out in full as above or focused in a Christ-centered summary ("Believe on the Lord Jesus, and you will be saved" [Acts 16:31]), has all four elements to it.

In the Reformation period, which was, as we have already observed, an era of great educational endeavor, all-age catechizing based on the four fixtures of the catechism—the Apostles' Creed, the Lord's Prayer, the Ten Commandments, and the Gospel sacraments as instituted by Jesus himself—was a major pastoral concern. In all age groups ignorance was to be banished and Gospel truth clearly grasped. Accordingly, as was noted in chapter 3, catechisms were composed and published in abundance. The catechetical method they serviced, however, was redolent of the schoolroom—answers to questions first being memorized, followed by question and answer viva voce to ensure that the memorizing had been done, leading to explanatory exhortation to live by the truths thus learned. This was the accepted style for catechizing both children and adults. But by the end of the seventeenth century adult catechesis had largely vanished.

In the parishes that made up the Anglican church, the supreme enthusiasts for such catechesis had been the Puritan pastors inspired by Richard Baxter's practice of family catechizing, which we considered earlier in the book. When they were ejected from the church in 1662 there was no one to carry the torch. It was assumed that the catechism included in the *Book of Common Prayer* was for the confirmation of children, and that after confirmation church people needed no further instruction beyond what Sunday sermons would give them— a view that Western Anglicans generally still take for granted. This is where persuasion has to start.

Let it be said at once that the schoolmaster style and the stress on memorizing are not integral to adult catechizing, and that some fruitful variants on the old austere procedure have recently been developed. We think, for instance, of the runaway global success story of the Alpha course emanating from Holy Trinity Church, Brompton, London, and of its counterpart Christianity Explored, developed in All Souls Church, Langham Place, London. The latter, which may not yet be as well known as it should be, is a ten-evening course based on Mark's Gospel, each session laid out as "an informal meal, a short Bible study, a talk . . . and a further discussion based on what the participants have just heard." Alpha is similar. These courses are in effect (though perhaps without their makers and devotees realizing it) first steps in reestablishing adult catechesis as a regular part of church life.

There is more than one way to skin a cat, and no limit should be set to human ingenuity in packaging the catechetical process—provided only that the syllabus of the Gospel doctrine gets fully and properly covered, and that the need for the fourfold response to it we described above remains in view.

11. Is the Traditional Question-and-Answer Format of the Reformation Catechisms Still a Wise Pattern to Follow?

In light of what we said in answer to question 10 above, we dare not suggest that the traditional question-and-answer approach must always be retained. In the first place this approach, popularized by Luther, was not so widely used in catechetical efforts prior to the Reformation. And there have been numerous catechetical works in the centuries since that have not adopted it. In general we suggest that flexibility and variety in the actual shape of catechetical materials is the best course. Sensitivity to developmental concerns—both in regard to natural abilities and spiritual progress—should be taken into account, as should the matter of cultural appropriateness. It may well be that the pattern deemed best for sixteenth-century Europeans in a broadly Christianized world may prove to be far less fitting for many of our ministry contexts today.

On the other hand we should not simply dismiss the suitability of a question-and-answer format for at least some of our instructional efforts. T. F. Torrance argued for the enduring value of the form traditionally found in the Reformation catechisms:

> It is an important step in any branch of scientific research to learn to ask the *right questions.* . . . Christianity does not set out to answer man's questions. If it did it would only give him what he already desires to know and has secretly determined how he will know it. Christianity is above all the question the truth puts to man at every point in his life, so that it teaches him to ask the right, the true questions about himself, and to form on his lips the questions which the truth by its own nature puts to him to ask of the truth itself that it may disclose or reveal itself to him. Now the Catechism is designed to do just this, and it is therefore an invaluable method in instructing the young learner, for it not only trains him to ask the right questions, but trains him to allow himself to be questioned by the truth, and so to have questions put into his mouth which he could not think up on his own, and which therefore call into question his own preconceptions. In other words it is an event of real impartation of the truth.[9]

Confrontation of Counterfeits

12. What Are the -isms of the Culture That Must Be Countered with the Truth? How Can We Do So?

As we suggested in chapter 8, catechesis typically has a built-in contrast: "You have heard that it was said . . . but I say to you." That is, in order to more clearly illustrate the truth of the Gospel we need to highlight

terclaims of the competing cultures. In every age and culture there are false
-*isms*—beliefs and worldviews that fly in the face of God's revelation in Christ.
Examples in our own age might include such -*isms* as materialism, godless
humanism, religious pluralism, and so on. In faithful and fruitful ministries
of preaching, teaching, counseling, and liturgy as well as through the hymns
and songs we sing, we must identify and challenge these with the potent,
liberating, universal, and unchanged truth of God's Word.

13. What Idols of the Culture Must Be Countered with the Life? How Can We Do This?

Another facet of this catechetical confrontation is to name and counter the
idols of the surrounding culture that would lure the hearts of men and women
away from the living God. Without question, even those in the believing community are not immune to the blandishments of these gods-that-are-no-gods
(see 1 Cor. 8:4–6). Thus Israel needed to hear perpetual warnings in this regard
(see, for example, the first two commands of the Decalogue [Exod. 20:3–6],
Joshua pleading with God's people as they were about to cross the Jordan into
the land of Canaan [Josh. 24:14–24], and the psalmists and prophets warning
against the idols of the nations, often with biting sarcasm [e.g., Psalm 115; Isa.
44:9–20]). John's warning too is as pertinent as it ever was: "Little children,
keep yourselves from idols" (1 John 5:21). A faithful catechist will be alert to
the shifting identities of the idols in the culture(s) in which the congregants
and their neighbors live.

14. What Perverse Practices of the Culture Must Be Countered with the Way? How Can We Do So?

Our third concern in confronting the cultural counter-catechesis is identifying and rejecting patterns of living that are plainly not-the-way. In his letters
to churches and church leaders Paul regularly cites examples of such and
continually calls for rejection, repentance, and return to the Way of the Lord.
One example of this is in 1 Timothy 1 where Paul lists a number of lifestyle
choices he describes as "contrary to sound doctrine in accordance with the
Gospel of the glory of the blessed God" (1 Tim. 1:8–11). As with -*isms* and
idols, the perverse practices we must confront will differ from context to
context. Again, therefore, careful catechists keep their fingers on the pulse
of the people.

Tragically, Christian history is replete with examples of church leaders not
only failing to confront the unholy habits of the day but explicitly or implicitly
endorsing them. We may think, for example, of pastors who have given aid
to such evils as slavery or other expressions of racism or classism by perverting biblical texts from the pulpit. Sometimes more subtly, perhaps, pastors
nowadays affirm practices in service of the cultural idols of wealth, beauty,

success, and much more. Far from affirming such values, we must assault them with the potent and penetrating light of the Gospel.

A Compelling Continuity

15. Do We Have a Clear Vision for Progress in Our Catechetical Journey?

In chapter 8 we considered the importance of "drawing lines" by separating primary doctrines from secondary or tertiary ones. Such distinguishing between doctrines is linked to spiritual development concerns. We then suggested that the imagery of a journey (what Webber called the "Journey to Jesus") is really essential as we envision and plan our ministries of catechesis and formation. Just as church leaders must come to consensus regarding what to teach, so also they should come to a clear vision of the faith journey they long to see their members take. A helpful resource for casting such a vision is the classic work of the Puritan John Bunyan, *Pilgrim's Progress*. This book—which is the second most popular book of all time in terms of sales (second only to the Bible)—is really a catechetical text of a different sort. In place of an overtly didactic approach it presents sound doctrine and spiritual progress through a powerful and evocative allegorical tale.

16. How Can We Encourage This Progress from Step to Step in the Journey of Catechumens?

Once we have established a vision for our catechetical journey toward maturity, we need to think in very practical terms about how to encourage movement "from strength to strength" until "each one appears before God in Zion" (Ps. 84:7). In chapter 9 we sketched out our vision for such progress. The key is that our catechetical scheme needs to have some "teeth" to it. There are many churches where serious, substantive teaching is available on a regular basis. But in too many of those cases members find ways simply to opt out. The vast majority, in many cases, do not seem to be persuaded that such instruction is a necessity for them. What, if anything, can we do about this?

We have used the language of a Compelling Continuity. To compel, in contemporary English at least, has mostly negative connotations of forcing, coercing, twisting a person's arm, and so on. Used as an adjective, on the other hand, to call something compelling is to suggest that it is convincing, persuasive, gripping. By appeal to this common adjectival sense of the word we suggest that we can and should in fact compel believers toward continuity in their journeys of faith. We envision at least three possible applications of these things.

First, by following something along the lines of what we have suggested in the previous chapter, a program should have built-in compelling components. The plan we put forth requires at least some catechetical experiences before baptism, communion, membership, and leadership. We might suggest, further, that some minimal catechetical experience also be required as one of the bases for annual or periodic review whereby to keep one's membership in good standing.

While some programmatic elements may be put in place that actually do compel in the sense of forcing people forward, there is another way to make catechesis compelling. Here we mean that a ministry of catechesis that is substantive, serious, well conceived, and carefully implemented will prove to be compelling on its own account. Whereas our previous suggestion speaks to an *external* compelling, we here have in mind an *internal* sort of compelling—the ministry itself and the fruit it bears will be so attractive and intriguing that people will find themselves drawn to it. May God grant that the testimony of catechized individuals and the fragrance of a well-catechized congregation will persuade others to joyously join the journey.

Finally, we would envision that both leaders and congregants alike would find that the love of Christ itself compels them to take this matter of catechesis seriously. Paul writes in 2 Corinthians 5:14 that "the love of Christ compels me" (NIV) to engage in the ministry of reconciliation. Paul is so gripped by, persuaded by, convinced of, and controlled by the love of Christ that he devotes himself completely to the Gospel ministry of helping men and women to be reconciled to God. We remember that Paul is writing to the believers in Corinth when he says, "We implore you on behalf of Christ, be reconciled to God" (2 Cor. 5:20). In our evangelical churches we often seem to think that pleading with others to be reconciled to God is only an appeal aimed at unbelievers. But here Paul is plainly pleading with Christians. Jesus died for them, becoming sin for them that they might become the righteousness of God (2 Cor. 5:21). He died for them so that they "might no longer live for themselves but for him who died for them and was raised" (2 Cor. 5:15). They had previously lived for themselves. Now in Christ they are created new: "The old has passed away; behold, the new has come" (2 Cor. 5:17). But the Corinthians—and there is lots of evidence in Paul's two letters to support this assertion—were not walking worthily of their calling. So it is that Paul would urge, persuade, and implore these often aimless, arrogant, antinomian Corinthians to be reconciled to God. It is precisely this at which a faithful ministry of catechesis aims. We pray therefore that the love of Christ would compel all God's people toward wholehearted participation in this pilgrimage toward confession, conversion, and conformity to Christ.

17. At What Age Should Our Catechetical Work Begin?

The question arises: How soon can we start? Can children, for example, be taught theology? If by theology we mean abstract, defensive, anti-heretical formulations, then the common response that children's minds cannot handle such abstractions until they are about ten would seem to be right. But if by theology we mean (as we always should) good news about what our heavenly Father and our heavenly friend Jesus were, are, and will be doing for us and for others; how they have shown us their love for us; what they have promised to do to look after us from now on; and what we must do to please them and why, the teaching and learning of theology can ordinarily begin at the age of about three. Certainly Bible stories should be taught in abundance in Sunday schools and other such settings from the start as is done now, but certainly also simple relational theology, based on and illustrated by the Bible stories, should be taught in an intentional way alongside the stories themselves. By doing so we can help tie the particular stories to the larger and great Story of God's redemptive dealings in Christ, and ensure that they not be reduced to moralistic tales that are disconnected from God's glorious Good News.

Cultivation of Catechists

18. Who Is Actually to Do the Work of a Catechist?

Throughout most of church history two figures have been most vital as instructors in the Faith. Concerning the catechetical work that is centered in the home there can be no question that the Bible puts the burden of instruction primarily on parents, and especially on fathers. In ancient Israel parents were to talk about God's commandments and his mighty saving deeds on behalf of Israel to their children and were to do so continually (Deut. 6:1–9; 11:18–21). This labor was to be supported by the entire community (Ps. 78:1–8). Paul, not surprisingly, casts the same vision, especially charging fathers with the responsibility to see that their children be raised "in the discipline and instruction of the Lord" (Eph. 6:4). In Jewish thought, the father is charged with final responsibility in these matters, as the head of the family. He may delegate responsibilities to the mother and even to others who may help with the instruction of his children. But the burden, finally, rests with him. The modern world may find this hard to believe, but the Bible is explicit.

Elsewhere, to be sure, the vital role of mothers in the formative task is clearly affirmed as well. Children are charged with obedience to both parents (Eph. 6:1; Col. 3:20), and the younger women are obliged to love their children to the end that the home be marked by godliness (Titus 2:4–5). We are reminded also of Paul's commendation of Timothy's mother and grandmother, who nurtured him in the faith (2 Tim. 1:5).

As exemplified by figures like Augustine, Luther, Calvin, Owen, and Baxter we see that pastors have historically assumed the primary responsibility for the catechizing of congregations. Like the father in the home, the pastor is a leader in the congregation. And, like the father, he may certainly call others into the catechetical work (he will, in fact, be wise to do so), but "the buck stops," so to speak, with the pastor. This notion too is biblically founded. Paul's call to his juniors Timothy and Titus to keep teaching and vindicating the Faith in the face of doctrinal confusion all around sounds like a constantly tolling bell in all three pastoral epistles: "Command and teach these things . . . devote yourself to public reading of Scripture, to exhortation, to teaching . . . keep a close watch on yourself and on the teaching" (1 Tim. 4:11, 13, 16). "Teach and urge these things . . . the teaching that accords with godliness" (1 Tim. 6:2–3). "What you have heard from me . . . entrust to reliable men who will be able to teach others also" (2 Tim. 2:2). "The Lord's servant must be . . . able to teach" (2 Tim. 2:24). "Teach what accords with sound doctrine" (Titus 2:1).

All of this will place one more burden on the shoulders of the pastor, who will need to persuade his people that this is the way to go, recruit catechists and oversee their preparation for this service, and form a plan for introducing the new procedures. Courses of sermons? Other courses? Pilot schemes? The pastor has to work it out. Our only excuse for burdening our fellow clergy is that we believe it will be a great gain for this to happen.

Although the majority of the biblical mandates and models point to parents and to pastors (elders) as the central catechists, others too share the responsibility to teach. The mature are to teach the less mature (Titus 2:3–4; Heb. 5:12). Some appear to have received the spiritual gift of teaching but may not hold the formal teaching office of pastor-elder (Rom. 12:7). All in the congregation are charged to teach and admonish one another (Col. 3:16) by, among other things, "speaking to one another in psalms, hymns, and spiritual songs" (Eph. 5:19). We all bear a personal duty to attend to our own souls also. "Grow in the grace and knowledge of our Lord Jesus Christ" (2 Peter 3:18) and "make every effort to supplement your faith" (2 Peter 1:5). And this applies to any would-be catechists. That is to say, before we would teach others, we must be learners.

Perhaps 2 Timothy 2:2 best portrays the idea of raising and cultivating catechists. Paul writes, "And what you have heard from me in the presence of many witnesses entrust to faithful men who will be able to teach others also." Paul plainly envisions that faithful ministries of catechesis will help to raise up more faithful catechists. This is intended, in other words, to be a reproductive work, as we normally understand all ministries of discipleship to be. As we catechize others we should ask God to make us aware of his gifts and calling to those learners. Certain ones among them, by God's grace and through our discerning encouragement and further equipping, will themselves in time become effective teachers of the Faith.

19. Why Is the Matter of Character So Critical for Would-Be Catechists?

Due partly to charismatic preoccupation with spiritual gifts and partly to the Western world's lack of interest in moral character as such, for the past half century the centrality of Christlike virtues (love, joy, peace, patience, kindness, goodness, faithfulness, gentleness, self-control—the fruit of the Spirit [Gal. 5:22–23]) in authentic Christian discipleship has been obscured. Catechizing, however, is a discipline which, when rightly managed, takes its recipients not only into orthodoxy but also into fellowship with God and, as one aspect of that fellowship, holiness of life. When Jesus said that a "fully trained" disciple will be like his teacher (Luke 6:40), he was referring to mental attitude and moral character, not just to skill in parroting off what the teacher taught. Most of his own specific teaching was on behavior, one way or another. The catechisms of history bring out the prominence of ethics in the life of faith and discipleship by their expositions of the Decalogue; here it is perhaps the *Heidelberg Catechism* and the *Westminster Larger Catechism* that lead the pack. We must never lose sight of the fact that discipleship means learning not only sound faith in Christ but also conscious obedience to Christ, conformity to his character, and a lifestyle that is conscientiously sin free, in purpose at any rate. A great deal depends on the character of the catechist as well as on his or her didactic competence. Paul, a catechist par excellence in our sense of the word, told those he discipled to "be imitators of me, as I am of Christ" (1 Cor. 11:1; see also 4:16–17; Phil. 3:17; 4:9; 1 Thess. 1:6; 2 Thess. 3:19). Today's catechist, like Paul, must be a convincing, winsome example of living by the truth being taught, in the power of the Spirit whose sanctifying work is being celebrated, and in a way that reflects the example of Christ. Catechizing seeks to transform weak and sinful beings such as ourselves into faithful worshipers of God in Christ, holy and disciplined followers of their Lord, self-denying servants of God and his church, clearheaded travelers through this often hostile world, and passionate outreachers to the needy and lost, and it is vital that in all these respects catechists themselves be good role models.

Catechists must know their theology before they start; they must, in other words, have been catechized themselves so that their minds are trained to communicate the saving truths they themselves live by. Then they need to be clear on what discipling is, that it is their precise job, and that it is not completed until those at the receiving end can and do, however simply, actively express in word and life the Faith their instructors have sought to share with them.

Commitment to the Cause

20. How Can We Lay Foundations for Long-Term, Faithful, and Fruitful Ministries of Catechesis in the Church?

When church leaders find themselves increasingly persuaded that our churches are in fact called to catechize, how should they proceed? Some might believe that fully implementing the broad outline of what we have been proposing would only be possible in the context of a new church plant. They may well be right. For those who are pursuing God's call to a church-planting ministry, we would strongly encourage building catechesis into the very foundations of the church. It is easier to do this than to try to change a church culture that has been in place for many years or many generations.

What shall we say to those who labor for the Lord in already existing churches, as, of course, most pastors do? We certainly do not need more initiatives that begin with enthusiasm only to fizzle out in short order. Nor do we simply need another program in any of our churches—no matter how "successful" it may appear. What we need is a commitment to the cause of catechesis that will have staying power. Reflecting upon Psalm 78 we mentioned earlier that we ought to strive for a multigenerational vision. This is precisely what we would wish for those churches that determine to adopt some serious system of catechizing. Toward this end we would suggest the following.

Accurately assess the current situation. From the table presented in chapter 9, a grid emerges that permits us to evaluate specific aspects of catechesis that are, or are not, presently at work in our churches. We reproduce that table here having removed our suggestions concerning proposed content. Working through this grid (or something like it), key leaders in the church can try to assess the strengths and weaknesses of their church's current practices, remembering that catechesis may well be occurring without it ever being called by that name and without many in the church being conscious of it. In the blank cells of the grid, evaluative remarks can be made, such as "strong," "weak," "non-existent," and so on.

	The Truth	The Life	The Way	
Procatechesis: First glimpses of the Gospel				*Formal*
				Non-formal
				Informal (and implicit)
Catechesis proper: Formal grounding in the Gospel				*Formal*
				Non-formal
				Informal (and implicit)
Ongoing catechesis: Further growth in the Gospel				*Formal*
				Non-formal
				Informal (and implicit)

In most cases we suspect that there will be areas of both weakness and strength. In some cases the picture may already be quite encouraging; in other cases, it may seem rather dismal and disheartening. Whatever our analysis may be, we can use this as a starting point for trying to strengthen the catechetical ministry of the church, then use this sort of grid again periodically to check on the progress of things.

Cast the catechetical vision. Next we can begin to sow seeds in the minds and hearts of congregants for a new or strengthened ministry of catechesis. This can be done in conversations, teaching venues, from the pulpit, and so on. Bringing before the people healthy examples from those eras of catechetical flourishing that we considered in chapter 3 can be helpful. So too can sharing the stories of contemporary efforts from churches near or far. Conversely we can also appeal from the unhappy consequences that emerge from our uncatechized or counter-catechized churches, such as widespread biblical illiteracy and the apparent disconnect between our profession and our practice. We may consider having others read this book (or something similar) to help at this stage.

Cultivate consensus among leaders. Because it will take a good deal of effort from a good many people to put in place a faithful and fruitful ministry of catechesis that has staying power, it is necessary that as many as possible of those who have key roles of official or unofficial leadership consent to the vision. This will take time and will require cultivation of healthy relationships. People will need to be given opportunity to voice concerns and offer suggestions about how best to proceed. We should be careful, though, not to try to form actual catechetical strategies by a "committee of the whole." A few people whose positions, passions, and gifts make them more or less obvious choices for leadership can serve the entire church by drafting and developing strategies and then tweaking them according to feedback received from others.

Start slowly but with resolve. We would suggest that movement toward a ministry of catechesis in a church where none has been in place previously be undertaken carefully. It is probably best not to attempt too much at once. Rather, small steps might be taken first. In one church the best beginning may be to establish a form of significant catechetical instruction for those who are already long-established members. Another congregation might determine that henceforth all who would be baptized or confirmed will have a catechetical experience along the lines we outlined in chapter 9. Still another church might decide to begin with a more rigorous membership training for future members. In these last two cases it will probably be necessary, as we said earlier, to "grandfather" in those who have already been baptized or are already members. But that should not discourage us from moving forward with resolve toward a more healthy future.

From Psalm 78 and other texts we are reminded that we need a long-range vision. Choices we make today may not bear much fruit in our own generation. But we may be planting seeds for healthy growth in future generations. The kingdom of God, Jesus said, is like a mustard seed—small and very unimpressive. But we dare not doubt what God can produce from the smallest and most humble of beginnings (Matt. 13:31–32). Churches often aim for big, showy, numbers-driven programs. But the biblical data certainly suggests that God's way is quite different. God's way is that of the seed (John 12:24) and of the meek (Matt. 5:5), that of making from foolish, weak, and lowly things—and from things that do not even exist—vessels that display his wisdom, power, and glory so that the only boasting that makes any sense at all is boasting in the Lord (1 Cor. 1:20–31).

Focus on families and children. While we are passionate about the need to restore a rigorous catechesis for adults, we also recognize that such efforts need to stand alongside similar efforts to faithfully catechize children, especially within the context of their families. Because of our failure to obey the biblical mandates about raising children of the covenant within the Faith, we wind up having to do far too much remedial work among adults. By the time they reach adulthood, many of our members have already been so thoroughly catechized in unbiblical thinking and values that our efforts to catechize them in the Faith of the Gospel become truly a steep uphill climb through very difficult terrain.

Aside from the obvious practical value that renewed attention to catechizing our children will have on our overall efforts to teach and feed the flock, there is simply the matter of our paying due attention to the biblical mandates and models. We have already seen how passages such as Deuteronomy 6:1–9, Psalm 78:1–8, and Ephesians 6:4 command us to raise our children in the Faith. There are also biblical examples of such faithful efforts. Paul wrote to Timothy with gratefulness for "your sincere faith, a faith that dwelt first in your grandmother Lois and your mother Eunice" (2 Tim. 1:5). And he went on to urge Timothy to "continue in what you have learned and firmly believe, knowing from whom you learned it and how from childhood you have been acquainted with the sacred writings, which are able to make you wise for salvation through faith in Christ Jesus." Churches wishing to push forward a ministry of catechesis need to urge and help equip parents to do their absolutely vital part in such work.

Hone the hymnody of the church. As we pointed out earlier, our hymnody has significant power as a catechetical tool, as Ambrose, Luther, the Wesleys, Watts, Toplady, and countless others have recognized. The truth of the Faith joined to suitable and singable melodies can work their way into our hearts as well as our heads.

Scripture itself points us toward the wisdom of utilizing our hymnody for formation as well as for worship. The Psalms of the Bible, for example—Spirit-inspired song-prayers each one of them—were plainly intended for such a twofold emphasis. On the one hand, our songs are often directed Godward as we sing. But, at the same time, they become a means of a mandated "speaking to one another" that facilitates in our midst both the fullness of the Holy Spirit (Eph. 5:18–19) and of the Word of Christ (Col. 3:16).

What we sing when we come together in congregational worship is not only a matter of our proper doxology. It also has power to help clarify for the congregation matters of doctrine, devotion, and duty, and to enhance our delight in the Lord. It is an unwise pastor who pays little attention to the song choices of the song leader (all too commonly called "the worship leader" in our day). When all is said and done, the songs of the saints in worship may well have more lasting, formative power than the sermons preached by the pastor. We had best choose our songs carefully.

Adjust appropriately as needed. New (ad)ventures such as the ones we are suggesting are major steps in transforming the culture and practices of churches. They cannot be effected quickly or easily. And they should not be undone quickly either simply because we may not see immediate returns on our investment of time, talent, and treasure. We should expect that there will be bumps in the road and that mistakes will be made. We learn as we go, and we need to remember that while there is joy in the journey there will also be times of sadness and confusion. We are unrealistic if we expect everything to go perfectly, and we are unwise if we quickly dismantle our initiatives because of difficulties. Regular evaluation should be built into our plans. In humility we adjust course when and where needed. But by all means we should resolve to stay the course, knowing that if we are not weary in doing the right thing we shall surely reap a harvest in God's good time (Gal. 6:9). Our labors in the Lord shall not be in vain (1 Cor. 15:58), and God's Word, faithfully proclaimed, shall not return void but will accomplish God's intended purposes (Isa. 55:11).

Share stories of formation. As we proceed with our new efforts, we should share our stories with one another and with the congregation. Not all our stories or experiences will be happy ones. Some of the formation that occurs through catechesis may prove to be painful or difficult. But we share these stories. Alongside them we share stories that we more easily recognize and readily accept as good. The many contours of our faith journeys—individually and corporately—may prove to be encouraging to other pilgrims who have just joined the journey, and may also move some to leave their places on the sidelines and begin a wholehearted engagement in their own pilgrimages.

Proceed with prayer. Finally, at every juncture let our efforts to catechize proceed with an abundance of prayer. Jesus prayed regularly as part of his own personal communion with the Father (Luke 5:16). He prayed as well for the spiritual well-being of his disciples (Luke 22:32; John 17). Paul's pattern, as evident from most of his letters, was to pray regularly and earnestly for the churches. Many of the prayers he prayed are recorded in the Scriptures (e.g., Eph. 1:17–19; 3:14–21; Phil. 1:9–11; Col. 1:9–12) and church leaders today would do very well to use these prayers for their own congregants.

We pray both for individuals who are being catechized and for the entire church as it seeks to deepen its experience of unity of the Faith and of the knowledge of the Son of God, and so become mature (Eph. 4:13). Jesus had been *the* Teacher of the Twelve (Matt. 23:10; John 13:13). To the Twelve, and for our sakes as well, he promised that another Counselor would come—the Spirit of Truth whom the Father would send to us in Jesus's name to be our Teacher and guide us into all truth (John 14:26; 16:13). It is by the work of the Spirit that lives are transformed and catechesis can be found faithful and fruitful. We may sow seeds or water them, but only God makes things grow (1 Cor. 3:6–7). Believing these things to be true, we pray. And as we pray, we labor in the Lord with all our might to the end that God alone would be glorified in our midst. May it be always so.

Appendix I

Examples of Catechetical Hymns

Christ We Proclaim!

Christ we proclaim, for we have heard	Colossians 1:28
no other certain, saving word.	John 1:1
In Jesus Christ, God became flesh.	John 1:14
No other name will we confess.	Isaiah 53:11; Acts 4:12
Christ we proclaim, the Righteous One,	1 John 2:1
for he alone God's will has done:	Romans 5:19
fully to love and to obey.	John 5:19; 17:4
Christ is the Truth, the Life, the Way.	John 14:6
Christ we proclaim: Christ crucified!	1 Corinthians 1:23
We live because our Savior died.	1 Peter 2:24
At the great price of his own blood,	1 Peter 1:18–19
Jesus has purchased us for God.	Revelation 5:9–10
Christ we proclaim, the Risen One:	2 Timothy 2:8
declared with pow'r God's mighty Son.	Romans 1:4
He conquered death, and doomed our foes.	1 Corinthians 15:20–28
Our hope was born when Christ arose.	Romans 6:5

Christ we proclaim, our great High Priest,	Hebrews 8:1
whose intercessions never cease.	Hebrews 7:25
And we ourselves are bold to pray	Hebrews 4:16
through Christ, our new and living way.	Hebrews 10:20
Christ we proclaim: our coming King.	Revelation 19:16
The Spirit stirs our souls to sing.	Revelation 22:17
The whole creation shall be healed,	Romans 8:21
when all God's children are revealed.	Romans 8:19

Christ we proclaim that every one	
may be perfected in the Son.	Colossians 1:28
Christ we proclaim from fervent hearts,	
with pow'r that God himself imparts.	Colossians 1:29
Christ we proclaim, and Christ alone,	1 Corinthians 2:2
until, at last, before the throne	Revelation 7:9
we cast the crowns his grace supplied,	Revelation 4:10
as God alone is glorified.	Revelation 4:11

Text: Gary A. Parrett (2009)

Tune: *Jerusalem* (Parry)[1]

On the Third Day

Hanged upon a tree, accursèd,	Galatians 3:13
buried in a borrowed tomb;	Matthew 27:59–60
is this whom the magi worshiped—	Matthew 2:1–11
offspring of the virgin's womb?	Isaiah 7:14
How could such a child of promise	Isaiah 9:6
come to such a dreadful doom?	Matthew 11:3
Yet Messiah had to suffer,	Luke 24:26–27
all the Scriptures to fulfill.	Luke 24:44–45
Now his earthly work is finished.	John 17:4; 19:30
He has done the Father's will.	John 4:34
Sabbath comes and so the Servant	Isaiah 52:13; Philippians 2:7
is at rest, his body still.	John 19:42
Have you searched the Scriptures further?	John 5:39
There is more the prophets say.	Luke 24:46
God would not let his Anointed	Psalm 16:8–11
see corruption or decay.	Acts 2:25–28
Our great God would work a wonder	Acts 2:24
before dawn on the third day.	1 Corinthians 15:4
Early in the morning darkness,	John 20:1
at the birth of a new week,	Matthew 28:1
come the women with their spices,	Luke 24:1
their beloved Lord to seek.	Mark 16:1
But an empty tomb amazes	Luke 24:2–3
as they hear the angels speak:	Luke 24:4
"He is not here. He has risen!	Luke 24:6
Why seek him among the dead?"	Luke 24:5
Now we live! Our sins forgiven,	Romans 4:24–25
our hopes raised in Christ our Head!	Romans 6:5–11
Hallelujah! He has risen	1 Corinthians 15:20
on the third day, as he said.	Matthew 16:21

The first day, the seed was planted,	Genesis 3:15; Galatians 3:16
lest it should remain alone.	John 12:24
Bursting forth upon the third day,	Acts 10:40
new life in its glory shone!	2 Timothy 1:10
From all nations, through all ages,	Revelation 7:9–10
see the harvest God has grown!	Hebrews 2:10
For all those who would see Jesus	John 12:21
we proclaim Christ crucified.	1 Corinthians 1:23
Grace and truth, and pow'r and wisdom,	Exodus 34:6; 1 Corinthians 1:24
in the Word-made-flesh abide.	John 1:14; Colossians 2:9
Lifted up, the Lord of glory	1 Corinthians 2:8; James 2:1
draws all people to his side.	John 12:31
He who bore our sins and sorrows,	Isaiah 53:4, 12
on the third day rose again!	1 Corinthians 15:4
To the Father, he ascended,	Hebrews 10:12
leading captives in his train.	Ephesians 4:8
Soon he shall return in glory	1 Thessalonians 4:16
and forevermore shall reign!	Revelation 11:15

Text: Gary A. Parrett (2008)

Tune: *Picardy* (verses 1–4), *Lauda Anima* (verses 5–8)[2]

Doxology

Each perfect gift from heaven's heights
comes from our Father, God of Lights,
who knows full well our ev'ry need
and ev'ry prayer of faith will heed.

(James 1:17)

When we were held by sin's fierce chain,
Heaven's great loss was our great gain,
for grasping not his throne above,
Christ came to us: redeeming love!

(Phil. 2:6–8)

You know the grace of Christ, our Lord:
though he was rich, he became poor,
that we, through his true poverty,
would be made rich eternally.

(2 Cor. 8:9)

To such a wondrous Servant King,
our worship we will gladly bring:
in sacrifice, henceforth to live.
As we've received, we freely give.

(Matt. 10:8; Rom. 12:1)

To God the Father, God the Son
and God the Spirit, Three-in-One,
Be all the glory, pow'r and praise
from ev'ry heart through endless days.
Amen.

(Rev. 5:13)

Text: Gary A. Parrett (2001)
Tune: *Old One Hundredth*[3]

How Great the Father's Love

Romans 8:28–30; Titus 2:11–14; 1 John 3:1–3

How great the Father's love,
so lavished upon us
that we should be one family
in Christ Jesus!
We have been saved!
Christ crucified has justified us.
God be praised!

When Jesus comes again
what will our glory be?
For by his grace, the Savior's face
our eyes shall see.
We shall be saved!
A glorified and spotless bride—
O, God be praised!

The Holy Spirit fills
our thirsting souls today.
He intercedes for us and leads us
in God's way.
We are now saved—
His sanctifying pow'r applying.
God be praised!

The grace of God appeared:
salvation from above!
In this faith and this hope we stand,
ablaze with love.
The God who saves—
the Father, Son, and Spirit,
One in Three—be praised!

Text: Gary A. Parrett (2001)
Tune: *Darwall*[4]

The Way, the Truth, the Life

In Jesus Christ the way is found!
His light illumines solid ground.
O Wisdom! Hallelujah!
To love our neighbor and our God,
we walk the path that Jesus trod.
O worship and adore him.
With your strength come, bow before him.
Hallelujah!

(Pss. 1; 32:8; 119:32; Isa. 30:21; Mark 12:28–34)

In Jesus Christ the truth is clear!
In Him the unseen things appear.
O Myst'ry! Hallelujah!
The sacred scroll is no more sealed;
God's deepest thought has been revealed.
O worship and adore him.
With your mind come, bow before him.
Hallelujah!

(John 1:1, 14, 18; Col. 2:3)

In Jesus Christ the life is ours!
Death's claim on us has lost its pow'rs.
O Fountain! Hallelujah!
The Spirit-waters in us spring,
and we cry, "Abba!" to the King.
O worship and adore him.
With your soul come, bow before him.
Hallelujah!

(John 7:37–39; Gal. 4:6; 1 John 5:11–13)

Jesus—the Life, the Truth, the Way!
In him the veil is torn away.
O Fullness! Hallelujah!
All deity in him abides,
and in our spirits, he resides.
O worship and adore him.
With your heart come, bow before him.
Hallelujah!

(2 Cor. 3:16; Col. 2:9–10; Heb. 1:1–3)

Text: Gary A. Parrett (1999)

Tune: *Lasst uns erfreuen*[5]

We Will Not Cease the Gospel to Proclaim

Romans 1:16–17

We will not cease the Gospel to proclaim.
Nor dare we ever turn from it in shame.
It is God's pow'r to save in Jesus' name.
Hallelujah! Hallelujah!

(1 Cor. 1:18–25; 9:16; 15:1–8; Gal. 1:6–9)

Both Jew and Greek, and all those who believe,
by faith alone the gift of life receive.
By grace alone to Christ alone we cleave.
Hallelujah! Hallelujah!

(Ps. 32:7–8; Acts 4:12; Gal. 3:21–28; 6:14; Eph. 2:1–22)

God's righteousness is in the Gospel shown.
Christ Jesus died for sinners to atone.
God is both just and justifies his own!
Hallelujah! Hallelujah!

(Rom. 3:21–26; Gal. 2:15–21; Heb. 4:10; 9:11–10:14)

From faith to faith this righteousness proceeds.
The child of God the Gospel ever heeds
as, in new life, the Holy Spirit leads.
Hallelujah! Hallelujah!

(Romans 4; Gal. 2:20; Phil. 3:7–16; Heb. 11:1–12:2)

At peace with God, by faith let us be bold.
Of his great pow'r for living we lay hold.
"The just by faith shall live!" It was foretold.
Hallelujah! Hallelujah!

(Hab. 2:4; Rom. 5:1–8:17; Gal. 3:11; 5:1, 22–25)

Text: Gary A. Parrett (2007)
Tune: *Sine Nomine*[6]

There Is None Good but God Alone

There is none good but *God alone*.
Not one of us is righteous.
We spurned God's way and sought our own,
and so have become worthless.
What hope, then, can we see?
Christ Jesus: only he
the path of life has trod,
to love both man and God.
Yes he alone is worthy.

(Isa. 53:6; Mark 10:18; Rom. 3:9–23; 1 John 2:1; Rev. 5)

Scripture alone reveals these things;
thus do the fathers witness.
Good news of life and light it brings
to those now lost in darkness.
For from this sacred Word,
what wonders we have heard:
God's grace in Christ revealed.
By his stripes we are healed.
We glory in the Gospel!

(Isa. 9:2; 53:5; Luke 24:25–27, 45; 1 Tim. 1:11;
2 Tim. 3:15–17; Titus 2:11; 2 Peter 1:19–21)

In *Christ alone* is all our trust
for full and free salvation.
With his own blood he ransomed us
from ev'ry tribe and nation.
For us he lived and died.
Now, at the Father's side,
full knowing all our needs,
our High Priest intercedes.
He lives to make us holy.

(Acts 4:12; Rom. 8:28–39; 1 Tim. 5–6; Heb. 2:11;
7:25; 9–10; 1 Peter 1:19; Rev. 5:9)

And now by faith alone we stand
in Christ, our risen Savior,
who has fulfilled each just command
and makes us just forever.
In him is all our peace
and life that cannot cease.

By no work of our own,
but all of *grace alone*,
have we become God's people.

(Rom. 3:28; 5:1–2, 15–19; Eph. 1:4–5; 2:5–10; 1 Peter 2:9–10)

For not by human pow'r or might,
but only by God's Spirit
Do we begin to glimpse the light
of all we shall inherit.
The new life he imparts
transforms our hardened hearts.
Our race, by faith begun,
in faith must still be run.
Christ set us free for freedom!

(Zech. 4:6; Rom. 8:2, 11; 2 Cor. 3:17–18; Gal.
3:2–3; 5:1, 7, 16–18, 25; Eph. 1:13–14)

Above all pow'rs abides the Word,
God's mighty Word that frees us.
Through prophets and apostles heard,
for us made flesh in Jesus.
No other word we speak,
nor human glory seek.
All earthly schemes must fail.
God's kingdom shall prevail.
To God alone be glory!

(Ps. 145:13; Isa. 42:8; John 1:1, 14; Rom. 11:36; Heb.
1:1–2; 2:1–4; 1 Peter 1:23–25; Rev. 4:11; 11:15)

Text: Gary A. Parrett (2008)

Tune: *Ein' Feste Burg*[7]

As a Witness

For the Gospel of the Lord
I would yield my grateful heart.
God saves sinners, first to last.
God alone can life impart.
As a witness to your grace,
help me serve you with my heart.

For the life of holiness
I would thirst with all my soul.
May your Spirit's cleansing pow'r
fill me till I overflow.
As a witness to your life,
help me serve you with my soul.

For the teachings of God's Word
I would humbly bow my mind.
God all-knowing would be known.
Those who seek the Lord shall find.
As a witness to your truth,
help me serve you with my mind.

For the oneness of the church
I would work with all my might:
joining Jesus in his pray'r,
loving all for whom he died.
As a witness to your love,
help me serve you with my might.

For the glory of our God
I would ever give my all,
till, confessing "Christ is Lord!"
on their knees all men shall fall.
Help me, as a witness, Lord,
for your glory give my all.

Text: Gary A. Parrett (2006, 2008)
Tune: *Dix*[8]

213

APPENDIX II

Resources for Further Study

Historical Introductions to the Ministry of Catechesis

Astley, Jeff, Leslie J. Francis, and Colin Crowder. *Theological Perspectives on Christian Formation: A Reader on Theology and Christian Education.* Grand Rapids: Eerdmans, 1996.

Augustine. *Instructing Beginners in Faith.* Edited by Boniface Ramsey. Translated by Raymond Canning. Hyde Park, NY: New City Press, 2006.

————. *The Enchiridion on Faith, Hope, and Love.* South Bend, IN: Henry Regnery, 1961.

Black, J. William. *Reformation Pastors: Richard Baxter and the Idea of the Reformed Pastor.* Carlisle, UK: Paternoster, 2004.

Green, Ian. *The Christian's ABC: Catechisms and Catechizing in England, c. 1530–1740.* Oxford: Clarendon, 1996.

Harmless, William J. *Augustine and the Catechumenate.* Collegeville, MN: Liturgical Press, 1995.

Osmer, Richard Robert. *A Teachable Spirit: Recovering the Teaching Office in the Church.* Louisville, KY: Westminster/John Knox Press, 1990.

Torrance, T. F. *The School of Faith: The Catechisms of the Reformed Church.* Eugene, OR: Wipf and Stock, 1959.

Van Engen, John, ed. *Educating People of Faith: Exploring the History of Jewish and Christian Communities.* Grand Rapids: Eerdmans, 2004.

215

Wengert, Timothy J. *Martin Luther's Catechisms: Forming the Faith*. Minneapolis: Fortress, 2009.

Westerhoff, John H. and O. C. Edwards, eds. *A Faithful Church: Issues in the History of Catechesis*. Eugene, OR: Wipf and Stock, 2003.

Historic Protestant Catechisms and Related Commentaries

Barrett, Lee C. III, trans. *The Heidelberg Catechism: A New Translation for the 21st Century*. Berea, OH: United Church Press, 2007.

DeYoung, Kevin. *The Good News We Almost Forgot: Rediscovering the Gospel in a 16th Century Catechism*. Chicago: Moody, 2010.

General Assembly of the Presbyterian Church. *The Westminster Confession of Faith, Together with the Larger Catechism and the Shorter Catechism, with the Scripture Proofs*. Lawrenceville, GA: Committee for Christian Education and Publications, 1990.

Hesselink, John. *Calvin's First Catechism: A Commentary*. Louisville, KY: Westminster John Knox, 1997.

Kolb, Robert, Timothy J. Wengert, and James Schaffer. *Luther's Small Catechism and Large Catechism*. In *The Book of Concord*. Minneapolis: Augsburg Fortress, 2001.

Torrance, T. F. *The School of Faith: The Catechisms of the Reformed Church*. Eugene, OR: Wipf and Stock, 1959.

Ursinus, Zacharias. *The Commentary of Zacharias Ursinus on the Heidelberg Catechism*. Translated by G. W. Williard. Phillipsburg, NJ: P&R, 1985.

Williamson, G. I. *The Heidelberg Catechism: A Study Guide*. Phillipsburg, NJ: P&R, 1993.

———. *The Westminster Shorter Catechism: For Study Classes*. Phillipsburg, NJ: P&R, 2003.

Catholic and Orthodox Catechisms

Aquinas, Thomas. *The Catechetical Instructions of St. Thomas Aquinas*. Manila, Philippines: Sinag-Tala Publishers, 1999.

Carlton, Clark. *The Faith: Understanding Orthodox Christianity—An Orthodox Catechism*. Salisbury, MA: Regina Orthodox Press, 1997.

Clement, Olivier. *The Living God: A Catechism for the Christian Faith*. Translated by Olga Dunlop. 2 vols. Crestwood, NY: St. Vladimir's Seminary Press, 2004.

Demetry, Rev. Constas H. *Catechism of the Eastern Orthodox Church*. Ft. Lauderdale, FL: Saint Demetrios Greek Orthodox Church, 1929. Available online at http://www.christusrex.org/www1/CDHN/catechis.html.

United States Conference of Catholic Bishops. *Catechism of the Catholic Church*. 2nd ed. New York: Doubleday, 2003.

Additional Catholic Catechetical Resources

The Companion to the Catechism of the Catholic Church. San Francisco, CA: Ignatius Press, 1994.

Connell, Martin. *The Catechetical Documents: A Parish Resource*. Chicago: Liturgy Training Publications, 2007.

de Cointet, Pierre, Barbara Morgan, and Petroc Willey. *The Catechism of the Catholic Church and the Craft of Catechesis*. San Francisco: Ignatius, 2008.

Kelly, Francis D. *The Mystery We Proclaim: Catechesis for the Third Millennium*. 2nd ed. Eugene, OR: Wipf and Stock, 2008.

Pope John Paul II. *On Catechesis in Our Time (Catechesis Tradendae)*. Washington, DC: USCCB, 1979.

Ratzinger, Joseph Cardinal. *Gospel, Catechesis, Catechism: Sidelights on the Catechism of the Catholic Church*. San Francisco: Ignatius, 1995.

USCCB Bishops' Committee on the Liturgy. *Rite of Christian Initiation of Adults*. Collegeville, MN: Liturgical Press, 1988.

USCCB Congregation for the Clergy. *General Directory for Catechesis*. Washington, DC: USCCB, 1998.

USCCB Department of Education. *The National Directory for Catechesis*. Washington, DC: USCCB, 2005.

Contemporary Catechetical Efforts and Related Proposals

"Alpha." http://www.alphana.org.

"The Anglican Catechism in Outline (ACIO)." Interim Report of the Global South Anglican Theological Formation and Education Task Force, January 6, 2008. http://www.globalsouthanglican.org/sse/aciointerimreport_1.pdf.

Benn, Wallace. *The Baxter Model: Guidelines for Pastoring Today*. Lowestoft, UK: Fellowship of Word and Spirit, 1993.

"Christianity Explored." http://www.christianityexplored.org.

Green, Michael. *After Alpha: You've Been on an Alpha Course—What Now?* Colorado Springs: David C. Cook, 2004.

Keller, Timothy J. "Gospel Christianity." New York: Redeemer Presbyterian Church, 2003. An overview and samples of the curriculum are available at http://www.redeemer2.com/websamples/GC1Sample.pdf.

Murphy, Debra Dean. *Teaching That Transforms: Worship as the Heart of Christian Education*. Grand Rapids: Brazos, 2004.

Osmer, Richard Robert. *A Teachable Spirit: Recovering the Teaching Office in the Church*. Louisville: Westminster/John Knox, 1990.

Packer, J. I. *Growing in Christ*. Wheaton, IL: Crossway, 1994.

Parrett, Gary A. and S. Steve Kang. *Teaching the Faith, Forming the Faithful: A Biblical Vision for Education in the Church*. Downers Grove, IL: IVP Academic, 2009.

Webber, Robert. *Journey to Jesus: The Worship, Evangelism, and Nurture Mission of the Church*. Nashville: Abingdon, 2001.

Catechetical Resources for Families and Children

"Catechesis of the Good Shepherd." http://www.cgsusa.org.

Engelbrecht, Edward. *The Lord Will Answer: A Daily Prayer Catechism*. St. Louis: Concordia, 2004.

Hunt, Susan, Richie Hunt, and Nancy Munger. *Big Truths for Little Kids: Teaching Your Children to Live for God*. Wheaton, IL: Crossway, 1999.

Meade, Starr. *Training Hearts, Teaching Minds: Family Devotions Based on the Shorter Catechism*. Phillipsburg, NJ: P&R, 2000.

Van Dyken, Donald. *Rediscovering Catechism: The Art of Equipping Covenant Children*. Phillipsburg, NJ: P&R, 2000.

Working, Randall. *From Rebellion to Redemption: A Journey through the Great Themes of Christian Faith*. Colorado Springs: NavPress, 2001.

Notes

Introduction

1. The collected papers of the conference have now been published under the title *J. I. Packer and the Evangelical Future: The Impact of His Life and Thought*, ed. Timothy George (Grand Rapids: Baker Academic, 2009).

2. The hymn—"As a Witness," now expanded to include a fifth verse—can be found in Appendix I, "Examples of Catechetical Hymns."

3. Thanks to Steve for his input on some of the notes in chapters 5 and 6.

Chapter 1 Building Believers the Old-Fashioned Way

1. What Gary's sister experienced is called the "Rite of Christian Initiation for Adults" (RCIA), a contemporary effort of adult catechesis for converts to the Catholic Church that was formally begun in 1972. The first stage of this four-stage process (which roughly corresponds to the catechumenal processes that were widely practiced in the churches of the second through fifth centuries), called the period of inquiry, can last anywhere from several months to several years. The second stage, the period of the catechumenate, is for those who already have faith in Christ; it involves more formal instruction, and generally lasts about twelve months for those who have not been baptized. The actual shape of the RCIA varies from diocese to diocese.

2. Both of these very contemporary ministries are in fact a sort of return to very ancient catechetical practice. Augustine, for example, has left us with instructions about catechizing "inquirers" in his book *First Catechetical Instruction*, trans. Joseph P. Christopher, Ancient Christian Writers (Mahwah, NJ: Paulist, 1978).

3. The story, as may be expected, is a complex one. We say more about this in chapter 3.

4. The historical content of catechesis which provided basic training in these areas included the Apostles' Creed, the Lord's Prayer, the sacraments, and the Decalogue. These *formulae* can be found in the majority of printed catechisms from the Reformation onward, Protestant and Catholic alike.

5. Quoted by William P. Haugaard, "The Continental Reformation of the Sixteenth Century," in John H. Westerhoff III and O. C. Edwards, eds., *A Faithful Church: Issues in the History of Catechesis* (Eugene, OR: Wipf and Stock, 2003).

6. This is clearly the understanding, for example, in Richard Baxter's classic work *The Reformed Pastor* (Carlisle, PA: Banner of Truth, 1979). The book is Baxter's passionate plea to

his colleagues to faithfully discharge their catechetical duties. On this book and Baxter's own catechetical practice in its broad Puritan context see J. William Black, *Reformation Pastors: Richard Baxter and the Ideal of the Reformed Pastor* (Carlisle, UK: Paternoster, 2004) and Ian Green, *The Christian's ABC: Catechisms and Catechizing in England, c. 1530–1740* (Oxford: Clarendon Press, 1996).

7. The movement away from the use of catechisms and toward Bible stories appears to have been a deliberate effort motivated in part by the desire to avoid doctrinal controversies. There are of course a number of other significant factors that contributed to the decline of evangelical catechesis, which we will explore in chapter 3.

8. There are, thankfully, a number of exceptions to this among evangelical Protestants, especially among evangelical Anglicans, Lutherans, Presbyterians, and other Reformed Christians.

9. C. S. Lewis, *God in the Dock* (Grand Rapids: Eerdmans, 1970), 201–02.

10. Gerhard Kittel, ed., *"katécheō,"* in *Theological Dictionary of the New Testament*, trans. Geoffrey Bromiley (Grand Rapids: Eerdmans, 1965), 3:638.

11. Zacharias Ursinus, *The Commentary of Zacharias Ursinus on the Heidelberg Catechism*, trans. G. W. Williard (Phillipsburg, NJ: P&R, 1985), 11.

12. John H. Westerhoff III, "The Present Situation," in Westerhoff and Edwards, *A Faithful Church*, 1.

13. John A. Berntsen, "Christian Affections and the Catechumenate," in Jeff Astley, Leslie J. Francis, and Colin Crowder, eds., *Theological Perspectives on Christian Formation: A Reader on Theology and Christian Education* (Grand Rapids: Eerdmans, 1996), 229.

14. Debra Dean Murphy, *Teaching That Transforms: Worship as the Heart of Christian Education* (Grand Rapids: Brazos, 2004), 112.

15. *National Directory for Catechesis* (Washington, DC: USCCB, 2005), 6.

16. Pope John Paul II, *On Catechesis in Our Time* (*Catechesis Tradendae*) (Washington, DC: USCCB, 1979), nos. 1, 2.

Chapter 2 Catechesis Is a (Very!) Biblical Idea

1. We have of course substituted the Hebrew *torah* for "law" and *derek* for "way." No one has continually meditated upon, nor fully obeyed, the Torah except the Lord Jesus Christ. We must also note that while the Torah points to life, it has no power to impart it. Thus the Torah points us finally to Christ alone (Gal. 3:21–25).

2. See Marvin R. Wilson, *Our Father Abraham: Jewish Roots of the Christian Faith* (Grand Rapids: Eerdmans, 1989), 216, 296.

3. What is described here is a variation on the argument set forth by Walter Brueggemann in his book *The Creative Word: Canon as a Model for Biblical Education* (Philadelphia: Fortress, 1982). For more on this, see chap. 6.

4. See Abraham Joshua Heschel, *God in Search of Man: A Philosophy of Judaism* (New York: Farrar, Straus, and Giroux, 1976), 31.

5. *The Apostolic Fathers*, ed. and trans. Michael W. Holmes, 3rd ed. (Grand Rapids: Baker Academic, 2007), 161.

6. We note as well Paul's language to Timothy that communicates similar convictions. He writes, "Follow the pattern of the sound words that you heard from me, in the faith and love that are in Christ Jesus. By the Holy Spirit who dwells within us, guard the good deposit entrusted to you" (2 Tim. 1:13–14). Furthermore, "the mystery of godliness" (1 Tim. 3:16) and "The [trustworthy] saying" (2 Tim. 2:11–13) could be confessional statements or early hymns that served, at least in part, a catechetical function. Other texts that may have served similar functions include Philippians 2:6–11 and Colossians 1:15–20.

7. See, for example, O. C. Edwards, "The New Testament Church," in Westerhoff and Edwards, *A Faithful Church*, 33.

8. R. V. G. Tasker, *The Gospel according to St. Matthew*, Tyndale New Testament Commentaries (Grand Rapids: Eerdmans, 1971), 19.

9. Ibid.

Chapter 3 The Waxing and Waning of Catechesis

1. Quoted in Westerhoff and Edwards, *A Faithful Church*, 127.

2. Among others, the Barna Group continues to provide research data on these unhappy trends. See their website: http://www.barna.org.

3. This is the title of an article posted on CSMonitor.com by Michael Spencer, March 10, 2009. Just around the same time period, articles and features suggesting significant decline in evangelical numbers and influence were common fare in major media throughout the United States. Spencer's article reminds us of the series of books that David Wells has written from the end of the twentieth century to the beginning of the twenty-first century, decrying the loss of Protestant and evangelical identity as many American Christians in these communities have consistently succumbed to such potent cultural forces as modernism, secularism, pragmatism, pluralism, individualism, postmodernism, and more. See his *No Place for Truth: Or, Whatever Happened to Evangelical Theology?* (Grand Rapids: Eerdmans, 1993); *God in the Wasteland: The Reality of Truth in a World of Fading Dreams* (Grand Rapids: Eerdmans, 1994); *Losing Our Virtue: Why the Church Must Recover Its Moral Vision* (Grand Rapids: Eerdmans, 1999); *Above All Earthly Pow'rs: Christ in a Postmodern World* (Grand Rapids: Eerdmans, 2005); and *The Courage to Be Protestant: Truth-Lovers, Marketers, and Emergents in the Postmodern World* (Grand Rapids: Eerdmans, 2008).

4. See, for example, Westerhoff and Edwards, *A Faithful Church*; Green, *The Christian's ABC*; and William J. Harmless, *Augustine and the Catechumenate* (Collegeville, MN: Liturgical Press, 1995).

5. As we saw in chapter 2, it might even be argued that some sort of catechumenate was already in place, at least in some churches, during the times of the New Testament.

6. Augustine argued that catechists should set before inquirers the great *narratio* of the Scriptures, the grand story of God's redemptive dealings with mankind.

7. What we know as the Apostles' Creed was not in its present form until about the seventh century. But it had taken almost complete shape centuries earlier. The Jerusalem Creed and the Old Roman Creed (both attested to by the fourth century) are examples of earlier predecessors of the Apostles' Creed.

8. Augustine, *Confessions*, trans. R. S. Pine-Coffin (New York: Penguin, 1961), 164.

9. Quoted in Harmless, *Augustine and the Catechumenate*, 69.

10. Ibid.

11. Ibid., 313.

12. John Bunyan's classic text, *The Pilgrim's Progress*, powerfully captures this sense of the Christian's journey. It really can be regarded as a wonderful and wise Puritan catechetical work.

13. John Meyendorff, quoted in Constance J. Tarasar, "The Orthodox Experience," in Westerhoff and Edwards, *A Faithful Church*, 242.

14. Ibid.

15. David C. Steinmetz, "Luther and Formation in Faith," in John Van Engen, ed., *Educating People of Faith: Exploring the History of Jewish and Christian Communities* (Grand Rapids: Eerdmans, 2004), 256.

16. William P. Haugaard, "The Continental Reformation of the Sixteenth Century," in Westerhoff and Edwards, *A Faithful Church*, 109.

17. Steinmetz, "Luther and Formation in Faith," 263. For an insightful treatment of Luther's catechetical work, see Timothy J. Wengert, *Martin Luther's Catechisms: Forming the Faith* (Minneapolis: Fortress, 2009).

18. Theodore Tappert, ed., *The Book of Concord* (Minneapolis: Augsburg Fortress, 1989), 357.

19. Ibid., 338.

20. T. F. Torrance, *The School of Faith: The Catechisms of the Reformed Church* (Eugene, OR: Wipf and Stock, 1959), xi.

21. Quoted ibid., viii.

22. Quoted in Haugaard, "The Continental Reformation of the Sixteenth Century," in Westerhoff and Edwards, *A Faithful Church*, 119.

23. Tappert, *The Book of Concord*, 356.

24. Josef Andreas Jungmann, *The Good News Yesterday and Today*, ed. and trans. William A. Huesman (New York: W. H. Sadlier, 1962), 102.

25. *Didache* 1:1.

26. Tappert, *The Book of Concord*, 363.

27. See Packer, *Rediscovering Holiness: Know the Fullness of Life with God* (Ventura, CA: Regal, 2009), 153 for a fuller explanation of how all three concerns are vital to our healthy spirituality.

28. *Our Hearts Were Burning Within Us* (Washington, DC: USCCB, 1999), 34. The quotation, including the italicized portion in parentheses, is from the *General Directory for Catechesis* (Washington, DC: USCCB, 1997).

29. I. John Hesselink, *Calvin's First Catechism: A Commentary* (Louisville: Westminster John Knox, 1997), 40.

30. What Luther considered the "first use of the Law"—that is, an evangelistic use—others would come to call the "second use of the Law." See Wengert, *Martin Luther's Catechisms*, 4–9, for more on Luther's primary catechetical use of the Law. For the majority of Protestants, the "first use of the Law" is a civil or governing use; that is, application of God's commands for the good and safety of societies.

31. Ursinus, author of the *Heidelberg Catechism*, speaks about this twofold use of the Law in the introduction to his commentary on the catechism.

32. *Reliquiae Baxterianae* [Baxter's autobiography] (1696), II.xli.180. Already in the dedication of *The Reformed Pastor* we find Baxter writing, "I find by some experience that this is the work that must Reform indeed; that must expel our common prevailing ignorance . . . and help on the success of our publike preaching; and must make godliness a commoner thing, through the Grace of God, which worketh by means. I find that we never took the rightest course to demolish the Kingdom of Darkness till now" (cited in Black, *Reformation Pastors*, 190).

33. J. C. Ryle, *Light from Old Times* (Hertfordshire, UK: Evangelical Press, 1980), 328.

34. Ibid.

35. Ibid.

36. Ibid.

37. Ibid., 328–29.

38. Ibid., 329.

39. Ibid.

40. J. I. Packer, "Introduction," in Baxter, *The Reformed Pastor*, 12.

41. Quoted in ibid., 12–13.

42. Ibid., 13.

43. Ibid., 12.

44. Ibid.

45. From a letter to the Massachusetts missionary John Eliot (N. H. Keeble and G. F. Nuttell, *Calendar of the Correspondence of Richard Baxter* [Oxford: Clarendon Press, 1992], 2:70, no. 768).

46. A first step toward its renewal was outlined by Wallace Benn, *The Baxter Model: Guidelines for Pastoring Today* (Lowestoft, UK: Fellowship of Word and Spirit, 1993).

47. *The Heidelberg Catechism: A New Translation for the 21st Century*, trans. Lee C. Barrett III (Cleveland, OH: The Pilgrim Press, 2007), 8.

48. Torrance, *The School of Faith*, xvii.

49. For an interesting example of a megachurch engaging in self-critique, see Greg L. Hawkins and Cally Parkinson's *Reveal: Where Are You?* (Barrington, IL: Willow Creek Resources, 2007).

50. David B. Barrett, Todd M. Johnson, and Peter F. Crossing, "Missiometrics 2008: Reality Checks for Christian World Communions," *International Bulletin of Missionary Research* 32.1 (January 2008): 30. See also http://www.gordonconwell.edu/ockenga/globalchristianity/resources .php. Thanks are due to Gary's colleague Todd Johnson for providing this information to us.

51. Thanks to Gary's research assistant Jang David Kim for suggesting the concerns we have explored in points 5 and 6 above.

Chapter 4 Sources and Resources for Catechetical Ministry

1. Martin Luther, "Letter to George Spenlein, April 8, 1516," in *Luther's Works*, ed. Jaroslav Pelikan and H. T. Lehmann (St. Louis: Concordia; Philadelphia: Fortress, 1966–1986), 48:12.

2. We are using the word *catechism* here not in the sense of a particular printed catechism. Rather we intend more generally that which comprises the biblical teaching in which we catechize.

3. Our use of the terms *traditionalists* and *progressives* is merely suggestive, not denotative. We are pointing out trends, not pointing at persons.

4. The five founts we have suggested are not to be taken as five distinct and authoritative sources for catechesis. Rather, we see Scripture alone as the final authoritative source. The other four elements represent the teaching of the fully inspired and fully authoritative Scriptures. Thus our approach is quite different from that of the Roman Catholic church, which acknowledges three sources for catechesis—Sacred Scripture, Holy Tradition, and the Magisterium (teaching office) of the Church. Of these three sources, the first two—Scripture and Tradition—are often presented in Catholic documents as being one, together constituting "the Word of God" (*General Directory for Catechesis*, 90). While Scripture is held to have primacy in this relationship, Tradition "transmits in its entirety the Word of God which has been entrusted to the apostles by Christ the Lord and the Holy Spirit" (*Catechism of the Catholic Church* [Washington, DC: USCCB, 1995], 31). The Magisterium is the Church's authority and obligation to faithfully preserve, interpret, and present this Word (*Catechism of the Catholic Church*, 91).

5. J. I. Packer, "Saved by His Precious Blood," in *A Quest for Godliness: The Puritan Vision of the Christian Life* (Wheaton, IL: Crossway, 1994), 125–48. The quotation comes from page 130.

6. This is unpacked further below. The outline is adapted from Gary A. Parrett and S. Steve Kang, *Teaching the Faith, Forming the Faithful: A Biblical Vision for Education in the Church* (Downers Grove, IL: IVP Academic, 2009).

7. *National Directory for Catechesis*, 83.

8. Ibid.

9. James B. Torrance, *Worship, Community, and the Triune God of Grace* (Downers Grove, IL: InterVarsity, 1997), 30.

10. This testimony is from Egeria, a late fourth-century pilgrim (from Spain or the south of Gaul) to the Holy Land who observed and noted these practices. See Harmless, *Augustine and the Catechumenate*, 62–65.

11. See James Choung's *True Story: A Christianity Worth Believing In* (Downers Grove, IL: InterVarsity, 2008).

12. For such language in the Bible, see Job 5:19; Proverbs 6:16; 30:15, 18, 21, 29.

13. This is the design of the 1549 and 1662 catechisms, as included in those editions of the *Book of Common Prayer*. The 1962 Canadian revision of 1662 augmented the catechism with a section on the church and its ministry, plus a suggested rule of adult Christian life.

14. This order is found in the 1995 *Catechism of the Catholic Church*, which incorporates the "four pillars" into four major sections that contain other teachings as well. The section headings are: "The Profession of Faith," "The Celebration of the Christian Mystery," "Life in Christ," and "Christian Prayer."

15. Jungmann, *The Good News Yesterday and Today*, 103.

16. Augustine does not exposit the full Decalogue in his *Enchiridion* (Chicago: Regnery, 1996) but rather deals with the double command of loving God and neighbor—regarded by both Jews and Christians as a summary of the Ten Commandments.

17. J. I. Packer, *Growing in Christ* (Wheaton, IL: Crossway, 1994).

18. "Anglican Catechism in Outline (ACIO): The Interim Report of the Global South Anglican Theological Formation and Education Task Force," January 6, 2008, http://www.globalsouth anglican.org/sse/aciointerimreport_1.pdf.

19. Though not captured by the majority of English translations, the third commitment in Acts 2:42 is, literally, "the breaking of the bread." Many scholars believe "the bread" here is a reference to celebration of the Lord's Supper, rather than to a more general "breaking bread" as found in Acts 2:46. Likewise, the fourth commitment is not simply to "prayer," but to "the prayers," language which may suggest more communal and/or more liturgical prayers, rather than a commitment to prayer in some general sense.

20. From the Preface to the Large Catechism, in Tappert, *The Book of Concord*, 363.

21. Jungmann, *The Good News Yesterday and Today*, 103.

22. Packer, *Growing in Christ*, xi.

23. The same language is adopted and explained in Parrett and Kang, *Teaching the Faith, Forming the Faithful*, 118–19.

24. This last pairing is from E. Stanley Jones, *The Way: 364 Adventures in Daily Living* (Nashville: Abingdon, 1946). The expression "not-the-way" reminds us also of the title and thesis of Cornelius Plantinga Jr.'s *Not the Way It's Supposed to Be: A Breviary of Sin* (Grand Rapids: Eerdmans, 1995).

25. For example, "Therefore . . . learn Christ, specifically, the Crucified. Learn to sing to him and in your despair at yourself to say to him, 'You, Lord Jesus, are my righteousness'" (Martin Luther, "Letter to George Spenlein: 'Learn Christ . . . The Crucified,'" in *Luther's Spirituality*, ed. and trans. Philip W. Key and Peter D. S. Krey, CWS [New York: Paulist, 2007], 4). Gary thanks his colleague, Gordon Isaac, for introducing him to this emphasis in Luther.

26. John Paul II, *Catechesis in Our Time*, 6.

Chapter 5 The Gospel as of First Importance

1. Robert W. Mounce, "Kērygma," in *The International Standard Bible Encyclopedia* (Grand Rapids: Eerdmans, 1982), 6:84.

2. To draw too fine a line between the New Testament concepts of *kērygma* and *didachē*, however, may well be overstating the case from the biblical data itself as it seems that, in some instances at least, the two terms are used interchangeably.

3. A similar listing of summaries of the Gospel appears in Parrett and Kang, *Teaching the Faith, Forming the Faithful*, 102–3.

4. The New Testament writers cite or allude to Isaiah 53 more than any other Old Testament prophecy. See, for example, Acts 8:31–35; John 12:38; Romans 10:16; 1 Peter 2:24–25.

5. Parrett and Kang, *Teaching the Faith, Forming the Faithful*, 103.

6. J. I. Packer and Mark Dever, *In My Place Condemned He Stood: Celebrating the Glory of Atonement* (Wheaton, IL: Crossway, 2008), 25.

7. See also Parrett and Kang, *Teaching the Faith, Forming the Faithful*, chap. 4.

8. For a helpful survey of the thinking of many leaders within this movement, see Eddie Gibbs and Ryan K. Bolger, *Emerging Churches* (Grand Rapids: Baker Academic, 2005). We should not make overly broad statements about "the emerging church(es)," however, since the movement—

if it can properly be called that—is still very dynamic, with churches and individual leaders moving in and out. Identifying those accepting the moniker "emerging" and those distancing themselves from it is not easily done. What is done under the name "emerging" is sometimes dangerous, and yet at other times and by other leaders, praiseworthy. In other words it reminds us at times of some of the same difficulties in our day of trying to pin down what is meant by use of the title "evangelical."

9. Anonymous quote in Gibbs and Bolger, *Emerging Churches*, 54.

10. Packer and Dever, *In My Place Condemned He Stood*, 18.

11. Charles Spurgeon, *The Treasury of David* (Grand Rapids: Kregel, 2004), 453. Duncan is John "Rabbi" Duncan, sometime professor at the Free Church College, Edinburgh.

12. Packer and Dever, *In My Place Condemned He Stood*, 21.

13. This time perhaps in the forms of modern-day "propositional" evangelicals versus postmodern, socially activistic postevangelicals.

14. D. A. Carson, *Becoming Conversant with the Emerging Church: Understanding a Movement and Its Implications* (Grand Rapids: Zondervan, 2005); Doug Pagitt and Tony Jones, eds., *An Emergent Manifesto of Hope* (Grand Rapids: Baker, 2007).

15. To call the "new perspective" a movement may not be fair. There is a great deal of diversity among scholars who have been associated with the "new perspective." The brief summary offered here, therefore, cannot possibly do justice to the full discussion. Many books have been written from various viewpoints on all these matters, and we ask readers to consult some of these texts. For an overview of the debate from differing standpoints we recommend Guy Prentiss Waters, *Justification and the New Perspectives on Paul: A Review and Response* (Phillipsburg, NJ: P&R, 2004); Stephen Westerholm, *Perspectives Old and New on Paul: The "Lutheran" Paul and His Critics* (Grand Rapids: Eerdmans, 2003); N. T. Wright, *Paul: In Fresh Perspective* (Minneapolis: Fortress, 2006).

16. This is the title of a book by N. T. Wright: *What Saint Paul Really Said: Was Paul of Tarsus the Real Founder of Christianity?* (Grand Rapids: Eerdmans, 1997).

17. Meaning, respectively: "Scripture alone, Christ alone, grace alone, faith alone, glory be to God alone."

18. See John Murray, *Redemption Accomplished and Applied* (Grand Rapids: Eerdmans, 1984), chap. 5.

19. See D. A. Carson, Peter O'Brien, and Mark Seifrid, eds., *The Complexities of Second Temple Judaism*, vol. 1, *Justification and Variegated Nomism* (Grand Rapids: Baker Academic, 2001) and *The Paradoxes of Paul*, vol. 2, *Justification and Variegated Nomism* (Grand Rapids: Baker Academic, 2004).

20. E. P. Sanders, *Paul, the Law, and the Jewish People* (Minneapolis: Augsburg Fortress, 1985).

21. See Steve Jeffery, Michael Ovey, and Andrew Sach, *Pierced for Our Transgressions: Rediscovering the Glory of Penal Substitution* (Wheaton, IL: Crossway, 2007).

22. Packer and Dever, *In My Place Condemned He Stood*, 35.

23. C. J. Mahaney in ibid., 16.

24. Ibid., 138.

25. Keller, by the way, has developed a three-part catechetical curriculum (intended for about thirty weeks of instruction) that is focused on grounding and growing God's people in the Gospel: Tim Keller, *Gospel Christianity* (New York: Redeemer Presbyterian Church, 2003). An overview and samples of the curriculum can be seen online at the church's website, http://www.redeemer2.com/websamples/GC1Sample.pdf.

26. For more on the notion of the Gospel as plumb line, please see the next chapter.

27. D. Martyn Lloyd-Jones exhorts us in *Spiritual Depression* to preach the Gospel to ourselves ([Grand Rapids: Eerdmans, 1965], 21). John Piper also picks up this theme when he says,

"When we preach the Gospel to ourselves, we are addressing every word of every enemy of every kind" (*When I Don't Desire God* [Wheaton, IL: Crossway, 2004], 82).

28. "The Gospel Way," in Arthur Bennett, ed., *The Valley of Vision: A Collection of Puritan Prayers and Devotion* (Carlisle, PA: Banner of Truth, 1975).

29. Chapter XVII of his Rule of 1221. See http://www.americancatholic.org/e-News/Friar Jack/fj092302.asp#F2.

30. Antinomianism has been defined as "the view that there is no need for the law of God in the Christian life" (Donald K. McKim, *Westminster Dictionary of Theological Terms* [Louisville: Westminster John Knox, 1996], 13).

31. Of course, a minority of evangelicals were not keen on Graham's ecumenical approach.

32. From the hymn "Rock of Ages, Cleft for Me" by Augustus M. Toplady, 1776.

33. *Xenophilia* is a word found in relatively few English dictionaries. It is defined in *The American Heritage Dictionary of the English Language*, 3rd ed. (New York: Houghton Mifflin, 1992) as attraction to "that which is foreign, especially to foreign peoples, manners, and customs." It thus stands in stark contrast with *xenophobia*, a sin that has too often characterized many churches. Gary has been using the word since the late 1990s in alphabets like this. He was not too surprised to see it used in an acrostic-based book by Leonard Sweet, Brian D. McLaren, and Jerry Haselmayer: *A Is for Abductive: The Language of the Emerging Church* (Grand Rapids: Zondervan, 2003). After all, there are relatively few words that begin with *x*!

Chapter 6 Three Facets of the Faith

1. Thomas à Kempis, *Of the Imitation of Christ*, III.56.1.

2. Parrett and Kang briefly introduce this idea in *Teaching the Faith, Forming the Faithful*, 110.

3. "The Love of God," by Frederick M. Lehman, 1917. The verse was apparently based upon the opening verses of a Jewish poem, *Akdamut*, written in Aramaic in the eleventh century by Meir Ben Isaac Nehorai. A tragic irony is that the poem on which the hymn was based was originally written against the backdrop of crusades that involved Christian hostilities and aggressions against Jews.

4. Surprisingly (and misleadingly) the ESV has as its heading over Titus 2 "Teach Sound Doctrine." Other major versions typically have done better with their headings. The NIV has "What Must Be Taught to Various Groups." The NASB is better still, with "Duties of the Older and Younger."

5. The Greek term used here literally means "right-footed" and implies walking correctly, that is, in the Way of the Gospel.

6. In the next chapter we explore this matter more fully.

7. This language is taken from the definition of teaching that is offered and explained in Parrett and Kang, *Teaching the Faith, Forming the Faithful*, chap. 10.

8. The remainder of the chapter represents an expansion upon ideas Gary first introduced in Parrett and Kang, *Teaching the Faith, Forming the Faithful*, chap. 4.

9. Elsewhere, J.I. has called these "the three formulae which have always been central in Christian teaching" (*Growing in Christ*, xi).

10. D. H. Williams has offered a provocative and often insightful introduction to these issues in *Evangelicals and Tradition: The Formative Influence of the Early Church* (Grand Rapids: Baker Academic, 2005).

11. Geoffrey Wainwright has offered a very helpful and extensive treatment of these things in his book *Doxology: The Praise of God in Worship, Doctrine, and Life* (New York: Oxford University Press, 1980). See especially chapters 7 and 8.

12. Heschel, *God in Search of Man*, 31. Heschel earlier identified these as (1) the way of sensing the presence of God in the world, in things; (2) the way of sensing his presence in the Bible; and (3) the way of sensing his presence in sacred deeds.

13. *Beit knesset* (house of assembly) is the Hebrew name for the synagogue. But it is also called *beit midrash* (house of study) and *beit tefilah* (house of prayer).

14. Brueggemann, *The Creative Word*.

15. *Cultus* here simply refers to rituals for religious life. We prefer to use the word *communion* for this category, emphasizing practices to deepen our communion with the living God.

16. Augustine, *Confessions*, 43.

17. Blaise Pascal, *Pensées*, trans. W. F. Trotter (Mineola, NY: Dover, 2003), 65.

18. C. S. Lewis, *Surprised by Joy: The Shape of My Early Life* (New York: Harcourt, 1955), 5.

19. Marva Dawn, *Is It a Lost Cause? Having the Heart of God for the Church's Children* (Grand Rapids: Eerdmans, 1997), 18–19.

20. John Stott, *Between Two Worlds: The Challenge of Preaching Today* (Grand Rapids: Eerdmans, 1994), 151.

21. Gene Edward Veith, *The Spirituality of the Cross: The Way of the First Evangelicals* (St. Louis: Concordia, 1999).

22. Another familiar division has metaphysics as the third category in place of ontology. This is also a significant witness to the human longing for transcendence.

23. The principle Hebrew word for "way" or "path" is *derek*.

24. Additional Old Testament uses of "the Way" suggest that it is associated with life (Prov. 10:17; 12:28) and salvation (Ps. 50:23). Since the people have rejected the Way (Isa. 59:8), God sends his messengers to preach repentance and thus prepare the Way by removing obstacles from the path (Isa. 40:3; 57:14). But God himself must remove the obstacles (Isa. 62:10–12) and bring salvation to the people (Isa. 51:5). So, at last, the Way of holiness (Isa. 35:8) is established among the redeemed, the ransomed of the Lord (Isa. 35:1–11). This pattern of preparing the Way before the coming of the Lord himself was manifest in the ministry of John (Mal. 3:1) preceding Jesus (Mark 1:1–11).

25. The Greek word for "life" is *zōē*.

26. See *ESV Study Bible* (Wheaton, IL: Crossway, 2008), notes on Acts 5:20.

27. This table is adapted from Parrett and Kang, *Teaching the Faith, Forming the Faithful*, chap. 4.

Chapter 7 Forward in the Faith of the Gospel

1. Ralph Venning, *Learning in Christ's School* (Carlisle, PA: Banner of Truth, 1999), 4. This book, written by Venning in 1675, is a study of spiritual maturing based upon John's three terms in 1 John 2:12–14: "little children," "fathers," and "young men."

2. For a consideration of these theorists and their implications for Christian education see Parrett and Kang, *Teaching the Faith, Forming the Faithful*, chaps. 8 and 9.

3. Charles Spurgeon, *A Puritan Catechism*, available at http://www.spurgeon.org/catechis .htm.

4. Gary heard this expression from Robbie Castleman in a lecture she gave at Gordon-Conwell Theological Seminary in May, 2007. See her book *Parenting in the Pew: Guiding Your Children into the Joy of Worship* (Downers Grove, IL: InterVarsity, 2002).

5. Ibid., xxvii–xxviii.

6. Ibid., xxix–xxx. Ironically, one of the most visible efforts in our time at catechetical renewal among children, *The Catechesis of the Good Shepherd*, very much has in view the vision of *educare* that Torrance is cautioning against. This ministry, established by Hebrew and Scripture scholar Sophia Cavaletti in the mid-1950s, now operates in more than thirty countries and is utilized by both Catholic and Protestant churches. It is, according to the official website,

"rooted in the Bible, the liturgy of the church, and the educational principles of Maria Montessori" (www.cgsusa.org).

7. Venning, *Learning in Christ's School*, 4.

8. For a helpful discussion of this intriguing passage see I. Howard Marshall, *The Epistles of John*, NICOT (Grand Rapids: Eerdmans, 1978), 134–38.

9. *Rite of Christian Initiation of Adults* (Collegeville, MN: The Liturgical Press, 1988), 16. Additional major resources regarding catechesis as envisioned in the Catholic Church include Pope John Paul II, *Catechesis Tradendae*; *The General Directory for Catechesis*; *The National Directory for Catechesis*; and *The Catechism of the Catholic Church*.

10. Robert Webber, *Journey to Jesus: The Worship, Evangelism, and Nurture Mission of the Church* (Nashville: Abingdon, 2001).

11. These are called, respectively, *Follow Me!*, *Be My Disciple!*, *Walk in the Spirit!*, and *Find Your Gift!* (Wheaton, IL: IWS Resources, 2001).

12. For more on Alpha, see www.alphana.org/Group/Group.aspx?ID=1000016933. Alpha has developed an official follow-up course entitled "A Life Worth Living" based on the biblical book of Philippians. Another sort of guide for follow-up is Michael Green's book, *After Alpha: You've Been on an Alpha Course—What Now?* (Colorado Springs: David C. Cook, 2004). For more on Christianity Explored, see www.christianityexplored.org. The Christianity Explored program also has a follow-up course based on Philippians, entitled Discipleship Explored.

Chapter 8 Drawing Lines and Choosing Sides

1. This saying has been variously attributed. Some have suggested it reaches back as far as Augustine. Others believe that it first came from the Puritan Richard Baxter. While Augustine would have agreed with the general spirit of the saying, and while Baxter helped this favorite saying of his to become popularized, the quote is most likely attributable to Rupert Meldenius, a pseudonym for Peter Meiderlin, an irenic Lutheran theologian of seventeenth-century Augsburg.

2. Parrett and Kang interact with the first three of these three terms in *Teaching the Faith, Forming the Faithful*, chap. 14.

3. See James Cutsinger, ed., *Reclaiming the Great Tradition: Evangelicals, Catholics and Orthodox in Dialogue* (Downers Grove, IL: InterVarsity, 1997) and Charles W. Colson and Harold Fickett, *The Faith: What Christians Believe, Why They Believe It, and Why It Matters* (Grand Rapids: Zondervan, 2008).

4. J. I. Packer and Thomas C. Oden, *One Faith: The Evangelical Consensus* (Downers Grove, IL: InterVarsity, 2004).

5. The sixteen topics actually represent the sixteen chapters in the book.

6. Some contemporary evangelicals, however, would protest the inclusion of one or more of these *solas*. For example, advocates of the so-called "New Perspectives on Paul" might protest, or seriously redefine, the doctrine of *sola fide*. Others would stumble over including *sola scriptura* as an "evangelical essential." See for example D. H. Williams, *Evangelicals and Tradition*, and Craig D. Allert, *A High View of Scripture? The Authority of the Bible and the Formation of the New Testament Canon* (Grand Rapids: Baker Academic, 2007). On our part, we wholeheartedly affirm each of the five *solas* and are quite unwilling to give ground on any of them. Indeed, we might say that we must not yield on these points because of a sixth implicit *sola* from which the others all derive: *solus Deus* (God alone). There is none good but God alone. This means that all of us are desperately in need of a saving work that must come from Another, and not from ourselves. Because we lack goodness in ourselves, we must depend upon faith alone (not in any work of our own) in Christ alone (the Righteous One and only Savior) for our salvation. We would not know these things if God did not reveal them to us in the testimony of Scripture alone (which is affirmed by the fathers). Thus all our salvation is of grace alone (purely God's gift to us). Obviously, then, all glory goes to God alone (who alone is worthy of such and will

never yield his glory to another). For a hymn that celebrates these *solas*, please see "There Is None Good but God Alone" in Appendix I.

7. See Gary Parrett, "The Wondrous Cross and the Broken Wall," in Elizabeth Conde-Frazier, S. Steve Kang, and Gary A. Parrett, *A Many Colored Kingdom: Multicultural Dynamics for Spiritual Formation* (Grand Rapids: Baker Academic, 2004), 75–78.

8. This language is from the Nicene Creed and is common in many historic confessions of the faith.

9. The use of the term *classes* is simply intended to use language that is familiar and common. It need not imply a lecture-driven experience or anything approximating a formal classroom setting. The form of such learning experiences can depend upon all sorts of variables—subject matter, the teacher, the learners, the venue, the schedule, and more.

10. These "Guidelines for Receiving Communion" were adopted by the United States Conference of Catholic Bishops in 1996. They can be found at www.cosmm.com/out/guide.html.

11. See, for example, http://rec.Gospelcom.net/index.php?section=57 regarding the decision of the Christian Reformed Church.

12. *National Directory for Catechesis*, 211.

13. Rev. Constas H. Demetry, *Catechism of the Eastern Orthodox Church*. This can be found online at www.christusrex.org/www1/CDHN/catechis.html.

14. *National Directory for Catechesis*, 215.

15. See the Barna Group's research at http://www.barna.org.

Chapter 9 Moving In and Moving On

1. Quoted in Harmless, *Augustine and the Catechumenate*, 381–82.

2. See chapter 5, note 34.

3. Evangelical educator Robert Pazmiño has offered a helpful discussion of the three forms of education we are referring to in *Principles and Practices of Christian Education* (Grand Rapids: Baker, 1992), 62–65.

4. See Eliot Eisner, *The Educational Imagination: On the Design and Evaluation of School Programs*, 3rd ed. (New York: Macmillan, 1994).

5. For a very helpful guide to the Heidelberg Catechism, see Kevin DeYoung, *The Good News We Almost Forgot: Rediscovering the Gospel in a 16th Century Catechism* (Chicago: Moody, 2010).

6. Some may wish to add another layer of formal catechesis that focuses on the meaning of "the mysteries"—that is, the sacraments of baptism and the Lord's Supper. This could occur after one's baptism, or confirmation, and before a first experience of the Lord's Supper.

7. See Andy Crouch, *Culture Making: Recovering Our Creative Calling* (Downers Grove, IL: InterVarsity, 2008).

8. Examples of Puritan commentaries, or "explanations," of the *Westminster Shorter Catechism* include Thomas Watson's *Body of Divinity* (Carlisle, PA: Banner of Truth, 1957) and Thomas Vincent's *The Shorter Catechism Explained from Scripture* (Carlisle, PA: Banner of Truth, 1980).

9. *The Mission of an Evangelist* (Minneapolis: World Wide Publications, 2001), 37–38.

Chapter 10 Championing Catechesis in Contemporary Congregations

1. Torrance, *The School of Faith*, xi.

2. For an extended discussion of biblical aims for our ministries of teaching, see Parrett and Kang, *Teaching the Faith, Forming the Faithful*, chap. 2.

3. For another look at questions 4–7, see ibid., chap. 5.

4. Again, see http://www.barna.org for examples.

5. See Appendix II for a list of resources for further reading and study.

6. Quoted in Frederic W. Farrar, *Lives of the Fathers* (London: Adam and Charles Black, 1907), 2:197.

7. Paul J. Grime, "Luther and the Church Song," http://www.lifeoftheworld.com/lotw/article .php?a_num=3&m_num=1&m_vol=8.

8. Gary has written numerous hymns for congregational worship, including a number that are explicitly intended as catechetical hymns. See Appendix I for a few examples. For more on this idea of the power of our hymnody for formation, see Parrett and Kang, *Teaching the Faith, Forming the Faithful*, chap. 12.

9. Torrance, *The School of Faith*, xxv–xxvi.

Appendix I Examples of Catechetical Hymns

1. The hymn is based on Colossians 1:28 and reminds us that the one focus of our catechetical ministry is to proclaim Christ alone. Most of the hymns in this appendix can be found in Gary Parrett and Julie Tennent, *Psalms, Hymns and Spiritual Songs* (Chicago: MorgenBooks, 2009).

2. The hymn is another Christ proclamation, this time in narrative form. The first four verses are to be sung to the tune *Picardy* (familiarly used with "Let All Mortal Flesh Keep Silence"). Then, with the help of a musical transition, the last four verses are sung to *Lauda Anima* (familiarly used with "Praise My Soul the King of Heaven").

3. A meditation upon Christ, God's perfect gift, this hymn aims to foster both orthodoxy and doxology.

4. The hymn aims to portray a holistic vision of the wonder of salvation, noting its "past, present, and future" aspects and attributing the work of our salvation to the Triune God.

5. A reflection upon what we have called the "Three Facets of the Faith."

6. This hymn is based upon the book of Romans, specifically upon 1:16–17. The complete hymn has sixteen verses and emerged from a sermon series Gary had preached on the book of Romans.

7. This hymn—which celebrates the Reformation *solas*—was written in honor of David Wells, to whom we have dedicated the book. The tune is familiar to most as that used with "A Mighty Fortress Is Our God."

8. Written by Gary in honor of J.I.'s eightieth birthday. The hymn celebrates what Gary sees as the biblically holistic, catechetical vision of J.I.'s ministry as churchman, professor, and author.

Subject Index

Scripture Index

235

237

J. I. Packer is Board of Governors' Professor of Theology at Regent College and executive editor for *Christianity Today*. Best known for his bestselling classic *Knowing God*, Packer is the author or editor of more than fifty books.

Gary A. Parrett is professor of educational ministries and worship at Gordon-Conwell Theological Seminary and the coauthor of *A Many Colored Kingdom* and *Teaching the Faith, Forming the Faithful*.